American psychologists have woken up to the fact that they cannot acquire a comprehensive and even legitimate understanding of people, both individually and in groups, unless they go global. Seeking global understanding is not only essential to successful research, teaching, therapy, counseling, and consulting, it is also the key to combating fear of foreigners, xenophobia, and even hate. This book provides penetrating, invaluable insights from diverse and distinguished world experts as to why we all need to go global—not only to enhance our own understanding but also to serve the world in the way psychologists should, and indeed, must, in the 21st century.

—**Robert J. Sternberg, PhD,** Professor, Department of Psychology, College of Human Ecology, Cornell University, Ithaca, NY, United States; Honorary Professor of Psychology, Heidelberg University, Heidelberg, Germany

This book is a great read for any educator, clinician, policy maker, and advocate interested in international psychology. It consolidates all themes that constitute the cornerstone of global psychology in the 21st century.

—**Brigitte Khoury, PhD,** American University of Beirut, Beirut, Lebanon

D1341687

Going Global

Going Global

How Psychologists Can Meet a World of Need

Edited by Craig Shealy,
Merry Bullock, and Shagufa Kapadia

 AMERICAN PSYCHOLOGICAL ASSOCIATION

The opinions and statements published are the responsibility of the authors, and such opinions and statements do not necessarily represent the policies of the American Psychological Association.

Published by
American Psychological Association
750 First Street, NE
Washington, DC 20002
https://www.apa.org

Order Department
https://www.apa.org/pubs/books
order@apa.org

In the U.K., Europe, Africa, and the Middle East, copies may be ordered from Eurospan
https://www.eurospanbookstore.com/apa
info@eurospangroup.com

Typeset in Meridien and Ortodoxa by Circle Graphics, Inc., Reisterstown, MD

Printer: Gasch Printing, Odenton, MD
Cover Designer: Gwen J. Grafft, Minneapolis, MN

Library of Congress Cataloging-in-Publication Data

CIP data has been applied for. Library of Congress Control Number: 2022943515.

https://doi.org/10.1037/0000311-000

Printed in the United States of America

10 9 8 7 6 5 4 3 2 1

CONTENTS

CONTRIBUTORS

Ezequiel Benito, PhD, Association for the Advancement of Psychological Science, Buenos Aires, Argentina

Devi Bhuyan, PsyD, Sheppard Pratt, Baltimore, MD, United States

Michael J. Bordieri, PhD, Murray State University, Murray, KY, United States

Lindy Brewster, PhD, ORConsulting Inc., Manassas, VA, United States

Thema Bryant-Davis, PhD, Pepperdine University, Malibu, CA, United States

Merry Bullock, PhD, Ahimsa International, Boulder, CO, United States

Paula Caligiuri, PhD, Northeastern University, Boston, MA, United States

Amanda Clinton, MEd, PhD, American Psychological Association, Washington, DC, United States

Melanie M. Domenech Rodríguez, PhD, Utah State University, Logan, UT, United States

Stewart I. Donaldson, PhD, Claremont Graduate University, Claremont, CA, United States

Christopher F. Drescher, PhD, Augusta University, Augusta, GA, United States

Pamela Flattau, PhD, The PsySiP Project, Washington, DC, United States

John Fulkerson, PhD, Fulkerson Consulting, New Canaan, CT, United States

Steven E. Grande, PhD, James Madison University, Harrisonburg, VA, United States

Elaine D. Hanson, PsyD, JD, Fielding Graduate University, Santa Barbara, CA, United States

William E. Hanson, PhD, RPsych, Concordia University of Edmonton, Edmonton, Alberta, Canada

Connie Henson, PhD, Learning Quest, New South Wales, Australia

Tor Levin Hofgaard, PhD, Norwegian Psychological Association, Oslo, Norway

Laura R. Johnson, PhD, University of Mississippi, University, MS, United States

Shagufa Kapadia, PhD, The Maharaja Sayajirao University of Baroda, Vadodara, India

Jacqueline P. Leighton, PhD, RPsych, University of Alberta, Edmonton, Alberta, Canada

Sherri McCarthy, PhD, (deceased) Northern Arizona University, Flagstaff, AZ, United States

Chandra M. Mehrotra, PhD, College of St. Scholastica, Duluth, MN, United States

Gwen V. Mitchell, PsyD, University of Denver, Denver, CO, United States

Bonnie Kaul Nastasi, PhD, Tulane University, New Orleans, LA, United States

Thomas Oakland, PhD, (deceased) University of Florida, Gainesville, FL, United States

Corann Okorodudu, PhD, Rowan University, Glassboro, NJ, United States

Craig Shealy, PhD, Western Washington University, Bellingham, WA, United States

Sandra L. Shullman, PhD, Executive Development Group, LLC, Columbus, OH, United States

Lee Sternberger, PhD, International Beliefs and Values Institute, Bellingham, WA, United States

Chris E. Stout, PsyD, Center for Global Initiatives, Chicago, IL, United States

Mark D. Terjesen, PhD, St. John's University, Jamaica, NY, United States

Richard Velayo, PhD, Pace University, New York, NY, United States

Randall P. White, PhD, HEC Paris, Jouy-en-Josas, France

Going Global

Introduction to *Going Global*

Why Psychologists Should Meet a World of Need

Craig Shealy, Merry Bullock, and Shagufa Kapadia

- It's 1991, and an unarmed Black man, Rodney King, is brutally beaten by Los Angeles police officers, an event that culminated in 6 days of riots and 63 deaths.

- It's 2001, and extremists, in the name of Islam and the Muslim people, deliberately crash two airplanes into the Twin Towers in New York, killing 2,753 people.

- It's 2005, and in a national forest in Northern Assam, India, a refugee mother and her squatter family from Bangladesh are fearing imminent deportation.

- It's 2009, and in Bonn, Germany, delegates to the Education for Sustainable Development conference are confronting issues such as climate change denial around the world.

- It's 2015, in Arusha, Tanzania, at the Education for All conference, where attendees are pleading with leaders in higher education to address the dire need for quality teaching across Africa.

- It's 2015 still, but now in the village of Aurdak, Afghanistan, and Rokhshana, a 19-year-old woman married against her will, is stoned to death for adultery by Taliban leaders.

https://doi.org/10.1037/0000311-001
Going Global: How Psychologists Can Meet a World of Need, C. Shealy, M. Bullock, and S. Kapadia (Editors)

- It's 2020, during a global viral pandemic that has killed millions, and the face mask in England has become "politically correct," a "muzzle," and a "mark of submission" (Blunt, 2020).

- It's class on Monday, and our students are asked if they've heard of the Sustainable Development Goals or Millennium Development Goals (the answer was "No").

And we wonder, for the thousandth time: Where in the world is psychology?

WHY THIS BOOK?

In these examples—and thousands more that we and our coauthors have encountered over the years—three overarching realities prevail. First, each of these events will not be sufficiently understood or addressed if psychology and psychologists are not involved. Second, psychology and psychologists are doing a great deal, locally and globally, but our students, colleagues, other disciplines, policy makers, and the public at large often appear unaware of our knowledge, skills, and values, which are needed more than ever around the world. Third, psychology and psychologists must elevate their profile and increase their presence to be taken seriously in the ongoing quest to illuminate causes and provide solutions to the global challenges that affect us all. In matters of policy and practice, we really don't have a seat at the global table, and we must if we're going to impact events that are clearly psychological in nature and require psychological expertise to address and resolve.

WHO IS OUR AUDIENCE?

Our audience is all who believe that psychology should have a seat at the global table. This includes students who will be the next generation of scholars, educators, practitioners, and leaders—whom we teach, mentor, and supervise—even as they show us what they need and want in order to address the many challenges we face, locally and globally. Along with students at whatever age and stage, we also seek to reach their teachers, supervisors, mentors, and collaborators—those who share a vision of psychology and psychologists "going global to meet a world of need." We need to amplify their voices; give them source materials upon which to draw; and support the discussion, internalization, and representation of these visions and values with others. Finally, we wish to engage our colleagues, early career to postretirement, who occupy all manner of roles and responsibilities in our broader field of inquiry and practice. If we are to pursue and realize our potential on the global stage—joining others as equals across the disciplinary and professional spectrum—psychology and psychologists must make their voices heard and their presence known.

GOING GLOBAL IN THE PAST, PRESENT, AND FUTURE

The good news is, as an international field of inquiry and practice, psychology has matured to the point where it may credibly identify and proactively address many of the most complex issues of our day, often referred to as "wicked problems," a term referring to complex challenges that require complex solutions (Alford & Head, 2017; Coffman et al., 2009; Kumlien & Coughlan, 2018), exemplified by the Sustainable Development Goals (SDGs; United Nations, 2022).[1] As Stevens and Wedding (2004) documented years ago in their seminal *Handbook of International Psychology*, such global challenges include, but are not limited to, "intergroup conflict, national transformation and development, threats to the natural environment, physical and mental health needs, and the struggles of disempowered groups" (p. 496). Likewise, in *Toward a Global Psychology*—another foundational book, edited by Stevens and Gielen (2007)—the authors sought to

> enhance communication and collaboration among psychologists worldwide through scholarship, advocacy, education, and networking . . . discover genuine universals through the study of psychological phenomena-in-context . . . [and apply] psychological science to pressing global concerns, such as overpopulation, global warming, HIV/AIDS, and human trafficking . . . concerns [that are] complex and multi-determined. (pp. xiii–xiv)

Going back even further in time, and as a final exemplar, *Human Behavior in Global Perspective*—written by Marshall Segall, Pierre Dasen, John Berry, and Ype Poortinga, with the first edition published in 1990—was among the first introductory texts on cross-cultural psychology. Their observations decades ago seem timelier than ever:

> From now on, educated persons everywhere need to cultivate a sense of their fellows everywhere—who we are, what moves us, and how we cope, both similarly and differently, with the problems we face. There is a crucial role for psychology in this increasing effort to globalize knowledge and understanding. For psychology to live up to the demands of this role, it must be a cross-cultural

---

[1]In reading *Going Global*, you may encounter terms, concepts, organizations, or movements that are new and may raise questions, as they are derived from disciplinary or epistemological perspectives that are different from those we typically encounter in psychology. The concept of "wicked problems" is one of many such examples in this book. We encourage our readers to explore terminology and paradigms that may be unfamiliar but are used by colleagues in other fields and systems. By expanding our understanding of such constructs and initiatives, we want to help facilitate further communication and engagement with scholars, educators, students, practitioners, and policy makers in allied professions around the world who also are "going global" in their lives and work.

psychology that is informed by the insights of several neighboring disciplines, preeminent among them anthropology. The four of us owe a debt to anthropology for pointing out to us the need to do research in societies other than our own. (pp. xvi–xvii)

These same themes—the urgent need to understand what makes us similar and different, apply what we know to the problems we face, learn from other disciplines, and engage peoples and perspectives from cultures different from our own—are expressed time and again in the chapters that follow. These activities, important for educators, scholars, practitioners, students, and leaders of psychology, will help create the dialectic bridges, dialogue, and self-reflection psychology needs to fulfill its promise.

Clearly, our colleagues have been writing about such matters for many years, a point that is worth emphasizing at the outset of this book, as a matter of respect and regard for those who came before us. The perspectives presented in *Going Global* rest on a mature and robust foundation, the same one that led George Miller, president of the American Psychological Association (APA), to rightly urge in 1969 that psychologists needed to figure out how to "give psychology away"—that is, to translate our theories, findings, and applications into accessible form for a nonpsychological audience (see also Evans, 2020).

Today, similar issues and concerns are highly resonant with the goals of current and future psychologists who wish to "internationalize their careers" and make a difference in the world (e.g., https://www.unpsychologyday.com/). Moreover, as is documented throughout *Going Global*, psychology and psychologists have abundant opportunities to "meet a world of need" across all nine of the areas that are our focus: advocacy, assessment, consultation, intervention, leadership, policy, research, service, and teaching. As we will see over the course of this book, psychologists increasingly are applying their knowledge, skills, and values to big picture issues such as sustainability, human rights, conflict resolution, global education, and religious and cultural understanding (United Nations, 2022).

Although many global organizations could be cited in this regard, from the standpoint of the APA, such activities are highly congruent with APA's mission ("To promote the advancement, communication, and application of psychological science and knowledge to benefit society and improve lives"; APA, 2020), vision (e.g., "The change APA aspires to create in the world" through "a strong, diverse, and unified psychology that enhances knowledge and improves the human condition"; APA, 2020), operating principles (e.g., "advance psychology globally through international engagement, association efforts, and meaningful collaborations"; APA, 2020), and ethical principles (e.g., for Principle D: Justice and Principle E: Respect for People's Rights and Dignities of the *Ethical Principles of Psychologists and Code of Conduct*; APA, 2017). In addition to these essential professional documents—and the many literatures that are cited in the chapters that follow—there is much material that we simply couldn't include for space reasons, although the chapters that follow do provide web-based links and other references, which are worthy of further exploration (e.g.,

Dana Dunn's, n.d., *Oxford Biographies* addressing international/cross-cultural psychology).[2]

This book is timely for another reason. For the first time, mainstream psychology is beginning to openly question its traditional narrow focus on Western norms, values, and perspectives. The increase in attention to decolonization is an important process for psychology (e.g., Adams et al., 2015; Okazaki et al., 2008), and the rise of robust Indigenous psychologies (e.g., https://www.indigenouspsych.org/; Allwood, 2019; Sundarajan et al., 2020) are creating powerful changes in the ways that psychologists think about and practice international engagement in a transculturally competent manner (Glover & Friedman, 2015).

So it's not that psychology or psychologists aren't engaged internationally. They are. It is just that, in our experience, psychologists as a whole still aren't seen—and don't see themselves—as indispensable to "meeting a world of need" despite the obvious psychological dimensions to many of these "needs." In other words, "thinking and acting globally" is not yet integral to our professional identity, which is not surprising given that such an identity typically is neither envisioned nor inculcated as a vital component of education, training, and professional development, both in the United States and in many other countries. From our perspective, that state of affairs is unfortunate but also rectifiable for good and important reasons, as we demonstrate in the chapters that follow.

GOING GLOBAL AS PSYCHOLOGY AND PSYCHOLOGISTS: REALIZING OUR PROMISE AND POTENTIAL

Many of the challenges that are addressed in this book—the "wicked problems," the global challenges that require collective action across individuals, groups, and disciplines—are the issues that are addressed by the SDGs of the United Nations. All psychologists who wish to "go global" should know about

---

[2]Although highly affirming of content and approach, one reviewer helpfully offered several additions that we rightly could have emphasized in greater detail and/or included such as the *International Psychology Bulletin of Division 52* (https://div52.net/newsletter/), source materials from kindred organizations such as the International Union of Psychological Science and its International Congress of Psychology (https://www.iupsys.net/events/international-congress-of-psychology/), and the International Association of Applied Psychology (https://iaapsy.org/). These are all excellent resources/organizations, and we encourage our readers to explore everything they have to offer. Of course, many colleagues also have made invaluable contributions to areas referenced in this book but may not have been included, mainly because we had to narrow our references to meet page requirements. As discourse continues, we see this process as a beginning, not the end, and we hope to widen our circle over time to include both individuals who were not referenced in this iteration of *Going Global* and colleagues from different parts of the world whom we haven't yet met but who are eager to connect with us as we are with them.

the SDGs, which were adopted by all member states of the United Nations in 2015 as the 2030 Agenda for Sustainable Development.

> At its heart are the 17 Sustainable Development Goals (SDGs), which are an urgent call for action by all countries—developed and developing—in a global partnership. They recognize that ending poverty and other deprivations must go hand-in-hand with strategies that improve health and education, reduce inequality, and spur economic growth—all while tackling climate change and working to preserve our oceans and forests. (United Nations, n.d.)

Even a cursory review of the SDGs reveals their deep relevance to psychology and psychologists by presenting questions of our age, like these, right before us:

- How can individuals, groups, organizations, governments, societies, and global regions with a chronic history of conflict come to terms with what is needed to resolve such conflicts and prevent their recurrence?

- How do we ensure access to quality education—perhaps the most powerful investment we can make in our future as a species—particularly by individuals and groups that historically have been denied such access?

- Why do we flagrantly continue to disregard the basic rights of human beings through all manner of justifications, all over the globe, and what can we do about that?

- What is the best way not only to enhance tolerance for cultures and religions that are different from our own but also to create greater understanding, respect, and engagement?

- Why do some people continue to deny the overwhelming evidence of environmental degradation, such as climate change, and what should be our response?

These are just a few big-picture questions that are fundamentally and ineluctably psychological in nature. How we ask and answer them cuts to the core of who we understand ourselves to be as well as what our responsibilities are to one another and to the living earth that sustains us (United Nations, 2022).

It is our contention that we—as psychology and psychologists—are not doing a good enough job to ask or answer questions of this nature or scope. To be clear, we love our field and have devoted our professional lives to it. We see the power of what we do in the research we conduct, courses we teach, training we supervise, and interventions we implement. These are good and necessary contributions to human welfare and the greater good, and we are *not* suggesting they should be abandoned or curtailed. But we can and must do more—much more—for as things stand, psychology really is not understood or often perceived to be an essential contributor to conversations about the "global crises" we face (United Nations, 2022). That is changing, as we document in the chapters that follow, but not nearly at the pace that local and global exigencies require (e.g., Moyer & Hedden, 2020).

So, the beating heart of *Going Global* is animated by a call to reform and refocus our educational, training, and professional systems so that our students might gain the necessary inclinations, competencies, and experiences to respond more effectively to the people and communities they serve. Right now, from survey data and anecdotal experience, they are both hopeful and fearful about what they are inheriting—with all its promise and peril—and are looking to us to help them find their way, and in so doing forge a more generative and responsive path for psychology and psychologists of the future (e.g., Smith, 2019; United Nations, 2020). It is in that spirit, toward those means and ends, that we offer this book.

The good news is, as observed at the outset of this chapter and throughout this volume, we are not alone in seeing or seeking the realization of a global future for psychology and psychologists (e.g., https://www.unpsychologyday.com/). In addition to the hundreds of psychologists and psychological initiatives and organizations that are cited in the pages that follow—in this book that is published by the APA—it seems especially fitting to describe how such matters are conceptualized and advanced by the one division of APA that is devoted exclusively to the internationalization of psychology and psychologists. Specifically, the mission of APA's Division of International Psychology (Division 52) states,

> Both at home and abroad, the Division of International Psychology (1) engages current and future psychologists who wish to think and act globally in their lives and work, (2) promotes ethically responsive and internationally informed education, training, research, practice, leadership, exchange, study, and service, and (3) fosters application of the essential knowledge, skills, and values of psychology to the most pressing issues of our day. (APA, Division of International Psychology, 2021, p. 1)

To operationalize this mission (i.e., to define and make it actionable), the Division also articulated a Vision Statement, provided in Exhibit 1. This statement is included for inspirational purposes—and for practical guidance—regarding why and how psychologists and psychology can meet a world of need.

As editors and authors of *Going Global*, we hope you will see, hear, and feel this mission and vision reverberating through the chapters that follow both in spirit and in letter via numerous real-world examples and practical guidance regarding how we can realize these aspirations. Our goal is to bring the world of psychology and psychologists to you via esteemed colleagues—pioneers on the frontiers of our field and profession—who are doing the work and showing the way across nine substantive areas of inquiry and practice: advocacy, assessment, consultation, intervention, leadership, policy, research, service, and teaching.

CONCLUDING BY BEGINNING: HOW WILL YOU MEET A WORLD OF NEED?

We began this chapter, and book, by asking a fundamental question: Where in the world is psychology? By now, it may be clear that although the need is great, the potential for us to meet that need is even greater. It's really up to all of us. Ultimately, it's really up to you. So, now that you have a sense of

---

EXHIBIT 1

Division 52 Vision Statement

Division 52 seeks to

1. become the primary or secondary professional "home" for current and future psychologists to engage in all things international;

2. encourage psychologists and students to direct their education, training, research, practice, leadership, exchange, study, and service activities and aspirations toward international emphases, populations, and needs;

3. openly explore and engage a globally inclusive and epistemologically diverse understanding of psychology as a discipline and profession, while (a) respectfully and credibly appraising established and emerging models, methods, and worldviews from the Global North, South, East, and West and (b) eschewing the reflexive and superficial embrace or rejection of any particular paradigm or approach, regardless of origin, culture, or context;

4. promote a globally inclusive and epistemologically diverse understanding of psychology within our affiliated organizations and systems as well as the programs, policies, and practices that we develop, implement, and review;

5. provide timely and relevant resources for personal and professional development that are aligned with our mission, vision, values, and strategic priorities;

6. create vibrant opportunities for collaboration and networking within psychology and with interdisciplinary colleagues and students around the world;

7. apply internationally informed psychological science and expertise to the global challenges we collectively face, exemplified by the Sustainable Development Goals of the United Nations; and

8. foster a culture of informed citizenry, ethical engagement, and social responsibility by the field and profession of psychology to address the global issues that affect us all.

Note. Reprinted from *Bylaws of the Division of International Psychology, American Psychological Association Division 52*, by American Psychological Association, Division of International Psychology, 2020 (http://div52.net/wp-content/uploads/2020/01/D52-Bylaws-final-Oct-2020.pdf). Copyright 2020 by the American Psychological Association.

"why" we must go global, the question is, How will you meet a world of need? We know that this question is daunting to ask, much less answer, which is why we conclude this chapter with the wisdom of Lao Tzu, who observed that "a journey of a thousand miles begins with a single step." We confirm this wisdom. From our experience, it feels right. The good news is, although the road is long, you are not alone. In fact, the best part of the journey is meeting new and old friends along the way. That is what we hope this book means to you. A chance to meet pioneers who have blazed paths to help you forge your own.

To start you on your way, this introductory chapter speaks to why we should go global—as psychologists and psychology—laying the groundwork for the journey to come. In our concluding chapter, we come full circle by offering personal insights and lessons learned from walking this walk in our own lives and work. It is our hope that these chapter bookends will give you hope, guidance, and inspiration as you navigate each of the nine paths before you.

So, as you prepare to go global, it might help to imagine you are standing at a crossroads, as we illustrate in Figure 1. Around you are nine life paths, pointing in different directions. Although we encourage you to walk them all, where do you want to start? You can always come back to the point you began, to take another road, but you won't be the same sojourner you were before you left. That's a good thing. It will help you to travel smarter, for sure, but also to appreciate the journey as much as the destination. You'll also discover, as we did and do, that these roads frequently connect and intersect, allowing you to veer off in any number of unanticipated directions. Sometimes that's great, as you discover amazing sites that weren't even on the map. Other times, you may hit a dead end, or two, or three. We sure have. But those won't stop you—not for long. With the help of your fellow travelers—all of us and so many more kindred spirits you'll meet over the years—you'll figure out where you made a wrong turn and set off again, a little older and a whole lot wiser.

Always remember, you are a psychologist. You possess indispensable knowledge, skills, values, and experiences. You are uniquely qualified to make sense of complexity because you have learned about, and examined, the nature of human nature through powerful models and proven methods that your

FIGURE 1. Nine Paths to Go Global

field invented. Through study, practice, and supervision, you have earned the right to wield them, ethically and humanely, with passion and purpose. Listen and learn from your interdisciplinary colleagues but contribute also as an equal member of any team. Be heard—with compassion, civility, conviction, and clarity. Your field of inquiry and practice started many years ago, in the late 1800s. It has been around a long time and has accomplished a great deal. It is thriving as one of the most popular areas of study in universities all over the world, for one fundamental reason: We cannot and will not solve the major challenges of our day without psychology and psychologists. So, with a proper balance between humility in the face of complexity and quiet pride in your intellectual and professional inheritance, take your rightful place at the table. As scholars and practitioners, as scientists and humanists, you explore and engage the deepest dimensions of the human heart and mind. You know what you need to do. You know why and how to do it. There is a world of need. The world needs you. It is time to go global.

REFERENCES

Adams, G., Dobles, I., Gómez, L., Kurtiş, T., & Molina, L. (2015). Decolonizing psychological science: Introduction to the special thematic section. *Journal of Social and Political Psychology, 3*(1), 213–238. https://doi.org/10.5964/jspp.v3i1.564

Alford, J., & Head, B. W. (2017). Wicked and less wicked problems: A typology and a contingency framework. *Policy and Society, 36*(3), 397–413. https://doi.org/10.1080/14494035.2017.1361634

Allwood, C. M. (2019). Future prospects for Indigenous psychologies. *Journal of Theoretical and Philosophical Psychology, 39*(2), 90–97. https://doi.org/10.1037/teo0000108

American Psychological Association. (2017). *Ethical principles of psychologists and code of conduct* (2002, Amended June 1, 2010, and January 1, 2017). https://www.apa.org/ethics/code/index.aspx

American Psychological Association. (2020). *Impact APA: American Psychological Association strategic plan.* https://www.apa.org/about/apa/strategic-plan

American Psychological Association, Division of International Psychology. (2020). *Bylaws of the Division of International Psychology, American Psychological Association Division 52* (Adopted 2018). http://div52.net/wp-content/uploads/2020/01/D52-Bylaws-final-Oct-2020.pdf

American Psychological Association, Division of International Psychology. (2021). *Bylaws of the Division of International Psychology, American Psychological Association Division 52* (Adopted 2018, revised July 2021). http://div52.net/wp-content/uploads/2021/08/BYLAWS-OF-THE-DIVISION-OF-INTERNATIONAL-PSYCHOLOGY-july2021.pdf

Blunt, D. G. (2020, July 31). Face mask rules: Do they really violate personal liberty? *The Conversation.* https://theconversation.com/face-mask-rules-do-they-really-violate-personal-liberty-143634

Coffman, J. E., Hopkins, C., & Ali, I. M. (2009). Education for sustainable development: Halfway through the decade of ESD and a long way from sustainability. *Beliefs and Values, 1*(2), 142–150. https://doi.org/10.1891/1942-0617.1.2.142

Dunn, D. (n.d.). "Psychology." In *Oxford bibliographies.* https://www.oxfordbibliographies.com/page/149

Evans, A. C. (2020). What does it mean to give psychology away? *Monitor on Psychology, 51*(8), 8. https://www.apa.org/monitor/2020/11/ceo

Glover, J., & Friedman, H. L. (2015). *Transcultural competence: Navigating cultural differences in the global community.* American Psychological Association. https://doi.org/10.1037/14596-000

Kumlien, A., & Coughlan, P. (2018, October 18). Wicked problems and how to solve them. *The Conversation.* https://theconversation.com/wicked-problems-and-how-to-solve-them-100047

Miller, G. A. (1969). Psychology as a means of promoting human welfare. *American Psychologist, 24,* 1063–1075. https://doi.org/10.1037/h0028988

Moyer, J. D., & Hedden, S. (2020). Are we on the right path to achieve the sustainable development goals? *World Development, 127,* Article 104749. https://doi.org/10.1016/j.worlddev.2019.104749

Okazaki, S., David, E. J. R., & Abelmann, N. (2008). Colonialism and psychology of culture. *Social and Personality Psychology Compass, 2*(1), 90–106. https://doi.org/10.1111/j.1751-9004.2007.00046.x

Segall, M. H., Dasen, P. R., Berry, J. W., & Poortinga, Y. H. (1990). *Human behavior in global perspective: An introduction to cross-cultural psychology.* Pergamon Press.

Smith, L. (2019, July). *Overcoming poverty of hope.* Barnardo's. https://www.barnardos.org.uk/sites/default/files/uploads/Barnardo%27s%20new%20report%20-%20Overcoming%20poverty%20of%20hope.pdf

Stevens, M. J., & Gielen, U. P. (Eds.). (2007). *Toward a global psychology: Theory, research, intervention, and pedagogy.* Lawrence Erlbaum Associates.

Stevens, M. J., & Wedding, D. (Eds.). (2004). *Handbook of international psychology.* Brunner-Routledge.

Sundarajan, L., Hwang, K.-K., & Yeh, K.-H. (Eds.). (2020). *Global psychology from Indigenous perspectives: Visions inspired by K. S. Yang.* Palgrave Macmillan.

United Nations. (n.d.). *The 17 goals.* https://sdgs.un.org/goals

United Nations. (2020, September 21). *One million people share hopes and fears for future with the UN.* https://news.un.org/en/story/2020/09/1072552

United Nations. (2022). *Make the SDGs a reality.* https://sdgs.un.org/

1

Advocacy

Global Opportunities and Responsibilities for Psychologists

Corann Okorodudu and Thema Bryant-Davis

Around the globe, certain pervasive social challenges have psychological dimensions, such as interpersonal violence, disease, disasters, lack of access to resources, armed conflicts, population displacement and migration, climate change, violations of human rights, and more. As scholars, educators, practitioners, and leaders, many psychologists across the world seek to address these and other challenges locally and internationally and to cultivate social change in the hopes of enhancing human life and well-being (Stevens & Gielen, 2007). As we are learning from such work, catalyzing effective social change requires engaging, assessing, and evaluating environmental contexts; preparing by acquiring relevant knowledge; and gaining necessary experience along the way, especially when working with people who have been marginalized, stigmatized, and disenfranchised. For psychologists and psychology, meeting a world of need is simply not possible without the inclusion of advocacy as a core area of emphasis. The focus of this chapter is to explore opportunities and responsibilities for the engagement of psychologists in global advocacy on a broad range of issues, in the belief that psychologists should embrace this area of competence as integral to their professional identity.

More specifically, our objectives in this chapter are to (a) define *advocacy* as it applies to psychology as a field of inquiry and practice in the international arena, (b) identify advocacy trends of global relevance to psychology, (c) discuss the ongoing debate about the place of advocacy in global psychology, (d) consider caveats about international advocacy, (e) describe the mechanisms of global

https://doi.org/10.1037/0000311-002
Going Global: How Psychologists Can Meet a World of Need, C. Shealy, M. Bullock, and S. Kapadia (Editors)

advocacy and various levels of action and organization through which global advocacy is undertaken, and (f) recommend practical steps and best practices for entering the world of global advocacy as psychologists. As we discuss, psychological advocacy within the global context covers a broad range of concerns and needs, including environmental degradation, climate change, systemic racism, organizational and societal governance, intergroup conflict and violence, health and mental health, decent work, and preparation for and recovery from disasters. Unfortunately, a sparse literature, combined with an insufficiently proactive stance by our accreditation, educational, and training systems, has had the net effect of underemphasizing all that we can and should do as psychology and psychologists to meet a world of need.

A DEFINITION OF GLOBAL PSYCHOLOGICAL ADVOCACY

At the outset, it may be helpful to contemplate the nature and scope of advocacy. In other words, what do we mean by this construct? At the most basic level, advocacy actions might include oral or written support for programs or policies to policy makers or the public, including encouragement and promotion of particular policy or program positions, or support for resource allocations that are intended to increase psychosocial well-being and promote social justice and human rights. The rationale for advocacy for resources may seem self-evident, as persons who are the focus of advocacy activities generally lack access to resources for a variety of reasons, including stigma, discrimination, poverty, distrust, geographical isolation, disaster, war, or a lack of knowledge. Such individuals include, but are not necessarily limited to, those typically characterized as "vulnerable," marginalized, or disempowered, including racial/ethnic minorities, children, older people, women, persons with disabilities, migrants, and sexual minorities (e.g., Action for Advocacy at https://www.actionforadvocacy.org.uk). To contextualize the discussion that follows, we offer a five-part definitional framework of advocacy for psychologists, followed by examples of psychological models that support this definitional framework.

As international advocates, psychologists (a) advance our discipline and profession through rigorous inquiry and thoughtful practice by (b) drawing deeply upon their knowledge, skills, experiences, and values to (c) promote empowerment, health, mental health, psychosocial well-being, and social transformation in a sensitive and informed manner across (d) multiple levels of analyses (e.g., individuals, families, groups, organizations, communities, societies) in (e) ethically grounded domains (e.g., conflict resolution, sustainability, global education, human rights, and religious and cultural understanding).

From the perspective of our definitional framework, international psychological advocacy is a process by which "citizen psychologists" (Henderson Daniel et al., 2021; Luis & Bruner, 2018) use their expertise and the expertise of others to work toward changes in global policies or programs, or changes in attitudes and behaviors, to promote social justice and social change. This process builds on the growing view that psychologists have an ethical and moral responsibility to address processes, circumstances, and events that impede the ability of human beings to achieve their full potential, thereby promoting the well-being of society and its members (International Union of Psychological Science, 2008; Kelman, 2010; Kiselica & Robinson, 2001). This view reflects the goals of several schools of thought and practice within the discipline of psychology. For example, it reflects the perspective of community psychology, which stresses the importance of research and social action, including advocacy, targeting inequities and oppressive conditions at various levels of society to bring about transformative change and empowerment in the broader community (e.g., Dalton et al., 2013). This perspective on international advocacy is also practiced explicitly in liberation psychology, which asserts that the purpose of psychology is to promote personal, community, and cultural transformation through liberation from oppressive structures and forces (Martin-Baron, 1994). Because international advocacy may require assessing impacts of conditions at multiple levels of the social environment, our definitional framework connects well with concepts and methodologies of an ecological systems model of human development (Bronfenbrenner, 1979).

ADVOCACY AND PSYCHOLOGY: GLOBAL AND HISTORICAL PERSPECTIVES

Psychologists have worked as advocates since the beginning of the discipline— as spokespersons for the mentally ill (Hooker, 1957), for children (Brooks-Gunn, 2004; Melton, 1985; Ramey, 1974; Zigler & Valentine, 1997), for women (Denmark, 1976; Payton, 1984; Raeburn et al., 2010; Tiefer, 1988), for families (Culp, 2013), for the aging (Antonucci et al., 2002; Smyer, 1989), and for human rights (Comas-Díaz et al., 1998; Lott & Bullock, 2001)—among other populations and areas of focus. Current global social justice research and advocacy by U.S. psychologists covers the broad scope of psychology's expertise, including international human rights concerns such as genocide, terrorism, intergroup conflict, racism, physical and mental health needs and disparities, violence against women and children, support for families, decent work, education, and climate change (Fisher, 1990; Landrine & Klonoff, 1996; Swim & Becker, 2012).

Moreover, psychologists in the United States and other countries have expanded the global relevance of psychology through their engagement in activities of international and intergovernmental agencies. Following World War II, the United Nations Educational, Scientific and Cultural Organization (UNESCO) encouraged international cooperation among psychologists and other social scientists who became involved with UNESCO because they believed that their scientific work could offer insights into how another atomic war could be prevented (Okorodudu et al., 2020). Between 1946 and 1960, Otto Klineberg, Gordon Allport, and other eminent U.S. psychologists felt the need to bridge psychological and social science research and United Nations (UN) policy making. They joined the International Tensions Project launched by UNESCO in 1946 and conducted psychological and social science research relevant to global conflicts, including national stereotyping, attitude change, and intergroup contact. After his term as president of the Society for the Psychological Study of Social Issues, 1942–1943, Klineberg served as director of the UNESCO International Tensions Project, 1948–1949, and later as director of UNESCO's Division of Applied Social Sciences, 1953–1955 (Cherry et al., 2011). Under his leadership during these years, the Tensions Project focused on the scientific conception of race and developed scientific facts to promote UNESCO's objective to combat racism and racial prejudice and to dispel stereotypic misconceptions among racial/ethnic groups in various countries (Klineberg, 1956).

Individual psychologists in the United States who contributed to building bridges between psychology and the UN include Roger W. Russell and Ed Hollander during the 1950s, Charles Osgood and Herbert Kelman in the 1960s, Henry P. David and Morton Deutsch in the 1970s, and Mark Rosenzweig and many others in the 1980s (Takooshian & Shahinian, 2008). Their legacy continues through psychology nongovernmental organizations (NGOs) working with UN intergovernmental organizations at UN headquarters in New York, Geneva, and Vienna, including the World Health Organization and the International Labor Organization, with government missions to the UN and with other NGOs affiliated with the UN. Examples of psychology NGOs that are carrying on the legacy of earlier U.S. psychologists by bringing the scholarship and practice of psychology to bear on the agenda of the UN include the American Psychological Association, Society for the Psychological Study of Social Issues, Psychology Coalition of NGOs having Consultative Status with the UN Economic and Social Council, International Council of Psychologists, International Association of Applied Psychology, International Union of Psychological Science, and the Society for Industrial-Organizational Psychology (Okorodudu et al., 2020).

In reflecting upon his career in psychology, Stuart Oskamp (2007) suggested that psychologists are uniquely qualified to address social concerns and policy issues because psychological processes impact all manner of human conduct and functioning. In addition, psychology has a significant literature base and diverse methodologies for examining and evaluating the effects of a variety of real-world problems and interventions. We suggest here the need for caution to be taken in psychological applications to non-Western cultural contexts. Since the origin of scientific psychology in 1879 in Leipzig, Germany (Wundt, 1873–1874), mainstream psychology has been a Western-dominated discipline (Bullock, 2013), supported by a research literature focused on finding universal principles of mind and behavior that is still 95% reflective of authors and samples drawn from the United States, Europe, or English-speaking countries (Arnett, 2008). However, as Bullock (2013) noted, in spite of the paucity of non-Western psychological research literature, the psychological literature outside North America and Europe is expanding with increasing attention to cultural context and Indigenous psychologies.

Yet psychology has not fulfilled the promise of its global relevance. For example, in his preface to *Toward a Global Psychology: Theory, Research, Intervention and Pedagogy*, edited by Stevens and Gielen, former president of the International Union of Psychological Science Kurt Pawlik (2007) noted that psychology has had less influence on international developments than the natural and social sciences. From our perspective, despite important activities by psychologists in advocacy arenas described in this chapter, this characterization remains largely true today and is a primary impetus for us to underscore the need for psychology and psychologists in the United States and globally to be engaged effectively in advocacy.

Debating the Place of Advocacy in Psychology

A degree of controversy regarding the place of advocacy has existed since the early development of psychology as a discipline. Some individuals have suggested that, as scientists, psychologists should ensure the highest degree of objectivity possible by maintaining a distance from any political concerns, fearing that taking a stand on social and political issues would reduce psychology's credibility both as a science and as a profession (Payton, 1984; Wright, 1992). For example, Elizabeth Loftus (1986) noted the pragmatic and ethical issues that become apparent when psychologists serve as advocates rather than impartial educators. Likewise, Sandra Scarr, a prominent developmental psychology researcher, held the view that "advocacy, even for the perceived public interest, is an uncomfortable companion to science, because it may pit social change against research findings" (Massey & Barreras, 2013, p. 618). Others have suggested that advocacy be limited to narrowly focused activities. For example, Craig Ramey (1974), a developmental psychologist whose work on early educational interventions and developmental outcomes has strongly influenced policies on children, suggested that psychologists should limit their professional comments only to those topics for which they have specific scientific expertise and for which there is a significant body of research.

In counterpoint, other psychologists have questioned the idea that science is or even can be apolitical and have argued that value-laden presuppositions underlie claims of scientific objectivity (e.g., Deacon, 2013; Fine & Barreras, 2001; Guthrie, 1998; Lewin, 1947; Martin-Baron, 1994). Some policy-minded psychologists have taken the position that psychology would not survive as a science if psychologists ignored the social implications of their work (Keita, 2001). Others, especially those whose research is oriented toward social justice issues, increasingly consider it their professional responsibility to show how findings from psychological and social science research can promote changes in policies and practices as well as changes in attitudes, beliefs, and behaviors (Goodman et al., 2004; Toporek et al., 2006).

In current discussions of the role and responsibilities of psychologists, an important consideration is the extent to which it is possible to separate our roles as citizens (whose primary goal is to maximize the implementation of their values in society) and scientists (whose primary goal is to observe and describe phenomena correctly and carefully) from advocates (who aim for societal transformation toward fulfillment of social justice, human rights, and other advocacy-based objectives). Although these roles are functionally different, we take the position that they are all values-based.

That said, it is important to be aware that psychology has been used to support both socially progressive and discriminatory policies. For example, psychological research on individual differences has been used to suggest that some groups are neurologically, intellectually, or morally inferior, including women, racial/ethnic minorities, sexual minorities, the disabled, and the mentally ill in the United States and the global community. Such uses have had grave consequences: support for eugenics movements, genetic discrimination, the construction of homosexuality as a mental disorder, and racial apartheid and discrimination, among other infamous manifestations (Jensen, 1969; Mallinckrodt et al., 2014; Rembis, 2004). In such instances, psychologists who claim to be functioning out of "scientific" or "professional" roles with the avowed neutrality of such positions have perpetrated damaging and discredited positions, which underscores the earlier point that there is no such thing as values-free conduct as psychologists (Shealy, 2016).

On the other hand, it also is important to remember the many examples where psychological research has been pivotal in advocating for democratic social change to advance social justice and well-being. One example of this work in the United States is Kenneth Bancroft Clark and Mamie Phipps Clark's 1940s "brown versus white" dolls experimental research on the psychological effects of segregation on African American children. The results of this research, which demonstrated children's prejudicial favoritism toward "whiteness," were pivotal in establishing the negative consequences of separate and unequal education cited in the 1954 Supreme Court decision in *Brown v. Board of Education* of Topeka, Kansas, which declared that the segregation of U.S. public schools was unconstitutional (Clark & Clark, 1940).

Analogous international advocacy work supportive of positive social change exists in other countries and cultures as well. For instance, Ajit Mohanty's seminal research on multilingual education was designed to highlight that dominant-language-only education for minority language students was not effective. His research in the tribal regions of India demonstrated the importance of using a child's home language ("mother tongue") as the language of early literacy and school learning and its positive impact on literacy and learning. This research evidence and sustained advocacy encouraged some Indian states to introduce structured programs of mother tongue–based multilingual education for tribal children (Mohanty & Skutnabb-Kangas, 2013).

Psychologists also have advocated for systemic change in how we conceptualize and intervene on issues that are of global relevance. To illustrate, psychologists have studied the impact and potential interventions for children and families living in the aftermath of war, conflict, displacement, and political transitions (Wessells, 1997). Based on his work in Africa, Wessells has described the need for psychologists to conduct and use research on the psychological consequences faced by war-exposed children to advocate for the United States to ratify the UN Convention on the Rights of the Child.

As another example of psychological advocacy of global relevance, in the 1980s the American Psychological Association (APA) Committee on International Relations in Psychology collaborated with the American Association for the Advancement of Science in advocating against apartheid in South Africa. The APA's Resolution on Apartheid supported efforts of institutions to divest their holdings from companies involved in business ventures in South Africa, advocated with the U.S. government to impose meaningful sanctions against the White minority government of South Africa, and urged U.S. psychologists to refrain from collaborating in projects sponsored by the South African government (APA, 1985). A further example of APA's successful international advocacy efforts involved a team of psychologists that includes the two authors of this chapter. The team utilized research on the psychological motives, effects, and solutions to racism and intolerance to first advocate for a resolution against racism for the APA (2001). After this research-based resolution was approved by the APA Board of Directors, the team used this document to collaborate with a Mental Health Caucus in advocating for the inclusion of mental health and psychosocial well-being in the outcome document of the 2001 UN World Conference Against Racism, Racial Discrimination, Xenophobia, and Related Intolerance in Durban, South Africa (APA, 2004).

During the intergovernmental negotiations (2013–2015) on the 2030 UN Agenda on Sustainable Development, the Psychology Coalition of NGOs having consultative status with the UN Economic and Social Council under the leadership of its president, Dr. Judy Kuriansky, launched a campaign to advocate for the inclusion of mental health and well-being into the Sustainable Development Goals (SDGs). Headed by Ambassador Otto of the Mission of Palau at UN Headquarters in New York City, the campaign engaged more than 80 missions in consultations as "Friends of Mental Health." These consultations succeeded in getting UN Member States to add "well-being" to the title of Sustainable Development Goal 3: "Ensure healthy lives and promote well-being for all at all ages" and contributed language for Target 3.4: "Promote mental health and well-being" (Okorodudu et al., 2020; UN, 2015).

CAVEATS ABOUT INTERNATIONAL ADVOCACY

The differences between local and global advocacy extend far beyond geography. Advocacy in international contexts requires layers of knowledge, cultural sensitivity, and collaboration in addition to what might be required of national or local advocacy. Why is that the case? Consider the following six specific reasons.

Understanding Etiology

First, to engage in advocacy-based activities globally, it is important to understand the cultural and historical factors that are etiologically relevant to the issue at hand (e.g., the factors that caused and perpetuate particular actions, policies, and/or practices). In most cases, global advocates must not only become familiar with this information but also learn from the experiences of individuals "on the ground" who are targets of, or participants in, advocacy efforts. For psychologists, such work may require altering an accustomed role as expert or cultural spokesperson. Wessells and Dawes (2007) cautioned that without clear knowledge of social, political, and historical alliances, U.S. international psychological advocates can unwittingly be perceived as supporting political, social, or cultural agendas or can be used to dominate vulnerable populations, in violation of the "Do No Harm" ethical principle of psychologists (APA, 2017a).

Appraising Scholarship

Along similar lines, when basing advocacy messages on psychological research, it is important to remember that most research in the published psychological literature has been conducted with U.S. or European populations (an overall minority of the world's population). Thus, it may not be clear how broadly such research generalizes to other cultures or contexts (e.g., Arnett, 2008; see also Chapter 7, this volume). Therefore, policy and practice recommendations based on the published psychological literature need to be developed with the active participation of local experts including Indigenous partners and local community members to ensure cultural relevance.

Appreciating Context

Advocacy always takes place within political, sociocultural, and economic contexts. Such contexts include the form of regional or national government, the kinds of intergroup struggles for political power and inclusion, power and resource struggles within communities and institutions, and the impact of policies and practices that promote or deny equity or access to resources. International psychological advocates need to be sensitive to and reflective about the potential impact of political, sociocultural, and economic concerns within communities where they work as well as the effects of their own cultural, economic, and political vantage points when advocating for others (APA, 2017b; Melton, 1985).

Assuring Transparency

International psychological advocates need to be as transparent as possible about their motives as well as the potential methodological and cultural limitations of research used as the basis of policy and advocacy recommendations. In advocating for specific actions, policies, practices, and programs, psychologists may wish to develop or cite cost analyses and outcome studies, including studies of the desirability and feasibility of various initiatives as well as the purported significance of anticipated outcomes (Massey & Barreras, 2013).

Adopting a Systems Perspective

Psychologists also need to understand the systemic implications of advocated actions, policies, or practices (e.g., how they may be experienced or how their anticipated outcomes will fit within the global or local society). In this regard, we believe that international psychological advocacy is well served by an ecological systems perspective, such as that proposed by Urie Bronfenbrenner (1979). According to the ecological systems model, behavior occurs within a nexus of interacting frameworks ranging from individual to societal levels. The American Counseling Association has developed social justice advocacy competencies on various levels of intervention within an ecologically embedded framework (see Bradley et al., 2012).

Embracing Interdisciplinarity

Sixth and finally, the complexity of global problems and the need for social transformation cannot be addressed by psychology alone. Effective international psychological advocacy requires openness and effectiveness in multidisciplinary partnership, collaboration, and the incorporation of local Indigenous partners (including community organizations) in decision making about policy and program approaches to development (e.g., Arredondo et al., 2004). Integrating scholarly knowledge with that of the community can enable a coconstruction of knowledge, which in turn may enhance the ecological validity of advocacy recommendations (Lerner et al., 2000).

INITIATING GLOBAL SOCIAL ADVOCACY

The mechanisms and processes by which psychologists engage in global social advocacy begin with identifying the targets of advocacy, including (a) the public (e.g., specific communities, groups, or populations); (b) international organizations of psychology and other disciplines or professions; (c) policy makers and decision makers such as intergovernmental organizations like the UN, regional organizations like the African Union, the Organization of American States, the European Union, or the South Asian Association for Regional Cooperation, and national governments; and (d) administrators and staff of local, national, or regional institutions or organizations. Psychologists also need to select the most relevant and effective communication modalities for global advocacy, depending on the target(s) identified. These modes might include advocacy statements; opinion editorials (op-ed pieces); articles in news media; letters via post, email, or fax; press releases; formal or informal talks;

briefings or educational reports with recommendations; educational programs; personal written communication or communication via social media; or meetings with key policy makers or policy institutions.

As initiators of advocacy, psychologists may engage in international advocacy in a number of roles, including representing professional organizations, NGOs, and civil society organizations, or as a member of grass roots movements concerned with particular social issues. Whatever the forum, we recommend that psychologists advocating with an organization recognize that the organization may have more than one level of accountability (i.e., individual advocates may need to ensure that stated or written positions are in fact congruent with and/or approved by the organization). As private citizens, psychologists may experience issues that are personally significant, compelling them to become active in advocacy with issues-based grass roots organizations. Although an individual's psychological background may inform and even enhance participation, these endeavors are likely to be quite different from international advocacy by a professional psychologist who centralizes psychological science and psychological benefits as the mobilizing focus. Therefore, we recommend that within a particular international advocacy project, psychologists who choose to be engaged strive to do so as professionals or as private citizens but not as both, even as we also recognize that in some circumstances such dichotomies may not be possible or even advisable.

Depending on the issues at hand, the initiation of global advocacy may take place domestically or internationally. However, regardless of its location, global advocacy requires a broad understanding of how issues cross national borders and are placed within an international context, such as the normative framework of UN resolutions, conventions, and human rights and humanitarian standards, or other international guidelines, treaties, or agreements. International advocacy requires thinking globally, even if acting locally, and is most effectively implemented in collaborations that cross borders and disciplines (Marsella, 2007). Informed by these overarching guidelines, global social advocacy may be initiated through national and international psychology organizations in consultative relationship with the intergovernmental organizations of the UN (Okorodudu et al., 2020), psychology coalitions and networks, other psychology organizations, and international organizations outside of the discipline of psychology.

ENTERING THE WORLD OF GLOBAL ADVOCACY

In this last section, we offer a five-point working blueprint for how psychologists may enter the world of global advocacy (Jimerson, 2012; Studwell, 2007).

Become Cognizant of Your Own Interests

Our first and most basic recommendation is to pay deep attention to your own reactions to the many local and global issues we collectively face. You undoubtedly will encounter "issues" that activate you intellectually, emotionally, ethically, and morally. To understand the sorts of issues that we believe may benefit from our particular areas of expertise, we offer the following broad categories for consideration along with some examples of each:

1. Human rights—for example, gender equity/empowerment of girls and women, human trafficking; the elimination of racial/ethnic discrimination; international migration/internal displacement

2. Criminal justice—for example, rehabilitation versus punishment, alternatives to incarceration, death sentencing, racial or economic disparities

3. Health and well-being—for example, disease prevention, disaster mitigation, trauma care/psychosocial recovery, access to physical and mental health care, the promotion of individual and community well-being

4. Education—for example, universal/global access to quality primary, secondary, and tertiary education; human rights and social justice education

5. Sustainability—for example, democratic governance, environmental justice, climate change

6. Conflict resolution—for example, peacemaking, peacebuilding, conflict prevention

7. Economic justice—for example, poverty eradication, income inequality, promotion of a living wage, entrepreneurial education/training

8. Religious and cultural understanding—for example, enhanced intergroup dialogue, promotion of religious and cultural tolerance, creation of effective partnerships

As Figure 1.1 illustrates, these eight broad categories of issues intersect well with the current UN 2030 Agenda of SDGs negotiated by UN Member States 6 years ago (UN, 2015). The SDGs are now the international focal point of projects and campaigns advocating for the implementation of the 17 goals.

Become Informed

Few graduate psychology programs offer training in advocacy as a specific track or focus. Lating et al. (2009) reported that less than 15% of programs offer advocacy training, with even lower rates for postdoctoral or internship positions. Most graduate programs that focus on advocacy are interdisciplinary master's programs, emphasizing areas such as global health, international development, or specialized areas such as peace studies or early childhood. This situation may change with increasing interest in the internationalization of the U.S. psychology curriculum (Leong et al., 2012; Marsella, 2007) and with the growth of professional psychology training programs that see continuing education and training on advocacy as an essential component of professional development in psychology (Burney et al., 2009). From our perspective, given

FIGURE 1.1. Sustainable Development Goals (SDGs)

student interests and evident need in the larger world, advocacy can and must become a more central component of our education and training programs, from secondary and undergraduate to master's and doctoral levels.

Psychologists may also seek formal or informal mentors and attend training and advocacy events at their graduate institutions or offered by civil society organizations at the state, regional, national, or international level. They may gain insights into the attributes of effective international advocacy by reviewing the careers of recipients of the APA International Humanitarian Award (APA, 2021) and similar awards by other psychology or professional associations. For example, Michael Wessells (Columbia University), APA International Humanitarian Award Recipient in 2008, has been an advocate for children and families in Africa, Asia, Central America, Europe, and South America, where he has applied his research to humanitarian services. Chris Stout (Center for Global Initiatives), recipient of the award in 2009, has been effective in integrating psychological principles into policy development, publishing the international work of the "new humanitarians" (Stout, 2006), and collaborating with other international advocates and service providers to address public health issues around the world (see Chapter 8, this volume, for more information). As a final exemplar, M. Brinton Lykes (Boston College), recipient of the award in 2013, has been a leader in participatory action research, combining research and advocacy to address the effects of state-sponsored violence on individuals and communities in Guatemala, Northern Ireland, and South Africa (Lykes, 2013).

As these pioneers demonstrate, psychologists aspiring to become engaged in international advocacy need to develop expertise about an international advocacy arena, map the major players and priority issues, and become familiar with international organizations and local NGOs engaged with these issues in specific countries of interest. Oftentimes, such information may be obtained through online research and through news media. Basic web-based searches also reveal myriad sites that link NGO employers with prospective employees, such as DevNetJobs Network (http://www.devnetjobs.org/) and the UN (https://www.un.org). Whatever the source, psychologists must develop mastery of the relevant body of psychological and related interdisciplinary research in their focus area(s), examining the gaps in and limitations of the literature and considering the policy implications of various findings for the public and for decision makers (Cohen et al., 2012).

In addition to knowledge of how the discipline of psychology can inform global advocacy, international psychologists need to understand current events—nationally, regionally, and globally—especially the history; political systems; and leaders of the country, region, or context in which they aspire to advocate. They also require an understanding of culture, cultural variations, cultural change, and how these factors shape social, political, and economic realities and human responses to them. According to the APA (2017b) *Multicultural Guidelines*, it is important for psychologists to recognize and understand the nuances and intersectionalities that exist in human interactions in sociohistorical and cultural contexts and shape our professional assumptions and practices. Therefore, it is important to analyze, understand, and frame psychological issues of a society or a community within a dynamic cultural systems framework and to propose solutions that are culturally congruent. For example, advocacy may include the promotion of gender equality and the elimination of gendered racism through a multicultural lens (e.g., analyzing expectations, roles, and rights of women and girls as well as men and boys of various socio-economic, racial/ethnic, and religious groups).

Practice Engagement

Psychologists involved in international advocacy should show that they have a passion for and sustained interest in global/international issues (Jennings, 1996). This interest might be demonstrated in their research, teaching, travel, humanitarian service, social policy experience, or projects in which they have applied psychological or social science theory, research, or practice to human issues or problems at the local, regional, or international level. Perseverance illustrates a commitment to advocacy in spite of inevitable challenges and obstacles. To cultivate such passion in an informed manner, we recommend immersion in seminal documents and materials, including the Universal Declaration of Human Rights (UN, 1948) and international human rights conventions (http://www.ohchr.org), the *Ethical Principles of Psychologists and Code of Conduct* of the American Psychological Association (APA, 2017a), and the Universal Declaration of Ethical Principles for Psychologists adopted in July 2008 by the International Union of Psychological Science, also adopted the same year by the International Association of Applied Psychology.

At any point in one's career, from student to advanced professional, those who have a passion for being international change agents can start "where they are." Beginning in familiar territory is useful for one to learn the advocacy "process," and this start can instill the confidence to reach out beyond borders. There are several ways to prepare for advocacy. For example, find opportunities to discuss the policy implications of research in course work, seminars, or professional conferences (see Chapters 6 and 7, this volume, for more information on policy and research); write letters to policy makers, outlining a local or global issue and proposing psychosocial solutions derived from psychological or biosocial science research; write commentaries or blogs to share policy implications of existing research on international advocacy issues, thereby building a network of psychologists with similar interests; join and become active in relevant APA divisions and/or other organizations that are pursuing advocacy; and contribute to leadership and communication about global issues (e.g., through professional newsletters; see Chapter 5, this volume, for more information on leadership).

At any career stage, aspiring global psychology advocates may have to start as volunteers with local or international civil society organizations or inter-governmental organizations. Accordingly, they might need to look for organizations that have volunteer positions advertised, or they might propose a volunteer position and educate the organizations with profiles of service that interest them about the ways in which they could assist the organizations to fulfill their missions. They also may want to look for full-time employment with organizations or find employment in the country of interest with an agency, that will allow time for them to volunteer as an advocate with an NGO. Many organizations engaged in global advocacy have project and staffing needs, ranging from volunteer to paid work. Our suggestion is: Do the research and reach out to organizations that match your personal and professional advocacy interests.

Cultivate Self-Awareness

It is crucial for psychological advocates in international contexts to cultivate a deep awareness of self (e.g., why you are motivated to engage in international advocacy). In many cases, our motives may have to do with wanting to play a constructive role in relieving human suffering, addressing injustice, and trying to make the world a better place. These commitments are at the very heart of who we are as a "helping profession," and psychologists need to celebrate and promote such values in themselves, others, and the larger world. At the same time, as psychologists we need to appreciate that our own histories can interact with our motives in such a way that we burn out by trying to only fix things "out there," when we also need to understand and take care of what is happening in or around ourselves. These concerns are not mutually exclusive but are often inextricably linked.

Cultivate Competence

With awareness that such competencies are earned over the course of one's professional life, it may be helpful to specify several that seem integral to the long-term effectiveness of the global psychology advocate. One critical attribute in working with diverse others is a collaborative rather than an authoritarian style, conversational skills that include listening and turn-taking, conflict management skills, and patience with the relatively slow pace of progress on international social issues. Similarly, effective international advocates build and maintain discipline-based and interdisciplinary collaborative relationships and networks, including but extending beyond psychology organizations. Networks may include local experts and Indigenous partners in decision-making about policy and advocacy approaches and connections with NGOs of similar advocacy goals or geographical focus. One person or one organization is likely to have minimal impact from an advocacy standpoint, especially within an international context. Thus, it is helpful for international advocates and advocacy organizations, especially those working on common issues, to work together to create an advocacy block that increases their potential influence. Equally important, collaborative relationships should include partnership with members of the community who are the potential beneficiaries of psychologists' policy or advocacy objectives. By dint of all that we do as international advocates—and the complexity of the issues at hand—it is inevitable that we will be working alongside individuals who come from different disciplinary traditions and backgrounds. Learning how to learn from, and contribute to, such diverse perspectives in a respectful and open manner is key to our success as advocates over the short term and long term (Arredondo et al., 2004).

Being a skillful communicator, able to communicate psychological science clearly, succinctly, and without jargon in written and oral form (e.g., Cohen et al., 2012), is another core competence for international advocacy. To increase oral communication skills, aspiring global psychology advocates may volunteer to provide talks on their developing areas of international advocacy expertise to diverse audiences. Greater engagement typically leads to greater skill. Such skill acquisition matters because persons in position to make policy decisions have limited time and typically limited knowledge of psychological science. Thus, psychologists must be able to communicate the main points of their advocacy including definitions, solutions, and the potential impact of the specific actions that are recommended. When this information is to be communicated orally, it is important for psychologists to be engaging and assertive but respectful when advocating with organizational staff (e.g., international agency, government, or civil society) regarding the usefulness of psychosocial and other behavioral strategies for dealing effectively with a particular issue.

As a final area of competence, being an international advocate requires high energy and expertise as well as some time spent overseas. As such, it is important for psychological advocates to take care of their emotional and physical well-being so that they can be best equipped to engage in this work effectively. They should remember that a part of self-care is safety, so it is important to research and develop a safety plan when engaging in advocacy in potentially dangerous locations, especially when addressing potentially high-conflict topics, such as human trafficking, sexual identity, children's rights, women's rights, reproductive rights, and climate change (e.g., Amnesty International, n.d.).

Develop a Plan

Recognizing the inevitability of modifications, it may be helpful to develop an "advocacy plan," with particulars drawn from personal experience and that of others (e.g., Cohen et al., 2012). This plan might include headings such as (a) Issue (e.g., what is the issue of emphasis and why is it important), (b) Background (e.g., from a scholarly and lay perspective, what essential literature or other facts/figures are available that speak to the actual work that psychologists might do in the area of focus), (c) Proposal (e.g., what specifically are you proposing you would like to do, where, with whom, for what purpose, and within what timeline), and (d) Outcomes (e.g., how will you and your collaborators know that the impact of the plan has been successful). From our perspective, the benefit of developing an *advocacy plan* is to sharpen your own thinking, at the level of not only "what is out there" in terms of informative literature but also what you wish to pursue. Such an exercise may also be useful in the context of a formal class on advocacy and/or as preparation for your own outreach to a specific organization of interest.

In developing and discussing an advocacy plan, it is important to be clear and succinct. Use an engaging interactional style, describing psychological science plainly in oral and written communication. Have someone you respect review and edit what you develop. The crux of what you have to say should fit on two or three pages with a clear takeaway message about the issue or problem that needs to be addressed and specific evidenced-based solutions. If you share your plan (e.g., with an organizational leader or staff member of a policy maker), consider what is important to the person with whom you are meeting and how that might interface with your issue. Share your advocacy plan with your contact before you meet so that you may have a more focused discussion at the meeting. Busy people are not likely to give you a lot of time, so make the most of the meeting. Remember that successful advocacy is built on relationships characterized by reciprocal understanding and assistance. Unless the situation feels unstable or untenable, if you are offered the opportunity to collaborate, find a way to say "yes." If you promise something, deliver it, remaining open to feedback and suggestions throughout the process. Finally, psychologists effective in international advocacy evaluate their interventions to assess their efficacy. In this way, successful psychological advocates learn from project experiences by evaluating the effectiveness of their international policies or advocacy strategies and the processes by which they are developed.

CONCLUSION

Through advocacy, psychologists have the opportunity—and responsibility—to expand the influence of our expertise for the benefit of human welfare. Psychologists have used individual and organizational advocacy to promote social justice and human rights, provide for humanitarian aid, and work for the betterment of society. Psychological advocacy has multiple content areas, methods, and outlets. Through education and training, psychological organizations, other NGOs, and intergovernmental organizations, psychologists can effect positive change to preserve human dignity. The ethics, values, and mission of our profession should compel each of us to reflect on the ways we can use our professional expertise to counter human suffering, promote sustainable development, and enhance quality of life and well-being.

Although many in other fields are working to address societal ills, effective solutions require an interdisciplinary approach that includes psychological interventions. Psychologists are needed to assist policy makers in understanding the causes and contributing factors associated with global problems, as well as how we may ameliorate or prevent them in the first place. In addition, there is an overarching need for ecologically valid research, assessment, and evidence-based solutions (Cohen et al., 2012) that illuminate not only what practices are needed but also how to best communicate them to persons in charge of making decisions, locally and globally. In the final analysis, then, as a discipline and profession, psychology may not be sufficient to address a world of need, but it most certainly is necessary. There is no other field that can contribute what we have to offer: an empirical, theoretical, and applied understanding of the reciprocal interaction between environmental conditions and our innate potential, which manifests in cognitions, affects, and behaviors that shape our interactions in our world, to one degree or another. In short, through the thoughtful integration of psychological science and advocacy, we psychologists can and must do our part to empower people and nations to engage productively in the enhancement of the human condition.

REFERENCES

American Psychological Association. (1985). *Resolution on apartheid.* APA Council of Representatives.

American Psychological Association. (2001, June). *Resolution against racism and in support of the goals of the 2001 UN World Conference Against Racism, Racial Discrimination, Xenophobia, and Related Intolerance.* https://www.apa.org/about/policy/racism.aspx

American Psychological Association. (2004). *Final report of the APA delegation to the UN World Conference Against Racism, Racial Discrimination, Xenophobia, and Related Intolerance.* https://www.apa.org/pi/oema/programs/racism/apa-delegation-report.pdf

American Psychological Association. (2017a). *Ethical principles of psychologists and code of conduct* (2002, Amended June 1, 2010, and January 1, 2017). https://www.apa.org/ethics/code/index.aspx

American Psychological Association. (2017b). *Multicultural guidelines: An ecological approach to context, identity, and intersectionality.* https://www.apa.org/about/policy/multicultural-guidelines.pdf

American Psychological Association. (2021, October). *APA International Humanitarian Award.* https://www.apa.org/about/awards/international-humanitarian

Amnesty International. (n.d.). *Safety during protest.* https://www.amnestyusa.org/pdfs/SafeyDuringProtest_F.pdf

Antonucci, T. C., Okorodudu, C., & Akiyama, H. (Eds.). (2002). Well-being of older adults on different continents. *Journal of Social Issues, 58,* 617–626.

Arnett, J. J. (2008). The neglected 95%: Why American psychology needs to become less American. *American Psychologist, 63*(7), 602–614. https://doi.org/10.1037/0003-066X.63.7.602

Arredondo, P., Shealy, C., Neale, M., & Winfrey, L. L. (2004). Consultation and inter-professional collaboration: Modeling for the future [Special series]. *Journal of Clinical Psychology, 60*(7), 787–800. https://doi.org/10.1002/jclp.20015

Bradley, J. M., Werth, J. L., Jr., & Hastings, S. L. (2012). Social justice advocacy in rural communities: Practical issues and implications. *The Counseling Psychologist, 40*(3), 363–384. https://doi.org/10.1177/0011000011415697

Bronfenbrenner, U. (1979). *The ecology of human development.* Harvard University Press.

Brooks-Gunn, J. (2004). Interventions and policies as change agents for young children. In P. L. Chase-Lansdale, K. Kiernan, & R. J. Friedman (Eds.), *Human development across lives and generations: Potential for change* (pp. 293–340). Cambridge University Press. https://doi.org/10.1017/9780511808302.012

Bullock, M. (2013). International psychology. In I. B. Weiner (Series Ed.) & D. K. Freedheim (Vol. Ed.), *Handbook of psychology: Vol. 1. History of psychology* (2nd ed., pp. 562–596). Wiley.

Burney, J., Celeste, B. L., Johnson, J., Klein, N. C., Nordal, K. C., & Portnoy, S. M. (2009). Mentoring professional psychologists: Programs for career development, advocacy, and diversity. *Professional Psychology, Research and Practice, 40*(3), 292–298. https://doi.org/10.1037/a0015029

Cherry, F., Ellingwood, H., & Castillo, G. (2011). "Cautious courage": SPSSI connections and reconnections at the UN. *Journal of Social Issues, 67*(1), 165–178. https://doi.org/10.1111/j.1540-4560.2010.01690.x

Clark, K. B., & Clark, M. K. (1940). Skin color as a factor in the racial identification of Negro preschool children. *The Journal of Social Psychology, 11*(1), 159–169. https://doi.org/10.1080/00224545.1940.9918741

Cohen, K. R., Lee, C. M., & McIlwraith, R. (2012). The psychology of advocacy and the advocacy of psychology. *Canadian Psychology, 53*(3), 151–158. https://doi.org/10.1037/a0027823

Comas-Díaz, L., Lykes, M. B., & Alarcón, R. D. (1998). Ethnic conflict and the psychology of liberation in Guatemala, Peru, and Puerto Rico. *American Psychologist, 53*(7), 778–792. https://doi.org/10.1037/0003-066X.53.7.778

Culp, A. M. (Ed.). (2013). *Child and family advocacy: Bridging the gaps between research, practice and policy issues in clinical psychology.* Springer Science & Business Media. https://doi.org/10.1007/978-1-4614-7456-2

Dalton, J., Hill, J., Thomas, E., & Kloos, B. (2013). Community psychology. In I. B. Weiner (Series Ed.) & D. K. Freedheim (Vol. Ed.), *Handbook of psychology: Vol. 1. History of psychology* (2nd ed., pp. 468–487). Wiley.

Deacon, B. J. (2013). The biomedical model of mental disorder: A critical analysis of its validity, utility, and effects on psychotherapy research. *Clinical Psychology Review, 33*(7), 846–861. https://doi.org/10.1016/j.cpr.2012.09.007

Denmark, F. L. (1976). *Who discriminates against women?* Sage Ethical.

Fine, M., & Barreras, R. (2001). To be of use. *Analyses of Social Issues and Public Policy, 1*(1), 175–182. https://doi.org/10.1111/1530-2415.00012

Fisher, R. (1990). *Teaching children to think.* Simon and Schuster Education.

Goodman, L. A., Liang, B., Helms, J. E., Latta, R. E., Sparks, E., & Weintraub, S. R. (2004). Training counseling psychologists as social justice agents: Feminist and multicultural principles in action. *The Counseling Psychologist, 32*(6), 793–836. https://doi.org/10.1177/0011000004268802

Guthrie, R. V. (1998). *Even the rat was white: An historical view of psychology* (2nd ed. rev.). Allyn & Bacon.

Henderson Daniel, J., Rozensky, R. H., Grus, C. L., Brown, K. S., Gómez, C. A., Bruner, L., Crawford, K. A., Hewitt, A., McQuaid, E. L., Mio, J. S., Montalvan, C., Reeb, R. N., Ruiz, A., Sheras, P., Siegel, W., Taylor, J. M., Williams, W., Ameen, E. J., & Andrade, J. (2021). The citizen psychologist curriculum—Preparing psychologists for public service: The 2018 APA Presidential Initiative. *Psychological Services, 18*(3), 328–334. https://doi.org/10.1037/ser0000402

Hooker, E. (1957). The adjustment of the male overt homosexual. *Journal of Projective Techniques, 21*(1), 18–31. https://doi.org/10.1080/08853126.1957.10380742

International Union of Psychological Science. (2008). *Universal declaration of ethical principles for psychologists.*

Jennings, T. E. (1996). The developmental dialectic of international human rights advocacy. *Political Psychology, 17*(1), 77–95. https://doi.org/10.2307/3791944

Jensen, A. (1969). How much can we boost IQ and scholastic achievement? *Harvard Educational Review, 39*(1), 1–123. https://doi.org/10.17763/haer.39.1.l3u15956627424k7

Jimerson, S. R. (2012, Fall). Triarchic conceptualization of advocacy: The confluence of science, practice, and policy. *The School Psychologist,* 4–9. https://doi.org/10.1037/e676222012-002

Keita, G. P. (2001). Carolyn Robertson Payton (1925–2001). *Feminism & Psychology, 28*(3).

Kelman, H. C. (2010). Interactive problem solving: Changing political culture in the pursuit of conflict resolution. *Peace and Conflict, 16*(4), 389–413. https://doi.org/10.1080/10781919.2010.518124

Kiselica, M. S., & Robinson, M. (2001). Bringing advocacy counseling to life: The history, issues, and human dramas of social justice work in counseling. *Journal of Counseling and Development, 79*(4), 387–397. https://doi.org/10.1002/j.1556-6676.2001.tb01985.x

Klineberg, O. (1956). The place of psychology in UNESCO's social science program. *Transactions of the New York Academy of Sciences, 18*(5), 456–461. https://doi.org/10.1111/j.2164-0947.1956.tb00468.x

Landrine, H., & Klonoff, E. A. (1996). The schedule of racist events: A measure of racial discrimination and a study of its negative physical and mental health consequences. *The Journal of Black Psychology, 22*(2), 144–168. https://doi.org/10.1177/00957984960222002

Lating, J. M., Barnett, J. E., & Horowitz, M. (2009). Increasing advocacy awareness within professional psychology training programs: The 2005 National Council of Schools and Programs of Professional Psychology Self-Study. *Training and Education in Professional Psychology, 3*(2), 106–110. https://doi.org/10.1037/a0013662

Leong, F., Pickren, W., Leach, M., & Marsella, A. (Eds.). (2012). *Internationalizing the psychology curriculum in the United States.* Springer. https://doi.org/10.1007/978-1-4614-0073-8

Lerner, R., Fisher, C. B., & Weinberg, R. A. (2000). Applying developmental science in the 21st century: International scholarship for our times. *International Journal of Behavioral Development, 24*(1), 24–29. https://doi.org/10.1080/016502500383430

Lewin, K. (1947). Group decision and social change. In T. M. Newcomb & E. L. Hartley (Eds.), *Readings in social psychology* (pp. 197–211). Holt.

Loftus, E. (1986). Experimental psychologist as advocate or impartial educator. *Law and Human Behavior, 10*(1-2), 63–78. https://doi.org/10.1007/BF01044558

Lott, B., & Bullock, H. E. (2001). Who are the poor? *Journal of Social Issues, 57*(2), 189–206. https://doi.org/10.1111/0022-4537.00208

Luis, A., & Bruner, A. (2018, September). Citizen psychologist initiative. *Psychology Teacher Network.* https://www.apa.org/ed/precollege/ptn/2018/09/citizen-psychologist-initiative

Lykes, M. B. (2013). Participatory and action research as a transformative praxis: Responding to humanitarian crises from the margins. *American Psychologist, 68*(8), 774–783. https://doi.org/10.1037/a0034360

Mallinckrodt, B., Miles, J. R., & Levy, J. J. (2014). The scientist-practitioner advocate model: Addressing contemporary training needs for social justice advocacy. *Training and Education in Professional Psychology, 8*(4), 303–311. https://doi.org/10.1037/tep0000045

Marsella, A. J. (2007). Education and training for a global psychology: Foundations, issues, and actions. In M. J. Stevens & U. P. Gielen (Eds.), *Toward a global psychology: Theory, research, intervention, and pedagogy* (pp. 333–361). Lawrence Erlbaum Associates.

Martin-Baron, I. (1994). *Writings for a liberation psychology.* Harvard University Press.

Massey, S. G., & Barreras, R. E. (Eds.). (2013). Impact validity as a framework for advocacy-based research [Special issue]. *Journal of Social Issues, 69*(4).

Melton, G. B. (1985). Training child clinicians as child advocates. In J. M. Tuma (Ed.), *Proceedings: Conference on training clinician child psychologists* (pp. 51–55). American Psychological Association.

Mohanty, A., & Skutnabb-Kangas, T. (2013). MLE as an economic equaliser in India and Nepal: Mother tongue based multilingual education fights poverty through capability development and identity support. In K. Henrard (Ed.), *The interrelation between the right to identity of minorities and their socio-economic participation* (pp. 157–187). Martinus Nijhoff. https://doi.org/10.1163/9789004244740_007

Okorodudu, C., Kuriansky, J., Walker, P. R., & Denmark, F. L. (2020). A historical narrative of psychology engaging human rights within the framework of the United Nations. In N. S. Rubin & R. I. Flores (Eds.), *The Cambridge handbook of psychology and human rights* (pp. 56–72). Cambridge University Press. https://doi.org/10.1017/9781108348607.005

Oskamp, S. (2007). Applying psychology to help save the world: Reflections on a career in psychology. *Analyses of Social Issues and Public Policy, 7*(1), 121–136. https://doi.org/10.1111/j.1530-2415.2007.00121.x

Pawlik, K. (2007). Preface. In M. J. Stevens & U. P. Gielen (Eds.), *Toward a global psychology: Theory, research, intervention, & pedagogy* (pp. xiii–xviii). Lawrence Erlbaum Associates.

Payton, C. R. (1984). Who must do the hard things? *American Psychologist, 39*(4), 391–397. https://doi.org/10.1037/0003-066X.39.4.391

Raeburn, C. A., Denmark, F. L., Reuder, M. E., & Austria, S. (Eds.). (2010). *A handbook for women mentors: Transcending barriers of stereotype, race and ethnicity.* Praeger.

Ramey, C. T. (1974). Children and public policy. A role for psychologists. *American Psychologist, 29*(1), 14–18. https://doi.org/10.1037/h0036055

Rembis, M. A. (2004). "I ain't been reading while on parole": Experts, mental tests, and eugenic commitment law in Illinois, 1890–1940. *History of Psychology, 7*(3), 225–247. https://doi.org/10.1037/1093-4510.7.3.225

Shealy, C. N. (2016). (Ed.). *Making sense of beliefs and values: Theory, research, and practice.* Springer.

Smyer, M. A. (1989). Nursing homes as a setting for psychology practice public policy perspectives. *American Psychologist, 44*(10), 1307–1314. https://doi.org/10.1037/0003-066X.44.10.1307

Stevens, M. J., & Gielen, U. P. (Eds.). (2007). *Toward a global psychology: Theory, research, intervention, & pedagogy.* Lawrence Erlbaum Associates.

Stout, C. E. (2006). *The new humanitarians: Inspirations, innovations, and blueprints for visionaries* (Vols. 1–3). Praeger.

Studwell, K. (2007). Influencing science policy through effective advocacy. *International Journal of Comparative Psychology, 20,* 1–4.

Swim, J., & Becker, J. C. (2012). Country contexts and individuals' climate change mitigating behaviors: A comparison of U.S. versus German individuals' efforts to reduce energy use. *Journal of Social Issues, 68*(3), 571–591. https://doi.org/10.1111/j.1540-4560.2012.01764.x

Takooshian, H., & Shahinian, S. (2008, October). Psychology at the United Nations: A brief history. *Psychology International.* https://www.apa.org/international/pi/2008/10/un

Tiefer, L. (1988). A feminist critique of the sexual dysfunction nomenclature. *Women & Therapy, 7*(2-3), 5–21. https://doi.org/10.1300/J015v07n02_02

Toporek, R. L., Gerstein, L. H., Fouad, N. A., Roysircar, G., & Israel, T. (Eds.). (2006). *Handbook for social justice in counseling psychology: Leadership, vision and action.* Sage Publishing.

United Nations. (1948). *Universal Declaration of Human Rights.* Office of the High Commissioner for Human Rights.

United Nations. (2001). *World Conference against racism, racial discrimination, xenophobia and related intolerance: Outcome document.*

United Nations. (2015). *Transforming our world: The 2030 agenda for sustainable development.*

Wessells, M. G. (1997). Armed conflict and children's rights. *American Psychologist, 52*(12), 1385–1386. https://doi.org/10.1037/0003-066X.52.12.1385

Wessells, M. G., & Dawes, A. (2007). Macro-social interventions: Psychology, social policy, and societal influence processes. In M. J. Stevens & U. P. Gielen (Eds.), *Toward a global psychology: Theory, research, intervention, & pedagogy* (pp. 267–298). Lawrence Erlbaum Associates.

Wright, R. H. (1992). The American Psychological Association and the rise of advocacy. *Professional Psychology, Research and Practice, 23*(6), 443–447. https://doi.org/10.1037/0735-7028.23.6.443

Wundt, W. (1873–1874). *Principles of physiological psychology.* Englemann.

Zigler, E., & Valentine, J. (1997). *Project Head Start: A legacy of the war on poverty.* National Head Start Association.

2

Assessment

The Power and Potential of Psychological Testing, Educational Measurement, and Program Evaluation Around the World

William E. Hanson, Jacqueline P. Leighton, Stewart I. Donaldson, Thomas Oakland,[1] Mark D. Terjesen, and Craig Shealy

As Ebbinghaus (1908) famously quipped, "Psychology has a long past but only a short history." The same is true of psychological assessment. It has a remarkably long past, dating back 4,000 years in China and Greece, yet a relatively short, formally documented history. Still, psychology's roots are grounded in assessment, constituting a core competency and day-to-day professional activity. Psychologists are leaders and experts in assessment, with specialized knowledge in research design; statistics; and, of course, psychological testing, measurement, and evaluation. Added to this leadership and expertise, psychologists also have specialized knowledge in diversity and multicultural issues as is documented throughout *Going Global* as well as advocacy (see Chapter 1, this volume), mental health and well-being (see Chapter 4), and many allied areas, which makes them major contributors on the worldwide assessment stage. Psychology, assessment, and research go hand in hand, fully informing—and perhaps even defining—psychologists' identities as scientist-practitioners. Thus, in meeting "a world of need," it is important to consider the full power and potential of assessment globally.

We were honored to write a chapter on assessment. We were also overwhelmed, as it is a daunting task. A typical Google Scholar or American Psychological Association (APA) PsycInfo database search yields literally hundreds of thousands of assessment hits. Moreover, there are hundreds of popular assessment books and scientific journals, including Geisinger's (2013) three-volume

---

[1]Tom Oakland was tragically killed during preparation of this chapter.

We thank Gauri Bhardwaj for helping reconcile references and in-text citations.

https://doi.org/10.1037/0000311-003

handbook series; APA's *Psychological Assessment*; and the *International Journal of Testing* (*IJT*), which is the journal of the International Test Commission (ITC; https://www.intestcom.org/). Today, thousands of tests circulate the globe, some clinically focused, some not. Alas, we faced many questions: Where do we start, given the field's lengthy history? What do we cover, given its broad, far-reaching size and scope? And in keeping with the book's focus on exemplary practice, what models do we highlight? We simply cannot cover it all in this relatively short chapter. So, after much deliberation, we took a bird's-eye view of assessment, a proverbial "lay of the land" perspective.

To begin, we discuss assessment broadly, focusing on its centrality to psychology and research. We also discuss contemporary national assessment practices considering the "big four" specialties: clinical, counseling, school, and industrial/organizational psychology (I/O; see also Chapter 3 on consultation and Chapter 5 on leadership). The first section discusses basic competencies, including what applied psychologists do in the United States. In subsequent sections, we discuss three important international assessment topics: psychological testing, educational measurement, and program evaluation. We also discuss cross-cultural issues in assessment, including test translation and adaptation. Throughout, we highlight challenges, opportunities, and cutting-edge exemplars, including Therapeutic Assessment (TA), formative educational testing and item development, and transformative program evaluation. To conclude, we offer practical suggestions for developing global assessment competencies and participating in the international assessment community.

ASSESSMENT-BASED RESEARCH AND PRACTICE

Assessment is a broad, overarching term and a multifaceted process. Arguably, it is the sine qua non of psychological research and practice. Without it, psychology's worldwide contributions to education, business, mental health, public policy, and other areas would be substantively diminished.

Although many people believe assessment, particularly testing, is a static, reductionist endeavor, this is not—or should not be—the case. Rather, at its best, assessment is a dynamic, excitingly rich process. Assessment reveals a great deal about people, cultures, decision making, and data processing, and it is inextricably linked to psychological research (Haynes et al., 2011). As parallel processes, assessment and research involve overlapping steps. This includes identifying problems, reviewing relevant literature and client or organizational histories, collecting and analyzing quantitative and qualitative data, measuring constructs of interest (i.e., the intended objective of the test), making reliable and valid inferences and attributions, and, in many cases, preparing formal evaluations and recommendations while answering questions that could not be answered without assessment.

Given psychologists' extensive research backgrounds and training in psychometrics, they are well qualified, highly capable, and professionally able to assess and evaluate, provided they know their limits; understand assessment theory, research, and practice; and appreciate how their beliefs and values affect their assessment models and methods, particularly across cultures. In fact, assessment and research/evaluation are core *functional competencies,* or necessary skills, of applied psychologists, and self-assessment/reflective practice and personal/ professional cultural awareness and sensitivity are core *foundational competencies,* or building blocks, of what psychologists actually do (e.g., Geisinger, 2013; Rodolfa et al., 2005). Psychologists should therefore nurture both types of competencies. In global contexts, psychologists should, for example, have the skills and wherewithal to select, administer, and interpret culturally appropriate, psychometrically sound tests and tools; provide meaningful test feedback; and use multiple data sources, while addressing basic and applied questions in an ecologically valid manner. Given that many tests are developed in Western society and adapted and modified for use globally (Muthukrishna et al., 2020), it is imperative that practitioners choose measures wisely and offer recommendations that reflect the psychometrics of the test while being culturally aware of the contexts in which recommendations are made. As described next, that is why competent psychologists understand why and how "equivalency of meaning" is a key practice and standard for the translation and usage of tests in different cultures and contexts.

Globally, assessment practices and contexts vary considerably, from mental health and psychoeducational assessments, for example, to asylum evaluations and assessments associated with migration and immigration to large-scale assessment of international programs. In almost all parts of the world, assessments are occurring. And although they occur in many specialty areas of psychology (e.g., health psychology, community psychology), this chapter focuses on the big four areas of applied psychology: clinical psychology, counseling psychology, school psychology, and I/O psychology.

Assessment Specialists: The Big Four and Beyond

Assessment competencies and skills are particularly important for clinical, counseling, school, and I/O psychologists, affectionately known as the big four. Clinical and counseling psychologists work mostly with adults, typically in applied settings (e.g., private practices, hospitals, community agencies). School psychologists work mostly with children, adolescents, and parents and teachers, typically in school settings. I/O psychologists work mostly with adults in business settings. Many psychologists work across specialty areas (Health Service Psychology Education Collaborative, 2013). They also work across settings and age groups, providing a variety of assessment services. In the mental health field, for example, clinical, counseling, and school psychologists use multiple assessment methods, including behavioral observations, interviews, group and individual testing, historical background data, and corroborative consultations with others. Haverkamp (2012, 2013) classified clinical, counseling, school, and I/O psychologists along two axes: the extent of client–clinician involvement/collaboration in testing (x axis) and the extent to which contextual data are considered in interpreting test results (y axis). As Figure 2.1 illustrates, psychologists vary across specialties.

Typically, mental health assessments describe current functioning, facilitate clinical hypothesis testing, assist in diagnosis and treatment planning, track/monitor client progress, manage risk and legal liability, and facilitate positive therapeutic change (Meyer et al., 2001). In non-mental-health capacities, I/O psychologists facilitate organizational and human resource decision making (e.g., employee selection, leadership development; see Table 2.1). Other specialty areas including, but not limited to, educational psychology, forensic psychology, and neuropsychology also engage in assessment research and practice. Examples include achievement testing, competency-to-stand-trial evaluations, and cognitive testing. To get a sense of the overall scope of psychological tests, readers are directed to the Buros Center for Testing (https://buros.org/), a prominent 90-year-old assessment and testing organization that classifies tests into 18 categories.

Assessment and psychological testing are not without criticism, especially early in their history. For example, in 1918 Yerkes ushered in intelligence testing en masse. The multiple-choice Army Alpha test determined "mental fitness" of literate World War I army draftees and, in turn, their prospective jobs (Gould, 1981). At the time, group-administered, multiple-choice standardized intelligence tests were new, efficient, and distinct from Binet's individualized testing of French children. From 1917 to 1940 in the United States, the ease and

FIGURE 2.1. Global Assessment Competencies and Practices

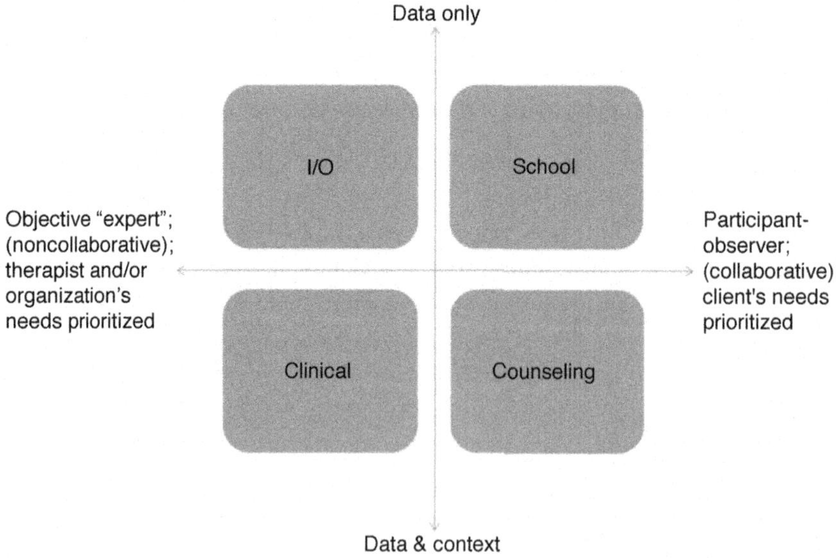

Note. Based on Haverkamp (2012, 2013).

TABLE 2.1. Common Psychological Tests Used Among Clinical, Counseling, School, and Industrial/Organizational Psychologists

Big 4 applied specialty areas	Psychological areas/constructs assessed	Commonly used tests
Clinical	Neuropsychological, Intellectual & Personality Functioning/ Psychopathology	WAIS-IV, WMS, MMPI-3, MCMI-IV, Rorschach Ink Blot Test, WRAT-4
Counseling	Intellectual & Personality Functioning, Career Interests, Strengths & Well Being, & Diversity Issues (e.g., ethnic identity)	WAIS-IV, MMPI-3, 16PF-5th ed., SII, SDS, Rokeach Values Survey, QoL
School	Intellectual, Academic Achievement, Social-Emotional Assessment, & Curriculum-Based Assessment	WISC-V, WIAT-III, BASC-3
Industrial/ Organizational	Job Analysis, Leadership, & Employee Selection & Development	Cognitive/Mental Ability Tests, KSAOs, LMX-7

Note. These tests are used in highly diverse settings, including child/school, psychiatric, community mental health centers, rehabilitation hospitals, university clinics, and forensic units. BASC-3 = Behavior Assessment Scale for Children–3; KSAO = knowledge, skills, abilities, and other; LMX-7 = Leader-Member Exchange-7 Questionnaire; MCMI-IV = Millon Clinical Multiaxial Inventory–IV; MMPI-3 = Minnesota Multiphasic Personality Inventory–3; QoL = Quality of Life measure; SDS = Self-Directed Search; SII = Strong Interest Inventory; 16PF-5th Ed. = 16 Personality Factors Inventory–5th Edition; WAIS-IV = Wechsler Adult Intelligence Scale–IV; WIAT-III = Wechsler Individual Achievement Test–III; WISC-V = Wechsler Intelligence Scale for Children–V; WMS = Wechsler Memory Scale; WRAT-4 = Wide Range Achievement Test-4.

speed of intelligence testing helped open the door, unfortunately, to a eugenics revival (Marshall & Robertson, 2019; Reddy, 2008). Although lessons were learned, such as the need to exercise sound and ethical test use, misuses should not be forgotten, especially as they relate to international testing practices. For example, in the late 1920s, dubious forms of "mental proficiency" testing were used in the Canadian provinces of British Columbia and Alberta to justify the sterilization of Indigenous women under the Sexual Sterilization Act (Province of Alberta, 1928). That such profound harm was perpetrated with the aid of psychological tests is a reminder that "scientific" tools can be abused to justify human rights violations.

Fortunately, testing has come a long way over the past century, evolving and advancing significantly, thanks mostly to advancements in human ethics and to psychologists' pioneering measurement concepts, such as *reliability* to quantify the consistency of test scores and *validity* to substantiate their interpretation, as well as improved norming and standardization procedures. That said, testing is not infallible; some amount of error always exists. The *Standards for Educational and Psychological Testing*, published simultaneously by the American Educational Research Association (AERA), the APA, and the National Council on Measurement in Education (NCME; 2014), is testament to present-day standards of test precision, rigor, and fairness, including validity evidence based on test/score content, response processes, internal structure, relations to other variables, and consequences.

INTERNATIONAL TEST USE AND DEVELOPMENT

Three factors affect test use internationally: (a) professional development, (b) presence of testing companies, and (c) a country's gross domestic product (GDP; Hu & Oakland, 1991). In a survey of 76 countries, Oakland et al. (2016) identified 606 tests used somewhat prominently in each country. These tests stood out and were used more than others. Intelligence tests (e.g., Wechsler scales, Ravens Progressive Matrices) and achievement tests were used most frequently, followed by measures of language, personality, neuropsychological qualities, school readiness, social-emotional, motor, and adaptive behavior. Although no group differences were found regarding intelligence testing, some countries (e.g., Argentina, Portugal, Latvia) used achievement, language, and motor skill tests more than other countries (e.g., Bulgaria, Cuba, Estonia). These same countries also used diagnostic, admissions, personal guidance, and career/vocational tests more. Finally, test use differed by age, with 6- to 12-year-olds tested most, followed by ages 12 to 18, 3 to 6, 19 and older, and finally 0 to 3.

In Oakland et al.'s (2016) survey, 11 professional groups were identified as using tests. Those who used tests most included, from high to low frequency, school and educational psychologists, clinical and counseling psychologists, general psychologists, school counselors, university researchers/professors, general education teachers, and special education teachers. Physicians, speech language therapists, nurses, and I/O psychologists rarely used tests in this sample. Professionals who have less academic training and experience were more likely to use outdated or obsolete tests. For example, some countries continue to use older versions of the Wechsler scales, some dating back to 1949, instead of the current version of the Wechsler Intelligence Scale for Children (WISC).

Recent survey results highlight several important international test use patterns. Going forward, it is important to consider variables that affect test use, and the role culture, language, politics, and economics play in the process. Much more research needs to be conducted and culturally appropriate practice guidelines developed. For example, training professionals to administer and interpret testing in a standardized manner may be more easily accessible to individuals in some countries than others. Furthermore, practitioners may find some tests do not take population characteristics or other cultural variables in their country into account, which may affect test norms, usage, and interpretation. Finally, the economic aspect of purchasing tests in countries with lower GDPs may preclude institutions and professionals from procuring updated versions of tests.

Importantly, since 1990, international test use has changed considerably, particularly regarding children, adolescents, and emerging adults. Several prominent programs and studies are underway currently, including the Program for International Student Assessment (PISA), Trends in International Mathematics and Science Study, and Progress in International Reading Literacy Study (see the TIMSS and PIRLS International Study Center at https://timss.bc.edu/). These programs rely heavily on testing, primarily to assess educational outcomes (Mateo et al., 2012; Pokropek et al., 2021; Rindermann, 2007). For practical reasons, such as the development, implementation, and refinement of policies, the evaluation and improvement of programs or systems, and the strategic allocation of resources, many countries need to know where their citizens are across multiple metrics. Consider the educational sector as one example. National educational attainment is associated with advances in science and technology and believed to make integration into the worldwide economy possible. Without assessment to appraise where the populace is at an educational level, from basic literacy to the mastery of sophisticated knowledge and skills, there is no way for a country to know where to go because it doesn't know where it is. This stark observation regarding education—just one of many societal sectors—illustrates the fundamental and ineluctable need to base policy and planning decisions on sound assessment data (e.g., Nishitani, 2020).

Many factors affect test development, including most prominently commercial marketing companies. For example, except for South Africa, companies that develop and market tests are uncommon in Sub-Saharan Africa. Test companies are also uncommon in the 22 Arab countries, a large region in which the testing industry is more or less absent. Most tests are developed in a few countries, including Canada, France, Germany, Italy, Mexico, Romania, Spain, and the United States (Oakland et al., 2013).

International Challenges, Opportunities, and Cutting-Edge Assessments

Many educational and psychological assessments have been adapted globally (Iliescu, 2017; Leong et al., 2016). To consider just a few examples, the WISC has been translated and adapted into multiple languages, with norms having been established for several countries, including France, Pakistan, Mexico, and Vietnam. A Spanish language version of the WISC also exists and has been adapted for international use. Similarly, many achievement batteries have been adapted and standardized globally. As an example, the Woodcock–Johnson Test of Achievement has been adapted and standardized for use in Australia and Brazil. Any adaptation and subsequent use of a measure needs to consider the varying degrees of cultural differences and linguistic variables that affect test performance. It is important, for example, for psychologists who administer these tests to determine whether differences in language or cultural background contribute to test performance difficulties over and above the presence of a true type of low-level outcome.

If tests developed in one country or culture are to be used in a different country and culture, important issues to consider include equivalency of meaning (e.g., constructs being assessed, item content) and underlying epistemologies (e.g., assessment and testing processes, interpretation of results). In their explication of a global psychology, Moghaddam and colleagues (2007) captured these concerns. In particular, outside the U.S. and Western contexts, "alternative psychologies" include countries seeking to "tackle questions left unaddressed by mainstream U.S. psychology" while generating "locally relevant knowledge rather than refashion imported knowledge" (Moghaddam et al., 2007, pp. 180–181). Even so, if basic principles of reliability and validity are followed, and cultural sensitivity and "equivalency of meaning" are maintained, there should not be regionally defined distinctions (i.e., this is a test "from the West"). From this perspective, a "good" assessment measure is just that, whatever its origins, because it adheres to best practices of development, validation, implementation, and adaptation.

On that point, it is important to understand that translation of an extant measure into another culture and context may be necessary but by no means sufficient. For example, the goal really is not translation but, as noted, equivalency through a process of adapting a measure into a form in which the underlying meaning processes are consistent across cultures and contexts. Resources and organizations such as the *Standards for Educational and Psychological Testing* (AERA, APA, & NCME, n.d.), the ITC, and the International Organization for Cooperation in Evaluation (IOCE; https://ioce.net/) provide key guidance in this regard. Additionally, two issues of the *IJT* (global norming: Bartram, 2008; advances in test adaptation research: Gregoire & Hambleton, 2009) further promote an understanding of how such rapprochement may be pursued conceptually, methodologically, and practically, demonstrating, for example, that there may be more within- than between-group differences around the world (e.g., Wandschneider et al., 2015). Next, we highlight a cutting-edge example of culturally appropriate assessment and testing: collaborative/therapeutic assessment.

Collaborative/Therapeutic Assessment: An Exemplary Approach to Psychological Testing

Regardless of the test used, developed, or adapted, careful attention should be paid to matters of usage.[2] In the mental health realm, for example, Poston and Hanson (2010) concluded that "assessment procedures—when combined with personalized, collaborative, and highly involving test feedback—have positive, clinically meaningful effects" (p. 1033). To that end, collaborative/therapeutic assessment (C/TA) represents a potentially beneficial and empowering paradigm shift in assessment internationally, from a traditional authoritarian, therapist-centric, information-gathering approach to a flexible, client-centered, therapeutic approach—one that is highly collaborative, empathic, and culturally sensitive (Finn et al., 2012). C/TA uses a collaborative, semistructured, theoretically based assessment approach in which psychological testing helps clients understand and overcome persistent problems in living (Finn et al., 2012). Specifically, C/TA helps clients develop more coherent, accurate, compassionate, and useful "stories" about themselves and the world. Client narratives

---

[2]Contributions to this section were made by Stephen E. Finn.

are changed through a collaborative process in which the client and assessment specialist are participant-observers. Because the core values of C/TA are collaboration, respect, humility, compassion, openness, and curiosity, C/TA is ideally suited to international contexts. Thus, C/TA can be transformative in nature, particularly at the individual level, which suggests it is a commendable and ecologically valid approach to assessment research and practice.

Perhaps not surprisingly, C/TA is practiced in many countries, including France, Italy, Sweden, the Netherlands, Japan, Finland, Argentina, and Mexico. To take any number of examples in this regard, professional deliberations among C/TA scholars and practitioners have included assessors' moderating their expression of positive emotion in Sweden, introducing Italian psychotherapists to the potential benefits of assessment consultation, speaking plainly and bluntly to clients in the Netherlands, and dealing with the highly abstract and philosophical ambience of psychology in France. Such adjustments are standard TA practice. Although TA typically uses a semistructured format, each assessment is tailored to the unique client and their context. Additional information, worldwide training opportunities, and international centers are described on the C/TA website (https://www.therapeuticassessment.com).

GLOBAL IMPACT OF EDUCATIONAL MEASUREMENT AND ASSESSMENT

Measurement is "at the heart of every science for, without measurement, meaningful research, both basic and applied, is impossible" (Haynes et al., 2011, p. xi). Psychologists and allied professionals across the globe create metrics for assessing student achievement within, as well as between, countries for comparison purposes. From South America to North America, Europe, Asia, and Australasia, psychometricians are employed by government ministries to evaluate learning outcomes in K–12 students and guide them into postsecondary institutions. For example, since 1988, students in Chile have been administered the *Sistema Nacional de Medición de la Calidad de la Educación* (SIMCE) assessment in certain grades (Meckes & Carrasco, 2010). The SIMCE is a government test designed to ensure that students learn the Chilean-designed curriculum in reading, math, and science, among other content areas. Further, since 2003, the *Prueba de Selección Universitaria* is used to guide Grade 12 students entering the country's universities (Mateo et al., 2012).

Testing is not only administered to K–12 students but also used to monitor and enhance student experiences at postsecondary institutions. For example, the European Higher Education Area, made up of 49 countries, is focused on attracting students by ensuring the compatibility of an integrated network of postsecondary institutions. In 1999, the Bologna Process was catalytic in the genesis of the European Higher Education Area to fulfill the goals of enhancing (a) the appeal of attending postsecondary institutions in Europe; (b) the educational experience, including improved mobility and employability, based on a system of accessible, understandable, and user-friendly undergraduate and postgraduate studies and degrees; and (c) the quality of their postsecondary education (Neave & Veiga, 2013). Likewise, the Aurora Network of European universities (https://alliance.aurora-network.global/) has adopted a multi-faceted Aurora Competence Framework, which relies on mixed-methods assessment to evaluate student learning processes and outcomes. This ambitious undertaking has many challenges, including assessing student outcomes or "qualification frameworks" and creating metrics to ensure the comparability of experiences at distinct institutions.

Although psychologists are often responsible for designing and administering tests to evaluate K–12 educational systems within countries, increasingly they also facilitate international tests to draw comparisons between countries. In these cases, international tests are not without controversy. For example, PISA provides country-by-country rankings of 15-year-old students. Large-scale tests such as PISA are controversial, in part, because there is debate about the nature of the schools that participate in the assessment and, thus, the sample of students compared across countries (e.g., such questions include whether participating students are from public or private schools and how much they represent the country's educational system).

The cost of administering any kind of large-scale test also receives significant scrutiny. In the United States and some other countries, large-scale test administrations cost less than 1% of total government expenditures for publicly funded projects (Clarke, 2012). However, the situation is different in other countries, where costs are significantly higher. In these countries, there is intense pressure to institute full-scale assessment systems into educational infrastructures. *Assessment systems* are "groups of policies, structures, practices, and tools for generating and using information on student learning" (Clarke, 2012, p. 1), and large-scale testing programs, including national and international assessments, are important system-related tools. Using cross-country growth regressions, consistent interdependence between acquisition of knowledge and skills and GDP growth has been demonstrated (Hanushek & Woessmann, 2012). "Benchmarking" a country's learning outcomes is vital to acquiring and maintaining a competitive edge in the global workforce. Along similar lines, Japan recently implemented a nationwide process of assessing the impact of international education in general and Collaborative Online International Learning or COIL in particular (e.g., the Institute for Innovative Global Education [https://www.kansai-u.ac.jp/Kokusai/IIGE/]).

Assessment systems also measure 21st-century skills. An example of this newfound focus is the Partnership for 21st Century Skills, sponsored by 32 organizations, including Apple Inc., Cisco Systems, Educational Testing Service, Microsoft Corporation, the U.S. National Education Association, and the Walt Disney Company. Such skills include foreign languages, creativity, and career and life skills, among others (e.g., Global Competency Standards for Students and Teachers). Binkley et al. (2010) outlined requirements for these assessments to be successful, such as aligning assessments with 21st-century knowledge and skills, transparency of constructs designed to capture them, use of performance-based items to enhance score validity, technical precision of score reliability, selection of appropriate measurement models, and assurance of fairness to diverse student groups.

Locally and globally, educational measurement faces many challenges and opportunities. One major challenge is properly capitalizing on technology advancements and digital environments to improve testing because traditional paper-and-pencil tests are becoming obsolete in many parts of the world. Another challenge is securing test items and testing environments from potential cheating as high-stakes assessment becomes digitized and more susceptible to hacking. A long-standing challenge with increased globalization is test translation from one language to another, normally from English to another language, and test equivalence (Leong et al., 2016). Although there are several challenges, there are also opportunities, such as cutting-edge assessments, including computer-based and adaptive testing (Mills et al., 2002; see also Gershon, 2005); cognitive diagnostic testing (Embretson, 2009); the assessment of international, multicultural, and transformative learning (Wandschneider et al., 2015); and serious games and stealth assessments (Mislevy, 2010; Shute & Ventura, 2013), which reflect new waves of assessment design for summative and formative purposes.

Formative Educational Testing Advancements Around the World

To thrive amidst the profound global and economic changes in the 21st century, countries require skilled workers who can think, reason, solve complex problems, adapt to novel situations, communicate, and collaborate.[3] Providing teachers and students with timely, detailed feedback is the norm, above and beyond a single final test score and performance evaluation. Thus, formative educational testing principles guide today's global assessment practices. Formative principles include any assessment-related activities—including administering tests more frequently—that provide process-altering feedback to teaching and other educational processes and, in turn, to improve desired outcomes.

With an increase in test usage comes requiring tests to be created more efficiently and economically, factors that are especially relevant in an international context. Fortunately, this requirement coincides with changes in educational technology, particularly computerized testing. Computerized testing supports and promotes formative assessment. For instance, computers permit on-demand testing, which allows students to take tests at any time and as often as they choose. Further, test items are scored instantaneously, thereby providing students with immediate feedback, and computers support the development of innovative item formats that allow educators to measure complex performances as well as a broader variety of knowledge and skills (van der Linden & Glas, 2010). The use of technology will provide greater access to testing for

---

[3]Contributions to this section were made by Mark J. Gierl.

students in remote settings and provides greater measurement precision. Of course, the drawbacks include access to device issues and the potential for the technology to unduly influence that format of the assessment.

Computerized testing can be expected to provide educators with local data as to student performance as well as to track and predict student performance over time and identify students who may warrant further intervention. As an example, computerized testing of reading performance at multiple points in kindergarten can be used to predict reading trajectories from first to fourth grade. In higher education, complementary research demonstrates that we can predict interest in, and satisfaction from, study abroad or multicultural education before a student has even taken his or her first class in university (Wandschneider et al., 2015). Despite these types of benefits, computerized testing can be challenging, particularly regarding large-scale item development (Downing & Haladyna, 2006) and automatic item generation (Gierl et al., 2021).

PROGRAM EVALUATION AND GLOBAL ASSESSMENT PRACTICE

Over the years, psychologists' expertise in assessment has been valued by scholars, practitioners, and leaders from a wide range of disciplines and professions outside of psychology. Program evaluation is one such area. Because psychologists design and evaluate social, educational, organizational, and community programs—which aspire to improve the human condition and make the world a better place—we can gather and analyze data to answer a wide range of questions, including the following: Was the program implemented well? Did the program achieve its goals? What works for whom, where, why, for what, and when (Gargani & Donaldson, 2011)? What was the overall impact of the program? Was the program cost effective? How can the program be improved?

Donaldson (2007, 2021) described common steps that evaluators go through to determine which questions to answer in a program evaluation: (a) determining the theory behind the program, (b) developing and prioritizing evaluation questions, and (c) designing evaluations to answer evaluation questions with credible and actionable evidence (Donaldson et al., 2015). More than 75 universities worldwide provide degrees and certificates in program evaluation, and more than 150 professional organizations provide evaluators with networking opportunities and professional development (LaVelle & Donaldson, 2021). A great deal of research shows that careers in program evaluation can be lucrative, fulfilling, and socially meaningful.

Psychologists evaluate programs in many countries and contexts. To consider just a few examples, applied social psychologists evaluate education, public health, drug abuse prevention, and a wide variety of workplace improvement programs and policies in the United States and abroad (Donaldson, 2021; Donaldson & Chen, 2021). Developmental psychologists enhance developmentally appropriate preschool services and education efforts. Health psychologists determine the effectiveness of obesity prevention and health promotion efforts. Organizational psychologists design and evaluate leadership development programs, policies, and problems. Clinical, counseling, and school psychologists design and evaluate mental health programs and services. In fact, across specialty areas, psychologists design, evaluate, and implement international programs focused on improving human welfare.

The quest for credible, actionable evidence fuels demand for program evaluation services. Approximately 150 national and regional program evaluation associations exist today. Furthermore, groups such as Eval Partners, the IOCE, and the International Evaluation Academy facilitate the development of the global evaluation community. Although, historically, evaluation methods relied largely on quantitative methods, they are now more diverse, with additional design choices and methods, including mixed methods.

Importantly, psychologists share many values and interests with evaluators. The APA's (2017) *Ethical Principles of Psychologists and Code of Conduct* emphasizes that psychologists should be socially responsible, concerned for others' welfare, respectful of people's rights and dignity, and adhere to scientific standards and professional ethics as they apply their assessment and evaluation expertise. Psychologists are well positioned to engage in such activity because they possess substantive knowledge about the phenomena under investigation as well as how to acquire such knowledge, as well as strong critical thinking skills and solid foundations in matters of methodology, design, and data analysis (Donaldson & Crano, 2011; Mark et al., 2011). That said, a successful career in program evaluation requires more than knowledge of psychology and social science research methods, especially in a global context. When juxtaposed with self–other awareness and cross-cultural competence, program evaluation knowledge, skills, and theory enhance dramatically the program offerings built into education and training in psychology.

Despite the great resonance of program evaluation for the professional identity of psychologists, more needs to be done vis-à-vis education and training to prepare psychologists to assume these roles internationally (Donaldson et al., 2013). Ofir and Kumar (2013) outlined some of the common challenges faced by Western evaluators commissioned to evaluate programs internationally. For example, to do such work, program evaluators should use varied lenses to frame evaluation questions and designs. Such an approach involves being aware of the following issues: getting good and sustained results are more complicated and unpredictable; deep cultural differences often persist; there are usually capacity and other serious constraints; and evaluators must address significant privilege and power differentials (e.g., Donaldson et al., 2013).

Given such complexities, mixed-methods research (MMR) is becoming increasingly popular for international program evaluation, particularly in the United Kingdom, Sri Lanka, Germany, Japan, and South Africa (see Mixed Methods International Research Association at https://mmira.wildapricot.org/). Essentially, MMR involves collecting, analyzing, and integrating or "mixing" quantitative and qualitative data in a single or multiphase study. Although complex, given the mixing of methodologies/paradigms, such an approach often enriches study findings above and beyond the use of quantitative or qualitative studies alone—and ultimately leads to better understandings, insights, and problem solving (Hanson et al., 2005; Mertens et al., 2010; Tashakkori & Teddlie, 2010; Wandschneider et al., 2015).

Transformative Program Evaluation

Transformative program evaluators view assessment and evaluation as contributing to positive social change, especially in marginalized communities (Mertens & Wilson, 2019).[4] To ensure that human rights and social justice are prioritized, these evaluators use MMR to understand the complexity of culturally diverse communities. Transformative evaluators question the assumption that evaluation questions can be predetermined and instead support the engagement of the full range of stakeholders in ways that are culturally respectful to reach better understandings of the culture, context, and challenges to develop appropriate questions for study. Thus, evaluators do critical preliminary qualitative work—prior to developing questions—to understand the community, build relationships, and ensure that appropriate groups are included and supported in respectful ways. Overall, transformative evaluators strive to identify the nature of power relationships and the implications of those relationships in terms of whose voices are given privilege in the planning of the evaluation and the program.

A transformative evaluation would use both quantitative and qualitative data from interviews, observations, and "hanging out" with the targeted population, as well as epidemiological data disaggregated by relevant dimensions of diversity. These evaluations may help promote an understanding of such issues as power relationships, the effects of poverty, and other issues that need to be incorporated into plans for an intervention intended to create desired changes (Chilisa, 2012). In short, program evaluation designs that use MMR have considerable potential to enhance evidence-based practices designed to provide appropriate, effective, and sustainable community support (Mertens & Hesse Biber, 2013). In other words, this work can increase the potential for systematic inquiry and enhancing human rights and social justice globally.

DEVELOPING GLOBAL ASSESSMENT COMPETENCIES

As assessment expands globally, a scientific acculturation process occurs (Berry, 2013). Whether you are interested in psychological testing, therapeutic assessment, educational measurement, formative testing, program evaluation, MMR, or some other aspect of assessment, you are encouraged to learn from past mistakes, controversies, and challenges, and use lessons to enhance future

---

[4]Contributions to this section were made by Donna Mertens.

interactions and collaborative projects. This learning may be facilitated—and cross-cultural integrity (and associated competencies) developed and maintained—by embracing the following exemplary practices (outlined in Exhibit 2.1).

Become Familiar With Academic Resources and Professional Opportunities

You should familiarize yourself with both relevant coursework and with tests, readings, conferences, and online resources. In addition to obtaining excellent training and firsthand assessment, measurement, and evaluation experience, you are encouraged to acquaint yourself with the ITC and IOCE. These organizations lead the way internationally in terms of exemplary assessment and evaluation practices.

Likewise, a key resource and publication outlet for assessment professionals is the *IJT*. First published in 2001, it is the flagship journal of the ITC. The journal is thriving, with contributions from hundreds of scholars and dozens of countries around the world. Along with other top assessment and measurement journals, such as *Applied Psychological Measurement* and *Educational and Psychological Measurement*, *IJT* is highly diverse, in both content and international scholarly affiliations.

From graduate students to established professionals, attending conferences is another useful step. In program evaluation, for example, four of the largest conferences are the American Evaluation Association (AEA), Canadian Evaluation Society (CES), European Evaluation Society (EES), and Australasian Evaluation Society (AES). The AEA is an international professional association of evaluators devoted to the application and exploration of program evaluation, personnel evaluation, technology, and many other forms of evaluation, with approximately 8,000 members representing all 50 states and more than 70 countries. AEA, CES, EES, and AES are equally devoted to the advancement of program evaluation. These organizations bring academics, practitioners, and the public sector together, thus creating a forum for bridge building and collaboration.

EXHIBIT 2.1

Global Assessment Competencies Around the World and Our Top Nine Most Important Skills

Become familiar with academic resources and professional opportunities
Know assessment theory
Understand test translation issues
Cultivate a "cultural self"
Collaborate with key stakeholders
Consider positives and assess/evaluate what is right with people
Think transformatively
Collect feedback and improve
Own your epistemologies

Training and employment opportunities can be found through various sources, both locally and abroad. Within the United States, for example, current and future psychologists interested in such work may wish to review the activities of APA Division 5, Evaluation, Measurement, and Statistics; Section IX on Assessment of APA's (n.d.) Division 12 (https://apadiv12secix.com), Clinical Psychology; as well as other divisions (e.g., 52, International; 13, Consulting; 14, Industrial and Organizational). Another productive way to become involved in international assessment is to engage with large-scale testing programs, such as the Educational Testing Service.

Know Assessment Theory

It is essential that competent developers and users of psychological tests and measures understand theories of assessment and evaluation, from different types of validity, reliability, and attendant statistical procedures to what is meant by concepts such as "true score" and "item response" theory, "operationalization of constructs," and "response set" and "confounding variables" such as "social desirability," as well as countervailing perspectives such as "dustbowl empiricism." Without sufficient theoretical knowledge, test developers and users may inadvertently engage in assessment research and practice that is conceptually inadequate and inappropriately conducted (e.g., AERA, APA, & NCME, n.d.; Alkin, 2012; Geisinger, 2013; IOCE; ITC; Wandschneider et al., 2015). Relatedly, test users are encouraged to carefully consider their assessment philosophies and underlying assumptions: Who am I as an assessor? What are my core beliefs and values? What are my primary goals of assessment? What is my primary role? And perhaps most important, What is my preferred assessment paradigm, and why? Wiggins (2005) provided a nice, easily accessible overview of assessment paradigms, including empirical, multivariate, interpersonal, personological, and psychodynamic. Paying close attention to assessment theory and paradigms enhances one's intentionality, competence, and ultimately one's positive results when testing and evaluating people around the world.

Understand Test Translation Issues

As noted previously, it may be possible to adapt, evaluate, and apply tests and measures developed in one country and culture to another. However, as indicated earlier (e.g., see "International Challenges, Opportunities, and Cutting Edge Assessments"), appropriate guidelines must be understood and followed. Such guidelines offer practical guidance when engaging in the complex process of test translation from one country and culture to another, which involves— as noted earlier—much more than translating an instrument from one language to another. Determining equivalency of meaning across languages and cultures is of paramount importance.

Cultivate a "Cultural Self"

Professionals engaged in transnational assessment work are encouraged to cultivate their cultural self while attending closely to personal beliefs, values, and worldviews and to better understand how these qualities affect their assessment and evaluation practices (Wandschneider et al., 2015). Such individuals acknowledge imposed and derived etics (i.e., wholesale application of Western concepts and measures to non-Western people and systems/organizations) as well as culturally appropriate emics (e.g., local, ingroup perspectives), value diversity and curiosity, are open-minded/committed to intellectual renewal, and immerse themselves in Indigenous cultures and traditions (Flores & Obasi, 2003).

Collaborate With Key Stakeholders

Collaboration is essential, in part because assessor–assessee power (and/or value) differences may be magnified in international contexts. Terjesen (2015) promoted the ABCs of developing global partnerships:

- **Adopt a shared vision.** That is, identify the key stakeholders and ascertain what they perceive to be the most important questions they want answered and what the implication of these results may be.

- **Be patient.** Like anything important, developing partnerships takes time, and there may be many detours throughout the process. Some of these detours can be anticipated, and having knowledge of the context that the partners are coming from may be helpful.

- **Collaboration, communication, and celebration.** Like any good partnership, the key is fostering effective collaboration through communication. Technology certainly has made possible collaborative global relationships that may have been a challenge 20 years ago, but even still, it is important to establish the best methodologies and patterns for collaboration. Finally, it is important to celebrate success throughout the partnership to provide intermediary reinforcement for the partners on their efforts at varied stages of the process.

Consider Positives: Assess and Evaluate What Is Right With People

Assessment and evaluation often focus on psychopathology and what is wrong, or "not working," with a person or group/organization. These are important foci, but when working in an international context, a focus on positive human strengths and attributes (e.g., hopefulness, problem solving, subjective well-being) is also important (Flores & Obasi, 2003). Furthermore, if your research examines assessment results cross-nationally, we recommend caution in interpretation of differences: Difference does not mean deficiency.

Think Transformatively

Assessment and evaluation can be transformative, especially when done collaboratively, empathically, and in culturally sensitive ways. Such practices are worth contemplating, if not modeling. Assessment and evaluation can assist the work of change agents that lead to the greater good and to advocate for others (e.g., the Summit Series at https://summitx.org/).

Collect Feedback and Improve

As you develop assessment- and evaluation-related experience and expertise, it is not okay to guess, or assume, you are "on track." It is a foundational competency to practice what you preach. Thus, it is incumbent upon the international assessor to constantly collect feedback to determine whether—and to what degree—they are on track (Miller et al., 2020). Guessing and assuming run counter to ethical principles, standards of practice, and general scientist-practitioner sensibilities—a point that should become evident to anyone engaged in assessment work internationally. Additionally, assessment- and evaluation-feedback can be transformative in and of itself, especially when approached collaboratively and humanistically (Hanson et al., in press).

Own Your Epistemologies

The question of pure "objectivity" constitutes one of the more epistemologically contentious debates in assessment and evaluation. This fundamental concluding point is implicit, if not explicit, in all preceding points and relevant to the entire chapter because our underlying assessment-related beliefs and values are culturally mediated (Shealy, 2016). Even though we strive for objectivity and all of its worthy concomitants in assessment research and evaluation, it behooves us to remember three final *Going Global* take-home points. First, clinicians may not be less biased than the clients we evaluate. Second, worthy standards of objectivity are more aspirational than fully realizable. Third, the privileging of data over engagement may have unintended negative consequences. Through ongoing reflection, we hope the local and global assessments we render—and the care we provide—evidence humility and integrity in the "realities" we apprehend and facilitate growth, healing, and meaning making. Such a process involves an active and ongoing commitment to ascertaining whether one's assessment-based conclusions and recommendations are ecologically valid, in that they not only resonate with clients but also are convincing to relatively impartial colleagues.

CONCLUSION

Assessment is a broad, globally relevant, and much-needed area of inquiry and practice—with tremendous power and potential. Without question, it has value and usefulness around the world. As should be evident, psychologists provide worldwide leadership in testing, educational measurement, and program evaluation, among many other applied areas. A prevailing theme is that when done competently and collaboratively, with keen alertness and responsiveness to cultural relevance, assessment and evaluation transform people's lives. Pragmatically, assessment is not only unavoidable at multiple levels of analysis (from individuals and communities to societies and nations) but also essential for understanding better who we are and how we may be more responsive to each other and our increasingly interconnected world. As such, it is time to expand and revise our understanding of assessment by contemplating the full spectrum of implications and applications in education, clinical practice, government, and policy making. To the extent that psychologists work across borders, disciplines, and specialty areas, they can make meaningful and measurable differences in the lives of many. As these important collaborations occur, let us first "do no harm." In so doing, the legacy of assessment—and its capacity to change lives for the better—will be appreciated and affirmed, both locally and internationally.

REFERENCES

Alkin, M. C. (Ed.). (2012). *Evaluation roots: A wider perspective of theorists' views and influences* (2nd ed.). Sage.

American Educational Research Association, American Psychological Association, & National Council on Measurement in Education. (n.d.). *Open access files.* https://www.testingstandards.net/open-access-files.html

American Educational Research Association, American Psychological Association, & National Council on Measurement in Education. (2014). *Standards for educational and psychological testing.*

American Psychological Association. (2017). *Ethical principles of psychologists and code of conduct* (2002, Amended June 1, 2010, and January 1, 2017). https://www.apa.org/ethics/code/index.aspx

Bartram, D. (Ed.). (2008). Global norming [Special issue]. *International Journal of Testing, 8*(4). https://doi.org/10.1080/15305050802434980

Berry, J. W. (2013). Global psychology. *South African Journal of Psychology, 43*(4), 391–401. https://doi.org/10.1177/0081246313504517

Binkley, M., Erstad, O., Herman, J., Raizen, S., Ripley, M., & Rumble, M. (2010). *Defining 21st century skills: The Assessment and Teaching of 21st Century Skills (ATCS 21) project* [White paper, draft 1]. University of Melbourne, Cisco, Intel, and Microsoft. https://oei.org.ar/ibertic/evaluacion/sites/default/files/biblioteca/24_defining-21st-century-skills.pdf

Chilisa, B. (2012). *Indigenous research methodologies.* Sage Publications.

Clarke, M. (2012, April 19). *What matters most for student assessment systems: A framework paper* (SABER Working Paper No. 68235). World Bank. https://documents.worldbank.org/curated/en/2012/04/16238771/matters-most-student-assessment-systems-framework-paper

Donaldson, S. I. (2007). *Program theory-driven evaluation science: Strategies and applications.* Psychology Press. https://doi.org/10.4324/9780203809730

Donaldson, S. I. (2021). *Introduction to theory-driven program evaluation: Culturally responsive and strengths-focused applications.* Routledge. https://doi.org/10.4324/9780429353277

Donaldson, S. I., Azzam, T. A., & Conner, R. (2013). *Emerging practices in international development evaluation.* Information Age.

Donaldson, S. I., & Chen, C. (Eds.). (2021). *Positive organizational psychology interventions: Design and evaluation.* Wiley-Blackwell.

Donaldson, S. I., Christie, C. A., & Mark, M. M. (2015). *Credible and actionable evidence: The foundation for rigorous and influential evaluations.* Sage Publications. https://doi.org/10.4135/9781483385839

Donaldson, S. I., & Crano, W. C. (2011). Theory-driven evaluation science and applied social psychology: Exploring the intersection. In M. M. Mark, S. I. Donaldson, & B. Campbell (Eds.), *Social psychology and evaluation* (pp. 141–160). Guilford Press.

Downing, S. M., & Haladyna, T. M. (Eds.). (2006). *Handbook of test development.* Lawrence Erlbaum Associates.

Ebbinghaus, H. (1908). *Psychology: An elementary textbook.* Heath.

Embretson, S. E. (Ed.). (2009). *Measuring psychological constructs: Advances in model-based approaches.* American Psychological Association.

Finn, S. E., Fischer, C. T., & Handler, L. (Eds.). (2012). *Collaborative/therapeutic assessment: A casebook and guide.* Wiley.

Flores, L. Y., & Obasi, E. M. (2003). Positive psychological assessment in an increasingly diverse world. In S. J. Lopez & C. R. Snyder (Eds.), *Positive psychological assessment: A handbook of models and measures* (pp. 41–54). American Psychological Association. https://doi.org/10.1037/10612-003

Gargani, J., & Donaldson, S. I. (2011). What works for whom, where, why, for what, and when? Using evaluation evidence to take action in local contexts. *New Directions for Evaluation, 2011*(130), 17–30. https://doi.org/10.1002/ev.362

Geisinger, K. F. (Ed.). (2013). *APA handbook of testing and assessment in psychology.* American Psychological Association.

Gershon, R. C. (2005). Computer adaptive testing. *Journal of Applied Measurement, 6*(1), 109–127.

Gierl, M. J., Lai, H., & Tanygin, V. (2021). *Advanced methods in automatic item generation.* Routledge. https://doi.org/10.4324/9781003025634

Gould, S. J. (1981). *The mismeasure of man.* W. W. Norton.

Gregoire, J., & Hambleton, R. K. (Eds.). (2009). Advances in test adaptation research [Special issue]. *International Journal of Testing, 9*(2). https://doi.org/10.1080/15305050902880678

Hanson, W. E., Creswell, J. W., Plano Clark, V. L., Petska, K. S., & Creswell, J. D. (2005). Mixed methods research designs in counseling psychology. *Journal of Counseling Psychology, 52*(2), 224–235. https://doi.org/10.1037/0022-0167.52.2.224

Hanson, W. E., Zhou, H., Armstrong, D. L., & Liwski, N. T. (in press). A humanistic approach to mental health assessment, evaluation, and measurement-based care. In J. J. W. Andrews, S. R. Shaw, J. F. Domene, & C. McMorris (Eds.), *School, clinical, and counselling psychology: Mental health assessment, prevention, and intervention.* Springer.

Hanushek, E. A., & Woessmann, L. (2012). Do better schools lead to more growth? Cognitive skills, economic outcomes and causation. *Journal of Economic Growth, 17*(4), 267–321. https://doi.org/10.1007/s10887-012-9081-x

Haverkamp, B. E. (2012). The counseling relationship. In E. Altmeier & J. C. Hansen (Eds.), *Oxford handbook of counseling psychology* (pp. 32–70). Oxford University Press. https://doi.org/10.1093/oxfordhb/9780195342314.001.0001

Haverkamp, B. E. (2013). Education and training in assessment for professional psychology: Engaging the "reluctant student." In K. F. Geisinger (Ed.), *APA handbook of testing and assessment in psychology: Vol. 2. Testing and assessment in clinical and counseling psychology* (pp. 63–82). American Psychological Association. https://doi.org/10.1037/14048-005

Haynes, S. N., Smith, G. T., & Hunsley, J. D. (2011). *Scientific foundations of clinical assessment.* Routledge. https://doi.org/10.4324/9780203829172

Health Service Psychology Education Collaborative. (2013). Professional psychology in health care services: A blueprint for education and training. *American Psychologist, 68*(6), 411–426. https://doi.org/10.1037/a0033265

Hu, S., & Oakland, T. (1991). Global and regional perspectives on testing children: An empirical study. *International Journal of Psychology, 26*(3), 329–344. https://doi.org/10.1080/00207599108246857

Iliescu, D. (2017). *Adapting tests in linguistic and cultural situations.* Cambridge University Press. https://doi.org/10.1017/9781316273203

LaVelle, J., & Donaldson, S. I. (2021). Opportunities and challenges ahead for university-based evaluator education programs, faculty, and students. *The American Journal of Evaluation, 42*(3), 428–438. https://doi.org/10.1177/1098214020937808

Leong, F., Bartram, D., Cheung, F., Geisinger, K. F., & Iliescu, D. (Eds.). (2016). *The ITC international handbook of testing and assessment.* Oxford University Press.

Mark, M. M., Donaldson, S. I., & Campbell, B. (Eds.). (2011). *Social psychology and evaluation.* Guilford Press.

Marshall, T., & Robertson, G. (2019, June 7). Eugenics in Canada. In E. Yarhi (Ed.), *The Canadian Encyclopedia.* https://www.thecanadianencyclopedia.ca/en/article/eugenics

Mateo, J., Escofet, A., Martínez-Olmo, F., Ventura, J., & Vlachopoulos, D. (2012). Evaluation tools in the European Higher Education Area (EHEA): An assessment for evaluating the competences of the Final Year Project in the social sciences. *European Journal of Education, 47*(3), 435–447. https://doi.org/10.1111/j.1465-3435.2012.01536.x

Meckes, L., & Carrasco, R. (2010). Two decades of SIMCE: An overview of the National Assessment System in Chile. *Assessment in Education: Principles, Policy & Practice, 17*(2), 233–248. https://doi.org/10.1080/09695941003696214

Mertens, D., Bledsoe, K., Sullivan, M., & Wilson, A. (2010). Utilization of mixed methods for transformative purposes. In A. Tashakkori & C. Teddlie (Eds.), *SAGE handbook of mixed methods in social & behavioral research* (pp. 193–214). Sage Publications. https://doi.org/10.4135/9781506335193.n8

Mertens, D. M., & Hesse-Biber, S. (2013). Mixed methods and credibility of evidence in evaluation. *New Directions for Evaluation, 2013*(138), 5–13. https://doi.org/10.1002/ev.20053

Mertens, D. M., & Wilson, A. T. (2019). *Program evaluation theory and practice: A comprehensive approach* (2nd ed.). Guilford Press.

Meyer, G. J., Finn, S. E., Eyde, L. D., Kay, G. G., Moreland, K. L., Dies, R. R., Eisman, E. J., Kubiszyn, T. W., & Reed, G. M. (2001). Psychological testing and psychological assessment: A review of evidence and issues. *American Psychologist, 56*(2), 128–165. https://doi.org/10.1037/0003-066X.56.2.128

Miller, S. D., Hubble, M. A., & Chow, D. (2020). *Better results: Using deliberate practice to improve therapeutic effectiveness.* American Psychological Association. https://doi.org/10.1037/0000191-000

Mills, C. N., Potenza, M. T., Fremer, J. J., & Ward, W. C. (Eds.). (2002). *Computer-based testing: Building the foundation for future assessments.* Taylor & Francis.

Mislevy, R. J. (2010). Design under constraints: The case of large-scale assessment systems. *Measurement: Interdisciplinary Research and Perspectives, 8*(4), 199–203. https://doi.org/10.1080/15366367.2010.526452

Moghaddam, F. M., Erneling, C. E., Montero, M., & Lee, N. (2007). Toward a conceptual foundation for a global psychology. In M. J. Stevens & U. P. Gielen (Eds.), *Toward a global psychology: Theory, research, intervention, and pedagogy* (pp. 179–206). Lawrence Erlbaum Associates.

Muthukrishna, M., Bell, A. V., Henrich, J., Curtin, C. M., Gedranovich, A., McInerney, J., & Thue, B. (2020). Beyond western, educated, industrial, rich, and democratic (WEIRD) psychology: Measuring and mapping scales of cultural and psychological distance. *Psychological Science, 31*(6), 678–701. https://doi.org/10.1177/0956797620916782

Neave, G., & Veiga, A. (2013). The bologna process: Inception, 'take up' and familiarity. *Higher Education, 66*(1), 59–77. https://doi.org/10.1007/s10734-012-9590-8

Nishitani, H. (2020). *English education reform-based on EBPM (Evidence-Based Policy Making).* https://www.openaccessgovernment.org/english-education-reform/79823/

Oakland, T., Douglas, S., & Kane, H. (2016). Top ten standardized tests used internationally with children and youth by school psychologists in 64 countries: A 24-year follow-up study. *Journal of Psychoeducational Assessment, 34*(2), 166–176. https://doi.org/10.1177/0734282915595303

Oakland, T., Wechsler, S. M., & Maree, K. (2013). Test use with children across cultures: A view from three countries. In K. F. Geisinger (Ed.), *APA handbook of testing and assessment in psychology: Vol. 3. Testing and assessment in school psychology and education* (pp. 231–257). American Psychological Association. https://doi.org/10.1037/14049-011

Ofir, Z., & Kumar, A. K. S. (2013). Evaluation in developing countries: What makes it different? In S. I. Donaldson, T. A. Azzam, & R. Conner (Eds.), *Emerging practices in international development evaluation* (pp. 11–24). Information Age Publishing.

Pokropek, A., Marks, G. N., & Borgonovi, F. (2021). How much do students' scores in PISA reflect general intelligence and how much do they reflect specific abilities? *Journal of Educational Psychology.* Advance online publication. https://doi.org/10.1037/edu0000687

Poston, J. M., & Hanson, W. E. (2010). Meta-analysis of psychological assessment as a therapeutic intervention. *Psychological Assessment, 22*(2), 203–212. https://doi.org/10.1037/a0018679

Province of Alberta. (1928). *The Sexual Sterilization Act of Alberta.* Statutes of the Province of Alberta. https://eugenicsarchive.ca/database/documents/5172e81ceed5c6000000001d

Reddy, A. (2008). The eugenic origins of IQ testing: Implications for post-Atkins litigation. *DePaul Law Review, 57*(3), Rev. 667. https://via.library.depaul.edu/law-review/vol57/iss3/5

Rindermann, H. (2007). The g-factor of international cognitive ability comparisons: The homogeneity of results in PISA, TIMSS, PIRLS and IQ-tests across nations. *European Journal of Personality, 21*(5), 667–706. https://doi.org/10.1002/per.634

Rodolfa, E., Bent, R., Eisman, E., Nelson, P., Rehm, L., & Ritchie, P. (2005). A cube model for competency development: Implications for psychology educators and regulators. *Professional Psychology, Research and Practice, 36*(4), 347–354. https://doi.org/10.1037/0735-7028.36.4.347

Shealy, C. N. (Ed.). (2016). *Making sense of beliefs and values: Theory, research, and practice.* Springer.

Shute, V., & Ventura, M. (2013). *Stealth assessment: Measuring and supporting learning in video games.* The MIT Press. https://doi.org/10.7551/mitpress/9589.001.0001

Tashakkori, A., & Teddlie, C. (2010). *Sage handbook of mixed methods in social and behavioral research.* Sage Publications. https://doi.org/10.4135/9781506335193

Terjesen, M. (2015, March). *Developing global partnerships for conducting research in schools: Closing the science-practice-culture gap* [Paper presentation]. Cultivating the Globally Sustainable Self Summit Series, Harrisonburg, VA, United States.

van der Linden, W. J., & Glas, C. A. W. (2010). *Elements of adaptive testing.* Springer.

Wandschneider, E., Pysarchik, D. T., Sternberger, L. G., Ma, W., Acheson, K., Baltensperger, B., Good, R. T., Brubaker, B., Baldwin, T., Nishitani, H., Wang, F., Reisweber, J., & Hart, V. (2015). The Forum BEVI Project: Applications and implications for international, multicultural, and transformative learning. *Frontiers: The Interdisciplinary Journal of Study Abroad, 25*, 150–228.

Wiggins, J. S. (2005). *Paradigms of personality assessment.* Guilford Press.

3

Consultation

Who Needs Psychological Expertise Around the World and Why?

Connie Henson, John Fulkerson, Paula Caligiuri, and Craig Shealy

Consulting psychology is a broad field of practice, including the application of psychological principles or processes to achieve a wide range of objectives with individuals, groups, organizations, systems, and communities (American Psychological Association [APA], 2017b). Psychologists within any subbranch of psychology, and even nonpsychologists, may provide psychological consultation in an array of fields. This perspective is congruent with the broader vision of the APA (2019) to be "a strong, diverse, and unified psychology that enhances knowledge and improves the human condition" (p. 4).

Despite a commitment by the consulting psychology field to diverse populations and needs, limited published literature is related specifically to international consulting psychology. These contributions are increasing, however, as globalization of businesses, increased interconnectedness between governments and nongovernmental organizations (NGOs), and an overall rise in the number of psychologists consulting internationally may prompt research and publications regarding international consultation. In the past several years, publications focused on issues related to international consultation have appeared more frequently. For example, the March 2020 special issue of the *Consulting Psychology Journal* featured five articles exploring the business application of consulting psychology. In one of these articles, Eyring (2020) described key lessons for a global consulting business: become fluent in multicultural interactions, balance cultural adaptation with personal and company values, embrace a global mindset, define your why, define your perfect client, find the right level of simplicity, learn how to scale yourself and your business, and pace yourself.

https://doi.org/10.1037/0000311-004
Going Global: How Psychologists Can Meet a World of Need, C. Shealy, M. Bullock, and S. Kapadia (Editors)

More comprehensively, the December 2012 special issue of the *Consulting Psychology Journal* focused explicitly on international consulting, including five articles featuring case studies and lessons learned as well as analyses and commentary on the current state of international consulting to organizations. The editors emphasized several key themes, highlighting the overarching importance of understanding the specific cultural context in which an organization is embedded. With the global rise and reach of organizations, traditional within-country boundaries for an organization may become quite blurred, and an organization's culture may have multiple and potentially conflicting facets that must be considered if an intervention is to be successful. The international consulting psychologist must be aware of cultural, economic, and political differences that exist across borders and that impact consulting interventions. Moreover, consultation by its very nature has the potential to drive social change in ways that may not be fully anticipated when an intervention is first conceived. For example, encouraging a more participative leadership style may be an effective intervention in some countries but may cause a leader to be perceived as weak and uncertain in others, which could result in confusion and reduced effectiveness (see Lowman, 2016).

This 2012 special issue also noted that although expert observations via case studies are important, an overarching need exists for more empirical research and theory development to inform consultative practice. This need remains and is more necessary than ever because although the majority of consulting psychologists may work exclusively in their home country, the continued globalization of the work and marketplace means that consultation is likely to touch on international issues, requiring all consulting psychologists to develop basic competencies in international consulting (APA, 2017b; Fulkerson, 2012; Lowman, 2012).

In this chapter, we first describe the fundamental competencies for international consultants—what consultants should do, know, and be—along with strategies for building these competencies. We then describe case studies illustrating how these competencies may be expressed. We next address those models and methods that may help bring a measure of coherence and direction to inquiry and practice within this field. We conclude the chapter with a summary of best practices and suggestions for how to advance international consulting practice and research over both the short term and long term.

COMPETENCIES OF INTERNATIONAL CONSULTING

From a practical standpoint—in terms of "what they do"—international consulting psychologists apply their knowledge, skills, and characteristics to a wide range of needs and opportunities, from the individual to the institutional level. That is, international consulting psychologists work "horizontally" across the spectrum of settings, issues, and populations: consultation regarding the impact of war trauma on refugees, human factor considerations for mechanical designs, promotion of an understanding of group dynamics in the pursuit of organizational goals, facilitation of mediation processes among conflicted parties, and a whole lot more. Additionally, they work "vertically," from the "micro" (e.g., cultivating self-awareness and leadership capacity via individual assessment and executive coaching) to the "macro" (e.g., designing interventions to promote behavioral, attitudinal, and structural change within and among groups, organizations, and governments). Against this backdrop, we suggest the following core competencies as integral to effective international consulting (see also APA, 2017b).

Awareness of Self, Others, and the Larger World

Although it is imperative that international consulting psychologists demonstrate skill in the practices and methodologies of the profession—the "doing" competencies—the key often is knowing how, why, and when interventions must be conceptualized, modified, and expressed through varied cultural frameworks. Not surprisingly, then, the international consultant needs to cultivate awareness at multiple levels from the "self" (e.g., appraising, understanding, and acknowledging one's own history, culture, stereotypes, and biases), to the "other" (e.g., what one does and does not understand about different cultures and systems), to the "larger world" (e.g., what one does and does not know about why the world works as it does). Thus, competent international consultants strive to know what they do not know while increasing their capacity to tolerate ambiguity and embracing a learning curve that never truly flattens (e.g., APA, 2017b).

In large part, the cultivation of such awareness has a practical intent, as the international consultant must be able to contemplate, design, implement, and evaluate highly complex interventions using an array of methodologies and tools. In this regard, Fulkerson (2012) illustrated the exponential complexity that can arise when attempting to adapt and apply interventions across countries and cultures. For example, an intervention such as "360 feedback," already complex, is fraught with additional promise and peril when implemented in cultures that do not value such processes or may even feel that such an exercise denigrates them and the organization. As Holt and Seki (2012) observed, practices in the Western, industrialized, and developed world may be experienced very differently in a culture that does share the same values, epistemologies, or practices vis-à-vis matters of leaders or the relationship of the individual to the group (see also Chapter 5, this volume, on leadership).

Although it is beyond the scope of this chapter to describe the full range of cultural dimensions that may exist when working with cross-national clients, psychologists who are considering international consulting work must be aware that their worldview may differ significantly from that of the client (Lowman, 2016). International consultants must be cognizant of their own beliefs and values and understand that these beliefs and values may not be self-evident or universally shared (Shealy, 2016). Clients may experience consultants who are without such an awareness of self, others, and the larger world as insensitive and superficial at best or self-serving and ineffective at worst.

At the same time, consultants must understand that broad cultural differences do not apply equally to all individuals within a culture. Fuqua and Newman (2002) called a tendency to use broad strokes of a culture to describe or attribute meaning to an individual's values and behaviors an "ecological fallacy." Vandaveer (2012) observed that individual differences may be a much stronger predictor of behavior than the stereotypic expectations of a given culture. Organizational context and contingencies also may exert a more powerful influence than culture or individual differences in terms of actual behavior.

A final consideration in regard to the overarching need for awareness of self, others, and the larger world is the caution from Leonard and colleagues (2012) that international consulting psychologists often "have fundamental assumptions not only about culture and the business environment, but also about leadership and learning" (p. 251). If unexamined, such assumptions may result in a misalignment between consultant interventions and client expectations, particularly in an international context. Leonard et al. specified three sets of assumptions as especially salient:

- assumptions about national and organizational culture
- assumptions about the relationship and expectations between international consulting psychologists and their clients
- assumptions that concern concepts related to leadership and learning

For the international consulting psychologist to reflect on all of these assumptions before working with an individual client seems a daunting task. However, as experience is gained with a particular client or national culture, assumptions may be tested and examined as the international consulting psychologist becomes more adept at understanding how these variables may help or hinder a given intervention.

In conclusion, international consultants must cultivate an awareness of beliefs and values of self and other, the national cultures in which they are consulting, the individuality of their clients, and the specific organizational context of the client. In so doing, they also must avoid the fallacy of overgeneralization even as they engage in reflection and evaluation of their consultative models and methods simultaneously. As consultation processes unfold, it is simply not possible to anticipate every variable that will need to be considered. Thus, it is helpful to be cognizant of not only different models of cultural development and change but also varying strategies for managing different contexts in real time (APA, 2017b).

Cultural Agility

The overarching self-management skill of cultural agility—the ability to understand the demands of cultural and business contexts and respond appropriately—has particular salience for international consultants in psychology (e.g., Caligiuri, 2021; Caligiuri et al., 2009). At times, the capacity for such agility may facilitate *cultural adaptation*, in which consultants adjust their behaviors to the expected norm within their clients' cultural context. At other times, the consultant may adopt a frame of *cultural minimization*, the need to override a cross-national difference in favor of an industry or organizational norm. In other consulting situations, such as team-based processes, the situation might benefit from *cultural integration*, the need for the client to apprehend that multiple cultural understandings are at play, which necessitates the deliberate explication of new cultural norms that are responsive to the characteristics and needs of the organization and its members. We offer the following examples of these three approaches.

Cultural Adaptation

Because most consultation work is client centered, as in business and educational contexts, understanding and mastering processes of cultural adaptation are key competencies for international consultants. Such adaptation could be as simple as understanding and engaging in culturally appropriate greetings or as complex as recognizing and respecting the underlying meanings that are attached to invitations to work as part of a specific group or participate in negotiations.

Cultural Minimization

At the other end of the continuum, cultural minimization is designed to control cultural differences to create consistency and limit variability in relation to a desired norm. Perhaps the clearest example of the need for cultural minimization is in the case of operating guidelines related to safety, ethics, quality standards, or human rights, which are common in many businesses that operate globally and are often not subject to negotiation or partial compliance. Of course, cultural minimization rarely happens in isolation. The ways in which consultants motivate, persuade, and influence others to support and maintain normative standards often require the core competencies of cultural adaptation, as described previously.

Cultural Integration

When international consultants work on global teams with colleagues from more than one country or culture, they may need to work across rather than within a particular cultural framework. Highlighting the need for cultural integration on heterogeneous or culturally diverse teams, Earley and Mosakowski (2000) found that, over time, teams functioned best when they had created a hybrid culture, which represented their team's aggregate norms for interactions, communications, and goal setting. In such contexts, consultants are actively encouraged to develop and foster their own rules for "interpersonal and task-related interactions, creation of high team performance expectations, effective communication and conflict management styles, and the development of a common identity" (Earley & Mosakowski, 2000, p. 36). Overall, then, culturally agile consultants possess a deep understanding of the cultural contexts in which they are working and can effectively execute the three response strategies as needed and when appropriate.

Affective Capacity

In addition to apprehending and adapting to varying cultural contexts, international consultants need to respond to the emotional challenges inherent in working internationally and out of one's comfort zone. Working internationally can be at once immensely rewarding and stress producing. For example, Anderzén and Arnetz (1999) found that, compared with those working in their country of origin, consultants living and working in foreign countries had measurable physiological changes in their levels of stress hormones, including increased prolactin and decreased testosterone levels. Among other implications, because familiar reinforcements and supports often are absent when consultants are working internationally—especially because environmental contexts and dynamics are often ambiguous—consultants must have the capacity and inclination to understand and manage their experience of stress.

An ability to recognize and regulate emotions may be key to our effectiveness as international consultants (Yoo et al., 2006). For example, Yoo and colleagues (2006) found that emotional regulation

> is important for positive adjustment because controlling one's negative emotions evoked during conflict and stress, which are inevitable in intercultural (and intracultural) life, allows one to not be overly influenced by negative emotions and instead think clearly and rationally, which then paves the way for using the other psychological skills important for intercultural adjustment such as openness, flexibility and critical thinking. (pp. 346–347)

The relationship between emotional regulation and adjustment has been demonstrated across a diverse range of expatriates. For example, Trejo and colleagues (2015) found a positive association between emotional regulation and the ability to adapt to unfamiliar cultures for military personnel. Similarly, Konanahalli and Oyedele (2016) found a positive relationship between both self-management and self-awareness and adjustment for British structural engineers working overseas.

Personality Variables: Stability, Sociability, and Openness

Related to the earlier points, our experience suggests that three personality variables may be especially conducive to international consultation effectiveness: stability, sociability, and openness. *Emotional stability* refers to a basic personality trait that allows individuals to respond to ambiguity and stressors while maintaining sufficient emotional well-being without heightened anxiety. Greater emotional stability enables consultants to manage the stress associated with the ambiguity and uncertainty of the foreign culture. Consultants who are more emotionally stable may have a greater tolerance of ambiguity in settings where full clarity is not present or possible. Professionals with a greater tolerance of ambiguity are rated by their supervisors as more effective in their global professional tasks (Caligiuri & Tarique, 2012).

Similarly, consultants who are inclined toward *sociability* may be more likely to seek and actively form relationships with colleagues and clients from diverse cultures. Actively forming relationships is important because such social networks offer consultants the opportunities to learn about dynamics and diversity from many different peers and clients. The rich relationships that emerge from such processes may be integral to in-country adjustment as well as to the breadth and quality of subsequent informational, instrumental, and emotional support networks. That said, extraversion—as a proxy for sociability—is neither necessary nor sufficient for success in international consulting. We know of many highly successful international consultants who are perhaps more introverted "by nature" but have successfully learned to push themselves beyond their natural comfort level when working cross-culturally (Caligiuri et al., 2009; Mol et al., 2005). Whatever one's predilections in this regard, international consultants must have a sufficient capacity and inclination for sociability if they are to succeed over the long term.

Finally, the personality trait of *openness*, which refers to the preference for novelty and variety as well as intellectual curiosity, may help international consultants to be more comfortable and better adjusted and to experience greater enjoyment when working in different cultures. Consultants with greater levels of openness are more inclined toward cross-cultural engagement, viewing such work as an opportunity for novel and satisfying experiences (Mol et al., 2005). Moreover, such individuals may be more receptive to experiencing different ways of working and interacting with their clients and tend to be more willing to adapt and modify methods and approaches when needed (Caligiuri et al., 2009; Mol et al., 2005).

Collectively, we offer these three personality variables as candidates for further inquiry vis-à-vis the competencies that are expected of international consultants. Affect labeling (Kircanski et al., 2012) and mindfulness meditation (Jacobs et al., 2013) are two strategies that could be used by consulting psychologists working in any environment. The availability and identification of strategies to attenuate the experience of stress further highlight the importance of the competencies of self-awareness and active self-management for anyone considering consulting internationally.

PUTTING KNOWLEDGE INTO PRACTICE: EXAMPLES OF INTERNATIONAL CONSULTATION

As noted earlier, the international consulting psychologist is likely to encounter greater complexity than they anticipate, which necessitates a deeper understanding of cultural foundations and differences, flexibility, and an ability to reflect on and test assumptions. The following five case studies illustrate how these competences were expressed in the real world.

Case Study 1: Adjusting to the Time Difference

In what initially seemed to be a rather straightforward coaching assignment, one of us (JF) was asked to coach and mediate the differences that an American chief executive officer (CEO) and a Dutch chief financial officer (CFO) were navigating. The original charge of the assignment was to coach the Dutch CFO, who was not getting reports done in a timely fashion that suited the American CEO. As the assignment unfolded, it was apparent that neither party understood the underlying cross-national dynamics at work. The American CEO wanted fast responses and quick answers even if the answers were not completely accurate. The Dutch CFO had a longer term view and believed that to get to an accurate report additional processes needed to be developed. A cross-national values assessment revealed that the source of the conflict lay in different cultural views of time between the United States (short term) and The Netherlands (long term). When the two parties realized and accepted this difference in national cultures and could label what was driving their respective positions, they successfully reconciled their differences.

Case Study 2: Learning by Teaching

One of us (CS) was asked to work with a group of master's- and doctoral-level human development counselors from India, providing them with content knowledge regarding the assessment and treatment of psychopathology. After these human development advocates and clinicians waded tentatively into prepared content—mindful that Indigenous and other perspectives on such matters definitely needed to be understood—it soon became clear that this group actually wanted real-world knowledge and skills to address the highly complex and gender-based dynamics that kept impeding the effectiveness of their marital, family, and community-level interventions. As the chasm between what was planned and what was needed became clear, all the prepared notes, lectures, and readings were jettisoned. Instead, over the next 10 days, the focus shifted dramatically to understanding the complex realities of attempting to intervene in highly traditional, often rural, and community-based contexts to promote healing, well-being, and change. From the fundamentals of marital and family therapy to the nature and role of "advocacy" within such a context, a balance was struck between imparting requested knowledge and skills that were unabashedly "Western" while learning from the unique "non-Western" roles and activities in which these individuals were compelled to engage as change agents facing highly complex dynamics in their "real world." An important take-home lesson was that the essential commitment to the non-imposition of beliefs and values on other cultures and contexts should not be so overlearned and overpracticed that we miss opportunities for in-depth sharing of what we do know or can do.

Case Study 3: Bridging Boundaries

Vandaveer (2012) described an example of two high-potential leaders who initially struggled to build an effective working relationship. One of the leaders was a male American CEO, and the other was a female Pakistani financial leader. The issues in this case involved cultural differences, including individualism versus collectivism, power distance, uncertainty avoidance, and paternalism, as well as misunderstandings and assumptions related to practical issues such as what leaders are expected to do. The consultant worked with her clients to test cultural assumptions previously not considered and to illuminate how these cultural differences manifest within the corporate culture for the specific organization. Through a series of coaching, mediation, and team-building sessions, the consultant assisted both parties in gaining a deeper understanding of differences in their expectations of each other and creating a platform for building an effective working relationship. Reflecting on her own insights gained through consulting internationally, Vandaveer (2012, p. 293) observed that working with two people from different cultures made her more aware of her own culture and the impact on the consulting process. Moreover, she examined the impact of her long-term relationship with both parties on the outcome of the interventions, highlighting her initial concern related to APA (2017a) Standard, 3.05, Multiple Relationships, from the *Ethical Principles of Psychologists and Code of Conduct*. By proactively addressing her concerns with her client, Vandaveer was able to avoid conflicts and ensure that her objectivity was maintained throughout the intervention. This case study illustrates cultural agility in that the consultant integrated her understanding of cultural difference and business needs to maintain her ethical standards while managing the expectations and needs of her clients.

Case Study 4: Handling Trauma

In this example, consultants worked with local counselors in an urban refugee environment, emphasizing from the outset the importance of context in delivering any sort of intervention while seeking to build upon the inherent strengths of the community (James, 2012). Here, the consultants sought to integrate Western knowledge with traditional approaches to healing, and so the felt experience of trauma was conceptualized as a normal reaction to extreme events. Moreover, a deliberate focus on connections to and among family and community members was emphasized in an attempt to call upon and leverage the latent strength and resilience of community members. Finally, real-world matters of safety were recognized and mitigated as was possible, including threats of violence, malnutrition, crowded work and living spaces with limited or no privacy, the presence of multiple relationships by the counselors, inadequate availability of support services including supervision, and the overarching challenge to retain hope for change given such circumstances.

Case Study 5: "Well, That Didn't Work"

Even with the best-laid plans, international consultation does not always unfold as intended, mainly because of the interacting and unknown complexities that are integral to such work. A large multinational corporation made an effort to standardize training for project managers and created a series of interactive e-learning courses, which enabled participants to work at their own pace, to self-assess, and to incorporate learning into aspects of their day-to-day work. The program was well received in the United States and Europe. A manager for this multinational organization was based in Hong Kong, managing Human Resources for the Asia Pacific region, and was given a requirement to implement the e-learning program throughout her region. Although the company had translated the courses into the needed languages, the internal learning and development consultants had not consulted with anyone in the region to determine receptivity to this mode of training.

The reaction from the local manager and from her internal customers was dismay. For example, the loss of personal contact from the facilitator led to program ineffectiveness: Although able to access and use the e-learning modules, managers in this region did not value information that did not come from a respected teacher. In another country, the opportunities to interact with peers had been a key motivator for participation in training, so the engagement with the new program was very low. The Hong Kong manager identified the most frustrating aspect of the intervention: When she and her colleagues raised the lack of effectiveness in the Asia region, they were told it was working in all other regions of the world and that they were expected to make it work in the Asian-Pacific region. Attempts to modify the program to deliver more culturally appropriate training were not supported by the home office. Although extreme, this example illustrates the importance of engaging in ongoing evaluation regarding whether interventions are experienced as effective by the recipients. In short, international consultants need to solicit relevant feedback that may lead to minor or substantial modifications in approach (Dyjak-LeBlanc et al., 2016).

Key Takeaways From the Case Studies

Each case study highlights the importance of integrating basic knowledge and expertise with an understanding of cultural differences and then developing, adapting, and/or selecting the most effective approach to meet the goals at hand. A few specific takeaways for international consultants follow:

- Be mindful of the level of analysis to which interventions are targeted.
- Frequently assess interests, beliefs, and needs, and be willing to set a new course when necessary.
- Approach cultural differences with sensitivity and sophistication, striving to facilitate understanding and find common ground.
- Always keep in mind the rights and responsibilities of different stakeholders, including aspects of confidentiality/privacy and informed consent.

In all such cases, an overarching commitment to the competencies described earlier—self-awareness, agility, openness, and tolerance for ambiguity, combined with ongoing and reflexive querying about the needs, beliefs, values, and goals of those with whom we are consulting—helps to "first do no harm" while offering knowledge and skills that genuinely are value-added and warmly received (APA, 2017b; Dyjak-LeBlanc et al., 2016; Lowman, 2016; Shealy, 2016).

INTERNATIONAL CONSULTING: THE NEED FOR MODELS AND METHODS

The competencies and case studies we offered earlier represent key pieces of the overall puzzle that is international consultation. However, consistent with calls for more theory and research in this regard (Fulkerson, 2012), models that can provide conceptual coherence regarding why and how such competencies exist in relation to one another as well as methods for evaluating and refining our models and attendant best practices over time are most needed at this time. These models need to account for the complexities that are inherent in practice of international consulting while helping the field identify and implement culture sensitive theoretically and empirically based strategies for understanding, appraising, and developing the competencies that are most central to this work. In addition to identifying essential competencies, models for international consulting need to also address behaviors and traits that are contraindicated for international consulting. For example, in a project that culminated in the EI Leadership Model of "doing, knowing, and being," Dyjak-LeBlanc et al. (2016) found that what leaders should do, know, or be is even more important than what they should not be. Citing observations from work in varying countries and contexts, subject matter experts concluded that leaders who were defined via critical incidents as "incompetent," "manipulative," "corrupt," "controlling," and "harassing" had a more pernicious impact on organizations and the people who worked within them than the salutary impact of leaders who displayed "integrity" and were "responsible, honest, trustworthy, and ethical" (Dyjak-LeBlanc et al., 2016).

In addition to understanding and developing explicit models of international leadership and consultation such as those described previously, it would serve the field well to engage in an ongoing conversation regarding who we are, what we do, and why we do it, as international consultants in psychology. For instance, when interviewing consultants and consultees in preparation for writing this chapter, we were struck by how frequently people provided examples of what could be thought of as minor acts of courage and compassion—or, conversely, acts of cowardice and insensitivity—that had a broader impact not just for the consultant but for those they represented wittingly or not. For example, one manager described the reduced trust that resulted when an American consultant did not follow through on an apparently accepted invitation to an important social function. Although the manager wondered if this oversight resulted from differences in cultural understanding and expectations, he nevertheless was offended by such behavior, which affected him personally and simply would not have happened within his own culture. This anecdote illustrates a fundamental point: As international consultants, who we are and what we do and know are seen through a lens that may be unknown to us and mediated by cultural values and personal beliefs that may never be knowable fully, even as such reactions may dramatically impact how we are experienced (Shealy, 2016).

LEAPING INTO THE FRAY OF INTERNATIONAL CONSULTING

Notwithstanding the stage of your academic, professional, or career development, if you are considering international consultation, the importance of self-awareness and self-management cannot be overemphasized. Working and living conditions can vary from location to location, and the individual psychologist can be isolated from colleagues and peer support. So, if you are contemplating working as an international consultant, we first suggest self-reflection vis-à-vis the earlier competencies and case studies. Although presently there are no formal specialty guidelines designed explicitly for international consulting psychologists, the Society for Consulting Psychology, Division 13 of the APA (2017b), developed the comprehensive document *Guidelines for Education and Training at the Doctoral and Postdoctoral Level in Consulting Psychology (CP)/Organizational Consulting Psychology (OCP)*. This document addresses many themes that are expressed in this chapter, as well as matters that are unique to a global/international context, and should be required reading for current or aspiring consulting psychologists. In particular, as Figure 3.1 illustrates (APA, 2017b, pp. 18–19), competence as a consulting psychologist requires knowledge and skill across an array of areas—individual assessment and coaching, group problem solving and team formation, an understanding of organizational design and change—across three interdependent levels of analysis: individual, group, and organization/system.

Complementary to these helpful guidelines, which are highly congruent with the competencies required for effective international consultation, we further recommend at the very least gaining supervised experience as well as participating in ongoing collaboration and consultation with colleagues who are successfully engaging in this work.

To summarize, on the basis of the competencies, case studies, and models and methods noted previously, we recommend the following best practices for psychologists who wish to consult internationally:

- **Know thyself.** Your personality characteristics will greatly influence how you are experienced internationally and will impact the quality and relevance of your interventions. Honest self-awareness, grounded in feedback from supervisors and colleagues, will help you identify blind spots, capitalize on strengths, and develop your competencies to their fullest capacity as you learn and grow in your knowledge, skills, and attributes.

FIGURE 3.1. Overview of Consulting Psychology/Organizational Consulting Psychology Guidelines

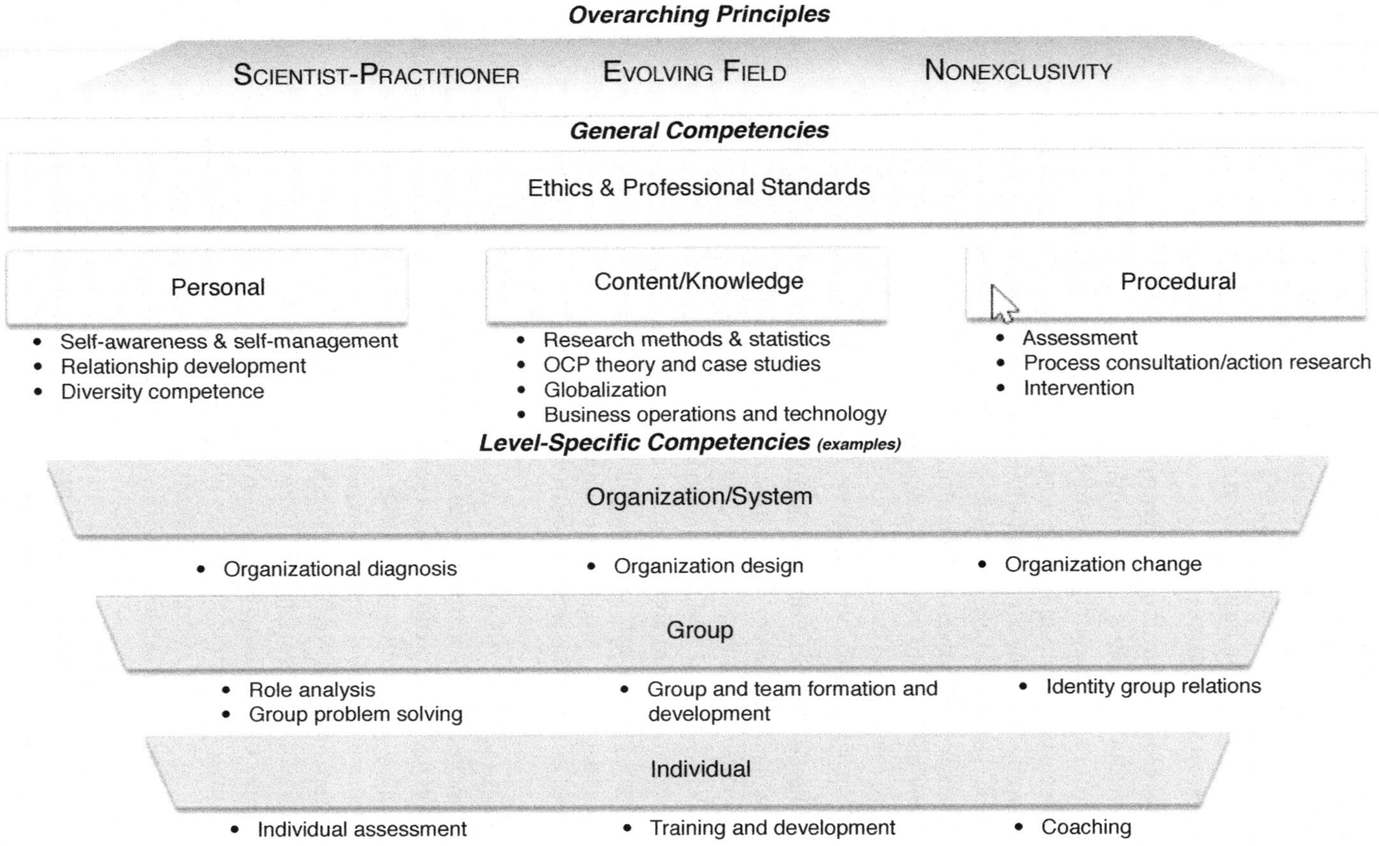

Note. Reprinted from *Guidelines for Education and Training at the Doctoral and Postdoctoral Level in Consulting Psychology (CP)/Organizational Consulting in Psychology (OCP)* (p. 19), by American Psychological Association, 2017 (https://www.apa.org/about/policy/education-training.pdf). Copyright 2017 by the American Psychological Association.

- **Develop cross-cultural knowledge.** Individuals who thrive in this work tend to be intrinsically curious about how and why different cultures and countries experience self, other, and the larger world as they do. Thus, we recommend a deliberate process of building your knowledge base about the larger world through deep and ongoing immersion in the news, identifying and making use of opportunities for connections with individuals from other cultures, and exploring the sorts of commitments that various stakeholders (e.g., higher education programs, NGOs, government, business) have in global events.

- **Develop cultural agility competence.** Informed by the competencies, case studies, models, and methods such as those noted earlier, international consultants ultimately must build the skills and experience necessary to be effective as agents of change. In addition to real-world experience, perhaps starting "at home" (e.g., volunteering with NGOs that are seeking to promote local/global change), reflect upon and further develop competencies such as perspective-taking, cultural humility, and tolerance of ambiguity. Seek opportunities to work collaboratively with peers from different cultures, where you can receive informal and formal feedback regarding your knowledge, skills, and values vis-à-vis cross-cultural consultation.

- **Engage early and often.** Consulting is as much about doing as it is knowing. Identify possible means for cross-cultural engagement and act on these opportunities. If you are a student, seek out faculty who seem to be invested in cross-cultural and international work. Offer to help on a presentation, publication, grant application, or another area of focus. If you are an early career professional, you might identify an NGO or commercial company devoted to the sorts of international activities that seem compelling to you. Examine the work of organizations such as Division 13, the Society of Consulting Psychology, of the APA, such as the previously referenced guidelines (APA, 2017b). Get in touch with relevant individuals and ask if, and how, you may help. In some cases, you may be able to spend time living and working in a new country. For example, many international consulting firms employ consultants who initially work domestically and gradually gain experience with global clients. Alternatively, many of the world's largest global companies, and NGOs, are headquartered or have major branches in the United States. Working as an internal consultant for one of these large companies or organizations may provide experience working with people from around the world and perhaps also provide opportunities to work or even live in another country. In short, as you gain knowledge and experience over time, you will better learn where your interests and skills best apply.

BEYOND THE HORIZON: THE FUTURE OF INTERNATIONAL CONSULTATION IN PSYCHOLOGY

As Lowman (2012) observed, international consultation is a distant frontier no more. Psychologists now work across national borders and will become only more diverse in their identities and activities as communication and information sharing become more commonplace and accessible around the globe (APA, 2017b). Even so, to get from here to there, we need to establish a field of international consultation that is grounded in real-world work and informed by competencies, models, and methods, such as those presented here, that can expand the breadth and depth of our inquiry and practice. Along the way, we need to examine a host of relevant issues, including but by no means limited to the relationship between national and corporate cultures; how individual differences among consultants interact with the varying needs and dynamics that they encounter internationally; and how best to access and cultivate the competencies that are integral to international consultation, to contemplate attendant ethical and moral principles of such international engagement, and to consider the relative universality of such principles and ways of working across countries and contexts.

In the final analysis, although global consultation is complex, anyone who has the capacity and inclination to undertake work in this area is likely to experience an overarching feeling of fascination because this work is so richly diverse—including individuals, dyads, communities, consortia, multinational initiatives, corporate endeavors, and stateless people, such as refugees and other highly marginalized groups. Remaining ever mindful of the potential downside of imposing beliefs and values on others, such essential sensitivity should not preclude us from offering desired knowledge and skills, even as we adapt our approach for doing so based upon the shared and unique needs and values of the individuals, groups, and constituencies we serve.

REFERENCES

American Psychological Association. (2017a). *Ethical principles of psychologists and code of conduct* (2002, amended effective June 1, 2010, and January 1, 2017). https://www.apa.org/ethics/code/index.html

American Psychological Association. (2017b). *Guidelines for education and training at the doctoral and postdoctoral level in consulting psychology (CP)/organizational consulting psychology (OCP)*. https://www.apa.org/about/policy/education-training.pdf

American Psychological Association. (2019, February). *Impact: APA and APA Services, Inc. strategic plan*. https://www.apa.org/about/apa/strategic-plan/impact-apa-strategic-plan.pdf

Anderzén, I., & Arnetz, B. B. (1999). Psychophysiological reactions to international adjustment. Results from a controlled, longitudinal study. *Psychotherapy and Psychosomatics, 68*(2), 67–75. https://doi.org/10.1159/000012315

Caligiuri, P. (2021). *Build your cultural agility: The nine competencies of successful global professionals*. Kogan Page.

Caligiuri, P., & Tarique, I. (2012). Dynamic cross-cultural competencies and global leadership effectiveness. *Journal of World Business, 47*(4), 612–622.

Caligiuri, P., Tarique, I., & Jacobs, R. (2009). Selection for international assignments. *Human Resource Management Review, 19*(3), 251–262. https://doi.org/10.1016/j.hrmr.2009.02.001

Dyjak-LeBlanc, K., Brewster, L., Grande, S., White, R., & Shullman, S. (2016). The EI leadership model: From theory and research to real world application. In C. N. Shealy (Ed.), *Making sense of beliefs and values* (pp. 531–574). Springer Publishing.

Earley, P. C., & Mosakowski, E. (2000). Creating hybrid team cultures: An empirical test of transnational team functioning. *Academy of Management Journal, 43*, 26–49.

Eyring, A. (2020). Global by design. *Consulting Psychology Journal, 72*(1), 58–67. https://doi.org/10.1037/cpb0000156

Fulkerson, J. R. (2012). Organizational consulting in international contexts: An integrative perspective. *Consulting Psychology Journal, 64*(4), 325–337. https://doi.org/10.1037/a0031663

Fuqua, D. R., & Newman, J. L. (2002). Academic perspectives on the principles for training in consulting psychology. *Consulting Psychology Journal, 54*(4), 223–232. https://doi.org/10.1037/1061-4087.54.4.223

Holt, K., & Seki, K. (2012). Global leadership: A development shift for everyone. *Industrial and Organizational Psychology: Perspectives on Science and Practice, 5*(2), 196–215. https://doi.org/10.1111/j.1754-9434.2012.01431.x

Jacobs, T. L., Shaver, P. R., Epel, E. S., Zanesco, A. P., Aichele, S. R., Bridwell, D. A., Rosenberg, E. L., King, B. G., Maclean, K. A., Sahdra, B. K., Kemeny, M. E., Ferrer, E., Wallace, B. A., & Saron, C. D. (2013). Self-reported mindfulness and cortisol during a Shamatha meditation retreat. *Health Psychology, 32*(10), 1104–1109. https://doi.org/10.1037/a0031362

James, K. (2012). Training Burmese refugee counsellors in India. *Intervention (Amstelveen, Netherlands), 10*(1), 4–16. https://doi.org/10.1097/WTF.0b013e328351d9df

Kircanski, K., Lieberman, M. D., & Craske, M. G. (2012). Feelings into words: Contributions of language to exposure therapy. *Psychological Science, 23*(10), 1086–1091. https://doi.org/10.1177/0956797612443830

Konanahalli, A., & Oyedele, L. O. (2016). Emotional intelligence and British expatriates' cross-cultural adjustment in international construction projects. *Construction Management and Economics, 34*(11), 751–768. https://doi.org/10.1080/01446193.2016.1213399

Leonard, H. S., Freedman, A. M., Hill, C. S., Warrier, J., & Chu, P. (2012). Consulting in international contexts: Examining and testing assumptions. *Consulting Psychology Journal, 64*(4), 250–267. https://doi.org/10.1037/a0031662

Lowman, R. L. (2012). Frontier no more: International consulting skills as necessary minimal competencies for consulting psychologists. *Consulting Psychology Journal, 64*(4), 338–343. Advance online publication. https://doi.org/10.1037/a0031676

Lowman, R. L. (2016). *An introduction to consulting psychology: Working with individuals, groups, and organizations.* American Psychological Association. https://doi.org/10.1037/14853-000

Mol, S. T., Born, M. P., Willemsen, M. E., & Van Der Molen, H. T. (2005). Predicting expatriate job performance for selection purposes: A quantitative review. *Journal of Cross-Cultural Psychology, 36*(5), 590–620. https://doi.org/10.1177/0022022105278544

Shealy, C. N. (Ed.). (2016). *Making sense of beliefs and values: Research, theory, and practice.* Springer.

Trejo, B. C., Richard, E. M., Van Driel, M., & McDonald, D. P. (2015). Cross-cultural competence: The role of emotion regulation ability and optimism. *Military Psychology, 27*(5), 276–286. https://doi.org/10.1037/mil0000081

Vandaveer, V. V. (2012). Dyadic team development across cultures: Case study. *Consulting Psychology Journal, 64*(4), 279–294. https://doi.org/10.1037/a0031652

Yoo, S. H., Matsumoto, D., & LeRoux, J. A. (2006). The influence of emotion recognition and emotion regulation on intercultural adjustment. *International Journal of Intercultural Relations, 30*(3), 345–363. https://doi.org/10.1016/j.ijintrel.2005.08.006

4

Intervention

Enhancing Mental Health and Well-Being Around the World

Laura R. Johnson, Christopher F. Drescher, and Michael J. Bordieri

A s a discipline, psychology is often thought to be synonymous with the *practice* of psychology in the form of clinical intervention or treatment. The prevailing image is that of a clinician engaged in talk therapy with a client, family, or group. Although such an approach has value, scholars and practitioners have emphasized that psychologists can and should broaden the nature and scope of their practice to effect positive changes in the lives of individuals, families, and communities beyond national borders (Berry, 2013; Stevens & Gielen, 2007). In this chapter, we discuss key conceptual and practical issues related to psychological interventions in a global context. In the Foundations section, we review the need for mental health services globally, highlighting the potential for psychologists to apply their knowledge and skills around the world and the competencies needed for such work. In the Applications section, we highlight diverse pathways to care and clinical service settings, such as health care settings, schools, families, and communities. We discuss levels of intervention (i.e., treatment, prevention, strengths based) and point out emergent areas of global concern in need of psychological interventions, such as the climate crisis and the COVID-19 pandemic. Along the way, we showcase eight diverse examples of intervention work in international psychology.

https://doi.org/10.1037/0000311-005
Going Global: How Psychologists Can Meet a World of Need, C. Shealy, M. Bullock, and S. Kapadia (Editors)

FOUNDATIONS

In this section, we highlight the need for psychologists and psychological interventions worldwide. Yet interventions in a global context requires that we first consider ethical issues, cultural competencies, and the World Health Organization's (WHO's; 2013) core competencies in global mental health.

The Need for Psychological Interventions Globally

Why should psychologists intervene globally? Worldwide, the need for mental health interventions is abundantly clear and largely unmet. WHO (2008) estimated that more than 450 million persons worldwide suffer from mental disorders. Depression accounts for more days of lost productivity from death and disability than any other condition (WHO, 2013). Alcohol dependence is among the top 10 causes of disability across all income groups, and substance abuse is recognized as a worldwide problem (Degenhardt & Hall, 2012). Moreover, 26 million people around the world are estimated to have schizophrenia, which is further associated with poor physical health, homelessness, and discrimination (WHO, 2008). Anxiety-related disorders remain a global problem, often in connection with stress, violence, poverty, and health problems (Baxter et al., 2013). Overall, mental health concerns account for 14% of the global burden of disease, which is likely an underestimation given the relationship between psychological health and chronic diseases (WHO, 2013).

Despite the prominence of mental health conditions globally, most people do not receive adequate mental health care (WHO, 2022). In low-income countries, less than $0.25 USD per person is spent annually on mental health, with the majority of such funds dedicated to inpatient hospitals (WHO, 2013). Complicating matters, low-income countries have a paucity of mental health workers, with the ratio of psychiatrists to persons estimated at 1:200,000 (WHO, 2013); other mental health professionals, such as psychologists, are even rarer. The COVID-19 pandemic has placed further stress and mental health strain on individuals worldwide, increasing the need for services, posing new barriers to treatment, and further exposing the harsh inadequacies of mental health services. Clearly, the field of psychology has not responded sufficiently to the vast need for mental health services around the world. In part, this response level is due to insufficient allocation of resources, limited education regarding global mental health, and a restricted sense of professional identity. Along with others, we contend that psychology has an ethical obligation to become more thoughtfully active on the global stage (e.g., Berry, 2013).

Rationale for Reaching Out: International, Transnational, and Global Intervention

WHO (2022) regards global mental health concerns as human development issues that warrant broad structural attention beyond traditional ways of intervening (Draguns, 2007). Public health concerns, poverty, population growth and mobility, human trafficking, intercultural conflict, gender and racial discrimination, social justice inequities, armed conflict, the climate crisis, and disaster preparation and mitigation, including the response to pandemics, are among the societal challenges with a direct relationship to mental health and well-being (Stevens & Gielen, 2007). Psychologists can and should consider engaging in such issues not only because there is so much need but also because our knowledge and skills may be of most use in these areas on a global stage (Waldorf, 2009). This does not mean that established intervention methods, including individual talk therapy, are irrelevant to global work, but expanded intervention competencies and roles for psychologists are needed. Education/ training, consultation, supervision, intervention research, and social advocacy are among the possibilities for international intervention (e.g., Draguns, 2007; Marsella, 2007; Moodley et al., 2013; Stevens & Gielen, 2007; Wedding & Stevens, 2004).

Given the diversity of roles for psychologists, providing a specific definition of intervention presents a challenge in a global context. Stevens and Gielen (2007) offered guidance by delineating between global and international psychology more generally, with *global* referring to universal applications and *international* meaning between nations. The word *transnational* is increasingly used to recognize interconnectivity between persons, groups, and organizations and the interactive influences of cultural, social, political, environmental, and economic realms within and beyond "the nation state." Transnational psychologists may work with diaspora communities and other socially constructed groups that span national borders (e.g., ethnic groups, immigrants and refugees; Bacigalupe & Cámara, 2012) and often fall outside any geopolitical or physical boundaries (e.g., transgendered persons, war veterans, religious minorities). Each perspective centers on collaborations among psychologists and/or allied service providers to broaden applications and multicultural competencies while enhancing the impact and effectiveness of psychological interventions.

Building upon the foundational perspectives of others (Stevens & Gielen, 2007), we offer the following aspirational definition of *intervention*: From a global perspective, psychological intervention includes collaborative activities engaged in by persons, groups, or organizations that are designed to (a) promote mental health, well-being, and the optimal development of individuals, couples, families, systems, communities, nations, and the world and/or (b) assess, prevent, ameliorate, mitigate, heal, or treat a wide range of individual, community, and social problems that affect the mental health, well-being, and development of persons, communities, systems, and societies, and which are (c) based on connected principles, theories, concepts, behaviors, and relationships that are considered "psychological" in nature.

What is considered an appropriate, ethical, effective, and competent psychological intervention will vary based on many dynamic factors. We are acutely aware that the terms *intervention* and *globalize* are culturally embedded and carry different meanings that may lead to misunderstanding and controversy.

Intervention in the global arena has long been associated with military actions, religious indoctrination, and oppressive control of resources. Moreover, efforts to "globalize" psychology may be seen as imperialist, dominating, oppressive, ethnocentric, and monocultural as well as potentially threatening to cultural autonomy and diversity. Therefore, as a matter of cultural competence, psychologists need to understand the unique settings in which they work, including relevant histories, sensitivities, and power differentials. This caveat holds true for work in areas of health and mental health, the environment, and economic development undertaken by well-meaning individuals and philanthropic nongovernmental organizations (NGOs). Although valuable in many contexts, some interventions further consolidate power away from the people they wish to serve and toward government elites, business, and NGOs themselves, while not producing satisfactory advancement toward development goals, such as food security (Abdul-Raheem, 2006).

Cultural Responsiveness in a Global Context

Culturally responsive intervention, by definition, varies across and within countries, nations, cultures, societies, communities, families, and persons, even as there are features that may cut across interventions. Culturally responsive interventions emerge from general, cross-cultural, and culture-specific competencies that facilitate effective functioning in diverse contexts (American Psychological Association [APA], 2017b). Self-awareness, other-awareness, cultural knowledge, and a range of practical skills, such as reflective thinking, intercultural communication, and flexibility, are key aspects (Hays, 2008). Cultural competence requires that psychologists be (a) aware of their own and others' cultural values, assumptions, biases, and behaviors; (b) knowledgeable about salient cultural and contextual factors, such as sociopolitical histories, worldviews, acculturation processes, identity and intersectionality, intergroup dynamics, communication styles, and kinship patterns; and (c) able to develop specific interventions and strategies that are appropriate for different cultures, contexts, and individuals. Marsella (2007) provided further guidance on specific global competencies needed by transnational psychologists, such as knowledge of common global challenges like poverty, disease, war, and climate change. Mindfulness of common cross-cultural issues, such as budget control and transparency, are needed, as is a willingness to examine the cultural encapsulation of the theories that drive professional activity, such as the emphasis on individualistic, reductionist, and decontextualized approaches, particularly when matters of "diagnosis" and "treatment" are involved (e.g., Deacon, 2013; Moodley et al., 2013).

Cultural mistrust and a lack of accessibility, affordability, applicability, or acceptability may have a negative impact on the help-seeking and treatment pathway even before interventions begin (Sue & Sue, 2008). Culturally responsive interventions thus account for cultural, social, and contextual factors, such as the goals, values, expectations, and perspectives of the intended beneficiaries.

However, no amount of planning can prepare one fully for the experiential aspects of international interventions, especially with vulnerable groups. As such, host country collaborators should be equal partners when assessing needs, developing and implementing interventions, and evaluating processes and outcomes. One should not assume that colleagues in a host country will be culturally competent or even aware of principles and practices of culturally responsive interventions. For example, it could be that host colleagues have been trained within a North American or European-based paradigm that focuses on biomedical conceptualizations and treatments while neglecting knowledge of and respect for Indigenous interventions (e.g., Deacon, 2013). Whereas consulting literature could provide some guidance, the available literature is limited in scope and generalizability to the majority world (Arnett, 2008; Thalmayer et al., 2021). Cultural brokers can help psychologists understand cultural and contextual concerns and within-group issues, such as taboos, the importance of gender matching, or communication norms that may not be obvious or understood by outsiders. In this regard, there are six core principles to consider.

Six Core Principles of Global Psychological Interventions

Psychologists may seek guidance from a WHO (2013) action plan emphasizing six cross-cutting principles and approaches for global mental health interventions.

Universal Access and Coverage

Universal access to mental health care is central to comprehensive interventions that are designed to improve well-being. Unfortunately, persons suffering from mental disorders are politically and economically disenfranchised in many countries, making it difficult for those who are most in need to access services. The denial of services to certain members of society based on a lack of economic power is fundamentally unfair and unethical. As Prilleltensky (2012) contended, wellness *is* fairness. Increasing public awareness of and access to health, mental health, and social welfare services is a worthy area for global psychological intervention. In particular, it is essential to strengthen the capacities of citizens to advocate for health and mental health care coverage from their government and other service organizations. The need for improvement in systems that "serve the underserved" is especially great, as is ensuring universal access to health and mental health care as a basic human right.

Human Rights

Any psychological intervention needs to respect human rights. Although such an assertion may seem self-evident, it is worth reflecting on the rights of persons suffering from mental health difficulties. With some exceptions, individuals have the right to make their own choices concerning mental health care (APA, 2010), including the decision to refuse an intervention or explore and pursue alternative treatment options. Furthermore, psychologists need to ascertain whether inclusion in an intervention could present a risk for being denied such rights. For example, interventions for certain stigmatized populations, such as lesbian, gay, bisexual, transgender, and queer or questioning persons, may inadvertently place participants at risk of losing their freedom or life (Semugoma et al., 2012). Moreover, certain psychological diagnoses may be so stigmatized in a culture that such a diagnosis (e.g., schizophrenia) effectively causes such a person to forfeit their right to make autonomous decisions.

Awareness of global human rights concerns is among the global competencies needed by psychologists (Marsella, 2007). Increases in human trafficking; marginalization of ethnic and religious minorities and persons with disabilities; gender inequities; sociopolitical conflict; and abuse and denial of rights to gay, lesbian, bisexual, intersex, transgender, and gender nonconforming persons are among the areas and populations that may benefit from the application of psychological knowledge. In so doing, caution is needed to attenuate the likelihood of psychologists' own complicity in rights abuses. Consider the ethical dilemma regarding the activities of psychologists who work to prevent terrorism or deal with armed conflict (Wessells & Edgerton, 2008). This fundamental point is illustrated by the APA Independent Review (the Hoffman Report), which concluded that psychologists had been directly and inappropriately involved in the development of interventions designed to torture captives of the U.S. government at Guantanamo Bay, Abu Ghraib, and other locations post–September 11 (APA, 2015).

Evidence-Based Practice

In line with developments in clinical psychology and the broader evidence-based medicine movement, evidence-based practice in psychology is an important principle (APA Presidential Task Force on Evidence-Based Practice, 2006). Defined as "the integration of the best available research with clinical expertise in the context of patient characteristics, culture, and preferences" (p. 284), *evidence-based practice* provides a framework for guiding culturally competent global interventions. Although we strongly endorse the principle of having evidence to support interventions, it is important to look critically at what constitutes the best available research evidence (Deacon, 2013). Given that the vast majority of psychological research is conducted with U.S. and Western European samples (Arnett, 2008), it is premature to assume that the existing literature on empirically supported treatments (ESTs) is applicable internationally. Moreover, debate is ongoing regarding the appropriate arbiter of what can and cannot be labeled "evidence-based" and the appropriate standards and criteria (e.g., APA, 2012). In fact, since Arnett's (2008) review of child and adolescent psychology research for majority world representation, small improvements have been seen in representation from European countries but no improvement in representation of majority world samples in low- and middle-income countries (Thalmayer et al., 2021).

Perhaps the greatest limitation regarding the EST movement has been its narrow focus on validating specific treatment manuals for specific disorders in rigorously controlled and replicated clinical trials. This strategy provides excellent evidence of efficacy but does so at the cost of external validity. Another limitation of the EST strategy is the extensive time and resources required to conduct clinical trials. Given the growing number of disorders contained in the fifth edition of the *Diagnostic and Statistical Manual of Mental Disorders* (American Psychiatric Association, 2013) and the abundance of treatment technologies available, it would take more than 500 years to conduct the research necessary to validate existing treatments (Wilson, 1997). From a global perspective, this 500-year problem quickly becomes a 5,000-year problem if researchers were to design clinical trials that take into account all the diverse client, therapist, and contextual factors that may interact with treatments to influence outcomes. As the efforts toward treatment development continue, the evidence base has broadened with examinations of therapy processes, which may be more closely aligned with the real-world exigencies that characterize global psychological intervention (Gaete et al., 2011).

Life-Course Approach

Knowledge of developmental issues and differences is essential for psychological interventions. For example, the unique needs of children often are not given sufficient attention within an international context or are simply tacked on to more general interventions (Wessells & Edgerton, 2008). Along similar lines, it should be noted that approximately 85% of youth today live in economically developing countries that are youth saturated, meaning that a large percentage of that country's population is aged 18 or younger (i.e., the "youth bulge"). The developmental and mental health needs of these youth must be addressed for a civil society to be sustainable. That said, there is incredible diversity in children's lives internationally in terms of their status in society, roles, rights, family structures, challenges, daily activities, and expectations for optimal development. Thus, any intervention for children must be adapted to meet not only their developmental level but also the cultural, social, political, and environmental contexts in which they reside. By understanding the multilayered developmental influences on youth and their developmental niches, psychologists can help shape effective interventions (Nayar, 2013). Some countries have high percentages of youth who are orphaned, living in poverty, and affected by war. Girls are subject to genital cutting each year (approximately 3.6 million in 2013), and multitudes face sexual and physical violence, corporal punishment, early marriage, and forced labor at home, in schools, or in institutions (UNICEF, 2014, 2017). In addition to considering diversity and cultural relativity, psychologists must know and respect universal child rights as outlined in the United Nations (1989) Convention on the Rights of the Child.

Psychologists must also be aware of unique issues facing older adults and understand that what is considered "old age" varies widely. For example, life expectancy as of 2016 is 83 years in Australia but only 64 in Afghanistan, where war is the fifth leading cause of death (UNICEF, 2017). Additionally, cultural attitudes toward older people vary. In the United States, for example, older adults may be viewed as challenges that need to be managed, often through professional services. However, older persons in Tanzania tend to be well respected and cared for by children, members, and even other elders (van Eeuwijk, 2014). Because there is a cultural norm to seek advice and permission from "the elders" in most matters of importance, successful interventions in such contexts would need the support of these valued community members (Johnson et al., 2019). At the same time, traditional cultural values of honoring and respecting elders are shifting in many parts of the world, causing a breakdown of traditional family supports. In Japan, for example, demographic changes and economic pressures increasingly discourage multigenerational living and associated caregiving. In short, contextual, cross-generational, and developmental issues should be known and addressed (Takagi et al., 2007).

Multisectoral Approach

When possible, interventions should be coordinated in partnership with existing systems so as to avoid conflict or confusion. Uncoordinated interventions may encounter difficulties at a structural, systemic, or political level, which can encumber interventions or render potential benefits moot. For example, a school-based intervention to enhance girls' attendance and participation that is approved by school officials may be stymied if other officials, such as regional or district officers or community leaders, are not consulted. Others may be "caught" between competing (often opposing) systems of care (e.g., hospital or traditional healer). Moreover, collaborating across multiple sectors affords excellent opportunities for intra- and interdisciplinary partnerships that can enhance cultural responsiveness and benefits of an intervention (Johnson et al., 2009; Nayar, 2013).

Empowerment of Persons With Mental Disorders and Psychosocial Disabilities

Insofar as possible, persons receiving an intervention should be involved in the planning, delivery, and evaluation of the intervention. They should be seen as resources to intervention developers, rather than as problems to be solved. Positively oriented paradigms, such as solution-focused, strengths-based, meaning-focused, community-based, and participatory action methods, may be especially useful and culturally appropriate (Johnson et al., 2009). For example, community systems strengthening in Afghanistan, which seeks to decrease domestic violence and reinforce the agency of women, has provided an important pathway to improving mental health in that area (van Mierlo, 2012). In situations in which persons have limited opportunities for expression, interventions that "give voice" to participants may be maximally empowering. The photovoice technique, for example, in which participants document and solve problems in their lives through photographic images and storytelling, has been used successfully with vulnerable groups, such as former child soldiers in Sierra Leone (Denov et al., 2012). Interventions should be culturally rooted and emphasize the empowerment of individuals through interpersonal relationships, community engagement, and social action. Ideally, mental health interventions will address real individual and community concerns, such as poverty and health access, and be built on empowerment frameworks, such as Yo Quiero, Yo Puedo, a psychosocial program to increase well-being in Mexico that has expanded into several other countries (Pick & Sirkin, 2010).

Ethics of International Psychological Interventions

Although considered throughout this chapter, the ethics of international interventions is an area that needs to be discussed explicitly. The issues are complex because the nature and scope of interventions includes a range of professional activities, from assessment and therapy to education, training, and policy-level activities. Various practice guidelines (e.g., the IASC Guidelines on Mental Health and Psychosocial Support in Emergency Settings; Inter-Agency Standing Committee, 2007) offer important cautions regarding direct intervention by nonnative psychologists. Most important, psychologists should avoid providing direct care clinical services in contexts and cultures that are unfamiliar; rather, they should focus on training and empowering local service providers. If psychologists are called upon to work directly with international clients, several caveats are worth emphasizing.

First and foremost, psychologists should not pursue treatment development or implementation independently. Instead, they should establish partnerships with existing international and local treatment developers, institutions, and resources. Second, psychologists should abide by and reflect on ethics. Although the APA (2017a) *Ethical Principles of Psychologists and Code of Conduct* provides an overarching framework for practicing psychology in the United States, many countries have their own ethics codes, licensure laws, and regulations that guide clinical practice; global principles also provide relevant perspective (International Union of Psychological Science, 2008). However, to date there are no universal global ethical standards for psychologists. Thus, before beginning any intervention, psychologists should review ethics codes and regulations that may be applicable to their work, both in their home country and in the location of the intervention.

Third, psychologists should be aware of practice parameters. They should not assume that their license to practice in their home country qualifies them to practice elsewhere. Educational and experience requirements for practice vary between countries, and no universal training standards exist. As such, we recommend (a) consultation with entities that are responsible for ethics and licensure in the home country, (b) engagement with host country practitioners and institutions, and (c) documentation of consultations as well as intervention activities.

Fourth, psychologists should understand cultural norms and practices. A variety of other ethical and practical considerations may arise, such as different norms and expectations regarding payment, bartering, and gift giving;

informed consent and confidentiality; preventing self-harm and duty to warn; supervision and training; gaining community support; providing referrals; managing multiple roles; and continuity of care (Johnson & Sandhu, 2010). For example, receiving gifts or attending social functions may be generally frowned upon by U.S. ethics, yet this action could be key to a trusting and reciprocal relationship in many cultural contexts, such as working with refugees (Johnson et al., 2009). In some cultures, it is taboo to mention suicide, which may hinder a practitioner's ability to assess suicidality directly. For example, in Brazil, suicide is considered to be a terrible sin, limiting its discussion despite a high suicide rate in the country (da Silva & Corrêa, 2015). Although a thorough discussion of such considerations is beyond the scope of this chapter, Hays (2008) provided useful guidelines for consideration during assessment and therapy within multicultural contexts.

APPLICATIONS: INTERVENTION SETTINGS

With foundations in place, it is now possible to consider the "how, when, and where" of doing this work. As becomes clear, the diversity of settings and types of intervention all bear directly on matters of application. When contemplating the possibilities for "going global," it is essential to understand how and where psychology is situated professionally as well as the vast diversity of settings in which interventions may occur. Stevens and Gielen (2007) provided an overview of some regional differences, and Wedding and Stevens (2004) offered several specific national examples in each region of the world. Here, we focus on some common intervention settings.

Mental Health Settings

Psychologists working internationally may find themselves within familiar mental health settings (e.g., inpatient and outpatient clinics and residential centers) that use a range of theoretical frameworks, systems of training, and intervention approaches. As clinicians, we must continually remind ourselves that any approach to thinking about and planning interventions is culturally embedded (Pedersen, 2004). Professionals in mental health settings may be educated in, and inclined toward, U.S.- and European-based models and theories. Although such congruence may be alluring, and some approaches quite relevant, it is important to account seriously for spiritual, religious, and cultural processes as well as contextual factors that bear directly on functioning (e.g., poverty, trauma, stigma). Because of a worldwide shortage of mental health practitioners, psychologists may play a role in helping colleagues in other parts of the world to gain familiarity and competence working with established psychotherapeutic approaches as long as the earlier caveats are openly addressed throughout education, training, supervision, and delivery (see the example by Sandhu in Exhibit 4.1; Sandhu, 2011).

EXHIBIT 4.1

From Suicidal Crisis to Support for Counseling Interventions in India

Daya Singh Sandhu

As a Fulbright-Nehru senior research scholar conducting research on suicide in India, I could not ignore the mental health crisis all around me. I was troubled to read news almost daily about students, farmers, and housewives hanging themselves, jumping in front of running trains, taking poisons, and killing themselves through self-immolation and drowning. As a part of the economic and social changes in India, people are experiencing multiple stressors. These stressors are causing serious mental health concerns, including clinical depression, anxiety, marital discords, domestic violence, alcoholism, and substance abuse, which in turn were the leading reasons for suicide contemplations and completions ("Suicides Rise," 2011). Witnessing the scourge of suicides imposing a huge emotional, social, and economic burden on the Indian society brought a dramatic change in my professional journey. From a research scholar, I became a social activist. In the spirit of preventing and addressing mental health problems throughout India, I collaborated with the United States–India Educational Foundation in New Delhi in 2010 to start the Association of Mental Health Counselors to combat mental health problems in India and to provide practical training. Tackling the suicide problem in India requires broad structural attention to societal problems and availability of counseling and mental health services.

Health Service Settings

Primary care is an obvious system through which psychological interventions may be delivered, and it is an appropriate venue in much of the world. Along these lines, behavioral health and health psychology are increasingly applied toward the treatment of conditions such as smoking, obesity, diabetes, substance disorders, and sleep disorders. The increasing relevance of concepts of "general practice," "primary care," and "health service psychology" to the roles and identities of psychologists is highly allied with international psychological interventions (e.g., Belar, 2012). Such disciplinary evolution also is consistent with the WHO initiative to integrate and decentralize mental health care services into primary care (WHO, 2008). Johnson et al. (2009) reported, for example, that in some countries, such as Uganda, most cases of depression could be treated by primary care staff at the local level, with only the more severe presentations requiring transfer to treatment centers. Thus, working within the existing primary care sector is essential to strengthening the ability of psychologists to bring mental health intervention to a broader public (WHO, 2008). Indeed, with an expected increase in health pandemics and zoonotic diseases, psychology will be increasingly called upon to play important roles in both shaping behaviors to prevent transmission and addressing the larger mental health toll of health disasters. Moreover, integrated services and interprofessional collaboration may be culturally responsive in many contexts, such as those less enmeshed in mind–body dualism or that stigmatize mental disorders (Moodley et al., 2013).

Couples and Families

Because couple and family work is such an important area of focus, it behooves psychologists to appreciate the vast diversity worldwide in how family units are organized. Such considerations apply to the definition of families (structure, roles, kinship patterns), how they are formed (marital arrangements, polygyny and polyandry, fertility beliefs and practices), and how they function (roles, gender dynamics, sexual practices, parenting, infidelity, divorce, concepts of health vs. dysfunction, and so on). Globally, the size of families and the relative importance of the family compared with the individual are key considerations. The size of the domestic unit is typically larger outside of the United States—including three or more children compared with 1.8 in the United States—with extended family members often playing key roles in childrearing (Arnett, 2008). Variations in sense of self and relations with others (e.g., individualism vs. collectivism, hierarchical vs. egalitarian) are among major differences to consider. Moreover, families in the majority world may disproportionately be affected by social trends, including changing sociocultural and sociopolitical conditions, evolving gender roles, rates of domestic violence, increased mobility and family separations, and cross-national adoptions. As such, both locally and globally, psychologists who work with couples and families should "expand the scope of our research and practice to encompass the larger socioeconomic and political contexts" that they face (Kaslow, 2001, p. 44).

Schools

Schools are an important setting for psychological interventions around the world. Across contexts, school-related concerns can center on increasing access, preventing dropout, ensuring student safety, addressing behavioral and learning problems, and promoting quality education. When working with schools, one must be aware of differences in practical and pedagogical approaches adopted toward education. For example, in the United States, teaching styles often are direct, favor critical thinking, and emphasize the uniqueness of each child. In contrast, other cultures may place a higher value on obedience, fitting in, and respect for authority (Nayar, 2013). Despite these differences, some school-based psychological interventions appear to be successful across cultures and contexts. For example, the Olweus Bullying Prevention Program, a comprehensive program designed to reduce bullying and achieve better peer relations in schools, has successfully been implemented in countries such as Norway, Sweden, England, Scotland, Ireland, Holland, Germany, Australia, Japan, and the United States (Olweus & Limber, 2010). Schools also are a natural setting to facilitate other youth-related goals, including elevating the rate of girls' education and overall literacy, enhancing civic engagement, improving intercultural relations, and cultivating youth leadership (Sustainable Development Goals [SDGs]; United Nations, 2021). Programs for parents, families, and community adults can also be housed in schools for ease of access, stigma reduction, and familiarity. For example, Parent Management Training has been successfully adapted for working with parents in the school setting in Mexico City (see Rodríguez et al.'s example in Exhibit 4.2; Baumann et al., 2014).

Communities

In many global contexts, a community-minded approach and social justice orientation are necessary for contextually relevant and durable mental health interventions (Nayar, 2013). Settings for community-based interventions may include government service-settings, such as agricultural or vocational centers; religious settings, such as churches or mosques; organizations, such as social or civic clubs; permanent or temporary settlements/camps, such as for refugees and displaced persons; rehabilitation or drop-in centers for street children, survivors of conflict, or disaster; and other "treatment" centers supported by hundreds of thousands of NGOs all over the world. Such services may shift in focus over time to meet changing needs of communities (see James & Bastien's example in Exhibit 4.3; James et al., 2012). As with all interventions, those at the community level must be sensitive to contextual variations, especially concerning conditions of justice and fairness (Prilleltensky, 2012). In this regard, psychologists working internationally should be aware of community psychology, which champions a holistic, ecosystems perspective that is particularly important when it comes to addressing broad societal issues, such as public health problems, poverty, conflict, and disasters, while taking interventions to people in need, wherever they are (see APA's Division 27, Society for Community Research and Action).

EXHIBIT 4.2

Benefiting Families in Mexico City: Adaptation of a Parenting Intervention in a School Setting

Melanie Domenech Rodríguez, Nancy Amador Buenabad, and Amanda Baumann

Evidence-based parenting interventions have provided an excellent support for families that have faced contextual, familial, and individual challenges that get in the way of achieving and maintaining harmonious relationships (e.g., Parent Management Training–Oregon model). With an existing relationship between the authors and a spirit of collegiality, research began in 2004, which led to collaborations for improvement of intervention efforts tailored to Latino families in the U.S. and Mexican families. Cultural adaptations to the treatment included surface adaptations (e.g., updated manuals with Mexican symbols and metaphors in collaboration with local design experts) as well as adaptations to fit to local structures (e.g., offering the intervention as one of the "parent remediation" classes offered by the school district). Work in Mexico with professionals and families supported the utility of Parent Management Training–Oregon model tools and the acceptability of the theory in the local context; with hundreds of families served, there are improvements for participating families across implementations (Baumann et al., 2014).

EXHIBIT 4.3

Empowerment in the Aftermath of an Earthquake: A Lay-Led Psychosocial Initiative in Haiti

Leah James and Gilberte Bastien

Soulaje Lespri Mou (SLM) is a collaborative group model designed to provide empowerment models of psychosocial support to Port-au-Prince residents displaced by the 2010 earthquake. First, residents are trained in evidence-based psychoeducation and culturally tailored coping skills to increase perceived safety, ability to self-calm, and social support. Second, SLM aims to enhance life meaning, hope, and collective efficacy by training workshop graduates to further disseminate coping skills to new participants. SLM is implemented by local young people as lay mental health workers who are themselves earthquake survivors. This two-level train-the-trainer model is a time- and cost-efficient approach that balances Indigenous and psychological perspectives and is suited to a low-resource postdisaster scenario (James et al., 2012). The structure of SLM evolved to accommodate shifting camp conditions and participant needs following the 2010 earthquake, with the trained young people leading groups framed as "seminars" to decrease stigma and capitalize on the value placed on education in Haitian culture.

Indigenous and Traditional Systems

Psychologists also may find avenues for intervention work within Indigenous or traditional healing sectors (Johnson et al., 2009; Sue & Sue, 2008). Indigenous approaches to care may include community service; prayer, meditation, chanting, or other types of devotion; purification rituals; reading or studying cultural or religious texts; veneration of god(s), spirits, or ancestors; and the creative and expressive arts (e.g., Hays, 2008; Johnson et al., 2017; Sue & Sue, 2008; Wessells & Edgerton, 2008). In some cases, Indigenous systems may not only run parallel to the "modern" system but also be equally if not better developed. For example, in many African countries the system of traditional healing is sophisticated and complex, including various training programs, certificates, and district-level councils for regulating herbalists, spiritualists, and other healers (Johnson et al., 2017; Wessells & Edgerton, 2008). Along these lines, governments and agencies such as the WHO contend that many mental health concerns may be treated by Indigenous healers, who are often more accessible (Ovuga et al., 2005). There is a need for knowledge sharing and collaboration among psychologists and traditional healers. Certain cultural rituals may readily be incorporated into standard interventions or used as adjuncts (see the example by Wessells in Exhibit 4.4).

APPLICATIONS: INTERVENTION TYPES

In addition to the rich array of settings in which global and international psychologists intervene, the types of intervention run the gamut from prevention to treatment and strength-based approaches.

EXHIBIT 4.4

Collaborative Healing in Postconflict Angola

Mike Wessells

Developing psychosocial interventions in postconflict contexts requires not only cultural sensitivity but also a willingness to suspend one's preconceptions, learn about local practices, and partner with local people. From 1995 to 2002, Angolan colleagues had been asked by USAID to support the reintegration of former soldiers, many of whom had been exposed to trauma. Western psychologists had advised addressing posttraumatic stress disorder, which did not address the main psychosocial problems. For example, a 14-year-old boy reported intense and powerful nightmares as the spirit of the man he had killed. Beyond poor sleep, his affliction was seen as communal in that the spirit also had the power to kill members of his family, cause crop failures, or otherwise harm members of the community carrying such spiritual pollution. The treatment team provided healers with the resources needed to conduct the purifying rituals, which typically involved the sacrifice of goats and ended with a communal meal. They also supported vocational training and income-generating activities, which enabled the boys to reduce their stigma and meet concerns over lack of necessities (Wessells & Edgerton, 2008).

Note. USAID = United States Agency for International Development.

Treatment

Psychologists interested in international work in standard clinical settings may consult, teach, train, monitor, and evaluate interventions derived from mainstream theories, integrated or eclectic theories, transtheoretical models, or culture-specific approaches. In addition to expanding our professional identities and paradigms when working internationally, there is a place for established approaches to intervention (e.g., assessment, therapy), as well as education and training in such methods, provided there is sufficient and ongoing attention to the cultural, collaborative, and ethical matters that have been described in this chapter (e.g., Chapter 2, this volume, for information on assessment). In this regard, intervention modalities across the spectrum of therapeutic orientations may readily be adapted, ranging from minor technical or practical adjustments (e.g., ethnic matching, reduction of jargon, translation of treatment materials) to major conceptual adjustments across multiple domains and culture-specific approaches. Verdeli, for example, discusses adaptations of interpersonal therapy for treating depression cross-culturally (see Verdeli's example in Exhibit 4.5; Patel et al., 2011; Verdeli et al., 2003). Incorporating cultural or religious material or strategies, adapting one's interpersonal style, and sensitively evaluating and using cultural beliefs and values are among the methods for increasing the effectiveness and relevance of treatment interventions (Johnson & Sandhu, 2010; Nayar, 2013).

Theoretical orientations vary across international regions and treatment targets, with no single dominant orientation (Draguns, 2007; Moodley et al., 2013; see also the Society for Psychotherapy Research [https://www.psychotherapyresearch.org/]). Not surprisingly, integrative, interdisciplinary, and third wave interventions may be quite useful in an international and global

---

EXHIBIT 4.5

Addressing the Global Crisis of Depression: Interpersonal Therapy

Helena Verdeli

My global mental health work has focused on rolling out psychosocial packages in diverse regions of the world by adapting core techniques, testing packages via rigorous research, and disseminating if effective (Verdeli et al., 2003). From 2002 to 2003, I participated in adapting and testing group interpersonal therapy (IPT) for depressed adults in rural Southwest Uganda. Group IPT was more efficacious in reducing depressive symptoms and dysfunction at termination and 6-month follow-up. We learned that the focus of IPT groups evolved from the treatment of depression per se, to encompass better education for their children, access to resources (e.g., material goods and services offered by NGOs), and involvement in community projects. From 2005 to 2007, I collaborated to adapt group IPT for adolescents suffering from depression and anxiety who lived in Internally Displaced Persons camps in Northern Uganda. Although the intervention was effective, acceptable, feasible, and adopted regionally, it did not scale up to a national level. I am convinced that the main reason was the lack of implementation of IPT in existing health care sites and lack of collaboration with the Ugandan Ministry of Health on a policy level. From 2005 to 2010, I joined the MANAS project in Goa, India, which focused on developing and testing a multicomponent intervention for anxiety and depression in primary-care settings. Preliminary results showed that patients had difficulty attending IPT appointments, primarily because of transportation costs they could not afford. After cultural and logistical adaptations of IPT were made for this population, significant beneficial effects were observed (Patel et al., 2011).

Note. NGOs = nongovernmental organizations.

context as they strive to bring together different levels of analysis, focusing on mechanisms of change. Acceptance and commitment therapy, for example, was developed in an international context (see Wilson & Bordieri's example in Exhibit 4.6; Wilson et al., 2013). Integrative practice also requires openness to the potential reconciliation of therapeutic methods and philosophies from Europe and North America with those from the Global South (e.g., Wachtel, 2008; see also the Society for the Exploration of Psychotherapy Integration [https://www.sepiweb.org/], as well as Chapter 2 on assessment in this volume, for a discussion of Collaborative Assessment and Therapeutic Assessment).

Prevention

Consistent with the health service delivery and integrative models of psychology intervention (e.g., Belar, 2012), numerous scholars and practitioners have called for preventative interventions across diverse areas, including infant health and development (see Black's example in Exhibit 4.7; Black & Nair, 2019). Moreover, a holistic model of mental health is predicated in part on the ability to meet basic needs and human rights (Prilleltensky, 2012). Thus, interventions that work to alleviate or prevent poverty, illness and disease, resource depletion, conflict, forced relocation, and rights violations, among other social ills, can prevent or ameliorate psychological problems.

EXHIBIT 4.6

ACT for All: A Contextual Approach to Acceptance and Commitment Therapy

Kelly Wilson and Michael Bordieri

Proponents of acceptance and commitment therapy (ACT) have taken a keen interest in broad international dissemination and collaborative treatment development. From a contextualist perspective, diverse science is simply better science, as research conducted from varied cultural perspectives increases our ability to generate effective interventions with broad applicability (Wilson et al., 2013). The Association for Contextual Behavioral Science (http://contextualscience.org) was founded in 2005 to facilitate the development of contextual science (including ACT) and has more than 9,000 members worldwide from more than 80 countries. Community building and mutually supportive collaboration is explicitly stated in the mission statement of Association for Contextual Behavioral Science, with multiple special interest groups, international chapters, and a developing nations committee dedicated to the global development of ACT. A substantial amount of ACT research has been conducted by investigators in countries outside of the United States, with a growing number of studies coming from low- and middle-income countries.

EXHIBIT 4.7

Investment in Early Child Development

Maureen Black

The first 1,000 days, representing conception through the second birthday, is recognized as a formative phase in children's early development (Black & Nair, 2019). Low access to adequate food has led to undernutrition as a major public health problem, keeping more than 220 million children younger than age 5 from reaching their developmental potential. As a result, psychologists and other professionals have called for the implementation and evaluation of integrated interventions that include opportunities for both child development and early nutrition interventions. In an example of an integrated intervention in India, we are conducting Project Grow Smart, in collaboration with the National Institute of Nutrition in India. Infants between 6 and 12 months of age are recruited to receive supplements and stimulation during a period of high vulnerability to iron deficiency and a period of rapid developmental growth in motor, cognitive, language, and socio-emotional development. Iron stores (ferritin) and home stimulation were independently associated with multiple areas of development, supporting the project. The nutrition-child development trial is conducted by Village Level Workers, thus facilitating the scaling up of the intervention.

Strengths-Based Approaches

Most big-picture frameworks (e.g., WHO core principles), community-based approaches (e.g., APA's Division 27, Society for Community Research and Action), and culturally responsive models tend to emphasize prevention-oriented aspects of intervention along with the cultivation of strengths. Such interventions capitalize on cultural, contextual, and personal assets to prevent problems and cultivate solutions, offering great applicability in many regions and cultures. This happens because wellness models, positive youth development (PYD) programs, and values-oriented methods may be more palatable in contexts where stigma related to psychosocial distress or help-seeking is high. From a global perspective, the PYD perspective is especially salient; as noted, about 85% of youth today live in low-income countries, where they face numerous threats to their communities and their own healthy development. Approaches grounded in PYD paradigms emphasize building behavioral competencies, interpersonal skills, efficacy, community connections, and a positive identity (Nayar, 2013). Indeed, PYD approaches have been successfully used in programming in low- and middle-income countries (Alvarado et al., 2017) and are considered a key strategy for achieving the SDGs (Olenik, 2019).

Global Concerns

As should be clear by now, psychologists who work transnationally have extraordinary opportunities to expand their professional identity and engage in interventions that include, but go beyond, problems and settings typically associated with clinical interventions. Documented throughout this chapter and elsewhere in *Going Global*, climate change, natural disasters, war, intergroup conflict, poverty, and forced migration are among the areas garnering more attention from psychologists. Consider first the role of psychologists in disaster mitigation and responsiveness. Psychologists began to assume a prominent role in disaster interventions during the 1990s, a process that culminated in the subfield of clinical-disaster psychology marked by networks of mental health professionals (e.g., APA's Disaster Response Network), handbooks (e.g., Reyes & Jacobs, 2006), and global efforts to train disaster mental health workers. Mental health professionals who practice in this area often work in collaboration with international agencies (see the example by Jacobs in Exhibit 4.8).

The climate crisis is germane to the issue of disaster response, as psychologists are increasingly conducting research and developing interventions to change behavior, policies, and social norms to prevent, mitigate, and adapt to climate change (APA, 2010). Engendering more sustainable behaviors and promoting care for the environment are crucial to addressing other societal problems, such as increases in natural disasters, forced population mobility, and scarcity of resources such as food and water, which are predicted to be main drivers of future conflict (United Nations, 2021). An increase in zoonotic diseases, such as COVID-19, H1N1, and SARS, is one negative effect of the climate crisis that demands transnational cooperation and presents multiple

EXHIBIT 4.8

Dealing With Disasters: International Interventions and Development of the Disaster Mental Health Institute

Jerry Jacobs

The Disaster Mental Health Institute (DMHI) at the University of South Dakota first worked internationally in 1995 when humanitarian workers returned from serving in the 1990 Persian Gulf War, having been exposed to extreme human suffering, harsh circumstances, and direct and immediate threat to their own lives and the lives of those they served. It was striking to learn that despite these traumatic events, their sponsoring agencies had provided them with no formal psychological support. It is easier to provide support to humanitarian staff than to those directly affected, because the staff can be provided with support in their countries of origin. When working in countries affected by disasters, the DMHI uses a model of psychological support known as community-based psychological first aid, which trains non–mental health professionals to support their families, neighbors, and colleagues and which promotes self-care. This model features adaptation to the local community with the collaboration of local residents, building on the strengths of the local culture. The DMHI has provided consultation and training in community-based psychological first aid, and/or disaster mental health through the WHO, the American Red Cross, the APA, the Asian Disaster Preparedness Center, and the International Union of Psychological Science and has worked with various organizations in more than 30 countries (Jacobs et al., 2016).

Note. WHO = World Health Organization; APA = American Psychological Association.

needs, roles, and avenues for psychological intervention. Psychologists continue to extend their skills to reduce intergroup conflict and to promote peace and human rights. For example, the Group on International Perspectives on Governmental Aggression and Peace is an interdisciplinary collective of researchers (more than 85 researchers from more than 20 countries) working on international perspectives on aggression, human rights, and peace (Malley-Morrison et al., 2006). Landis and Albert's (2012) edited handbook on ethnocultural conflict includes practical suggestions for preventive and corrective interventions and roles for psychologists in these domains. Finally, as noted previously, all global psychologists should be aware of the SDGs, which include multiple opportunities for intervention education, research, and practice (see United Nations, n.d., 2021). These are just a few big-picture interventions of relevance to psychology and psychologists, a list that will only expand as we increasingly strive to meet a world of need.

CONCLUSION

We have covered a great deal of terrain in this chapter. In the Foundations section, we reviewed the need for mental health services internationally and highlighted the potential of psychologists to apply their knowledge and skills around the world. We discussed cultural competence, caveats and ethics regarding intervention, and the WHO's (2013) core principles of global competence in mental health. In the Applications section, we considered diverse pathways to care and an array of settings in which psychological interventions occur, such as health service settings, schools, and communities. We discussed types of intervention (e.g., strengths-based approaches) and pointed out emergent areas of concern (e.g., the climate crisis) that present clear opportunities for psychologists to intervene across multiple settings and levels. We hope that current and future psychologists will dialogue further by sharing their own global perspectives and international experiences in scholarly and professional forums so we may continue to grow our collective understanding of this emerging, exciting, and essential area of intervention research and practice. Although the landscape of global psychology is vast and diverse, we hope this chapter illuminated the extraordinary opportunities and possibilities for psychologists to identify and meet a world of need.

REFERENCES

Abdul-Raheem, T. (2006, February 2). *Head-to-head: Africa's food crisis.* http://news.bbc.co.uk/2/hi/africa/4670744.stm

Alvarado, G., Skinner, M., Plaut, D., Moss, C., Kapungu, C., & Reavley, N. (2017). *A systematic review of positive youth development in low- and middle-income countries.* YouthPower Learning, Making Cents International. https://www.youthpower.org/systematic-review-pyd-lmics

American Psychiatric Association. (2013). *Diagnostic and statistical manual of mental disorders* (5th ed.). https://doi.org/10.1176/appi.books.9780890425596

American Psychological Association. (2010). *Psychology and global climate change: Addressing a multifaceted phenomenon and set of challenges.* https://www.apa.org/science/about/publications/climate-change-booklet.pdf

American Psychological Association. (2012). *Recognition of psychotherapy effectiveness.* https://www.apa.org/about/policy/resolution-psychotherapy.aspx

American Psychological Association. (2015, July). *Report of the independent reviewer and related materials.* https://www.apa.org/independent-review

American Psychological Association. (2017a). *Ethical principles of psychologists and code of conduct* (2002, amended effective June 1, 2010, and January 1, 2017). https://www.apa.org/ethics/code/index.html

American Psychological Association. (2017b). *Multicultural guidelines: An ecological approach to context, identity, and intersectionality.* https://www.apa.org/about/policy/multicultural-guidelines.pdf

APA Presidential Task Force on Evidence-Based Practice. (2006). Evidence-based practice in psychology. *American Psychologist, 61*(4), 271–285. https://doi.org/10.1037/0003-066X.61.4.271

Arnett, J. J. (2008). The neglected 95%: Why American psychology needs to become less American. *American Psychologist, 63*(7), 602–614. https://doi.org/10.1037/0003-066X.63.7.602

Bacigalupe, G., & Cámara, M. (2012). Transnational families and social technologies: Reassessing immigration psychology. *Journal of Ethnic and Migration Studies, 38*(9), 1425–1438. https://doi.org/10.1080/1369183X.2012.698211

Baumann, A. A., Domenech Rodríguez, M. M., Amador, N. G., Forgatch, M. S., & Parra-Cardona, J. R. (2014). Parent Management Training–Oregon model (PMTO™) in Mexico City: Integrating cultural adaptation activities in an implementation model. *Clinical Psychology: Science and Practice, 21*(1), 32–47. https://doi.org/10.1111/cpsp.12059

Baxter, A. J., Scott, K. M., Vos, T., & Whiteford, H. A. (2013). Global prevalence of anxiety disorders: A systematic review and meta-regression. *Psychological Medicine, 43*(5), 897–910. https://doi.org/10.1017/S003329171200147X

Belar, C. (2012). Reflection on the future: Psychology as a health profession. *Professional Psychology, Research and Practice, 43*(6), 545–550. https://doi.org/10.1037/a0029633

Berry, J. W. (2013). Achieving a global psychology. *Canadian Psychology, 54*(1), 55–61. https://doi.org/10.1037/a0031246

Black, M., & Nair, M. K. (2019, August 16). *Project Grow Smart: Intervention trial of multiple micronutrients and early learning among infants in India* (NCT01660958). https://clinicaltrials.gov/ct2/show/NCT01660958

da Silva, A. G., & Corrêa, H. (2015). *Suicide: It's time to break taboos.* https://www.psychologytoday.com/us/blog/update-brazil/201508/suicide-it-s-time-break-taboos

Deacon, B. J. (2013). The biomedical model of mental disorder: A critical analysis of its validity, utility, and effects on psychotherapy research. *Clinical Psychology Review, 33*(7), 846–861. https://doi.org/10.1016/j.cpr.2012.09.007

Degenhardt, L., & Hall, W. (2012). Extent of illicit drug use and dependence, and their contribution to the global burden of disease. *The Lancet, 379*(9810), 55–70. https://doi.org/10.1016/S0140-6736(11)61138-0

Denov, M., Doucet, D., & Kamara, A. (2012). Engaging war affected youth through photography Photovoice with former child soldiers in Sierra Leone. *Intervention, 10*(2), 117–133. https://doi.org/10.1097/WTF.0b013e328355ed82

Draguns, J. G. (2007). Psychotherapeutic and related interventions for a global psychology. In M. Stevens & U. Gielen (Eds.), *Toward a global psychology: Theory, research, intervention, and pedagogy* (pp. 233–266). Lawrence Erlbaum Associates.

Gaete, J., Clickman, K. L., & Hill, C. E. (2011). Developing and delivering practice-based evidence: A guide for the psychological therapies. *Psychotherapy Research, 21*(6), 732–734. https://doi.org/10.1080/10503307.2011.611544

Hays, P. A. (2008). *Addressing cultural complexities in practice: Assessment, diagnosis, and therapy* (2nd ed.). American Psychological Association. https://doi.org/10.1037/11650-000

Inter-Agency Standing Committee. (2007). *IASC guidelines on mental health and psychosocial support in emergency settings.*

International Union of Psychological Science. (2008). *Universal declaration of ethical principles for psychologists.* http://www.am.org/iupsys/resources/ethics/univdecl2008.html

Jacobs, G. A., Gray, B. L., Erickson, S. E., Gonzalez, E. D., & Quevillon, R. P. (2016). Disaster mental health and community-based psychological first aid: Concepts and education/training. *Journal of Clinical Psychology, 72*(12), 1307–1317. https://doi.org/10.1002/jclp.22316

James, E. J., Noel, J. R., Favorite, T. D., & Jean, J. S. (2012). Challenges of postdisaster intervention in cultural context: The implementation of a lay mental health worker project in postearthquake Haiti. *International Perspectives in Psychology: Research, Practice, Consultation, 1*(2), 110–126. https://doi.org/10.1037/a0028321

Johnson, L. R., Bastien, G., & Hirschel, M. J. (2009). Psychotherapy in a culturally diverse world. In S. Eshun & R. A. R. Gurung (Eds.), *Culture and mental health: Sociocultural influences, theory, and practice* (pp. 115–148). Wiley-Blackwell. https://doi.org/10.1002/9781444305807.ch7

Johnson, L. R., Chin, E., Kajumba, M., Kizito, S., & Bangirana, P. (2017). Patients and their healers: Differing perspectives on the path to treatment for depression in Uganda. *Journal of Cross-Cultural Psychology, 48*(2), 243–261. https://doi.org/10.1177/0022022116675424

Johnson, L. R., Drescher, C., & Assenga, S. (2019). Street-connected youth in East Africa: New angles with participatory methods. *Journal of Adolescent Research, 34*(5), 619–651. https://doi.org/10.1177/0743558418822334

Johnson, L. R., & Sandhu, D. S. (2010). Treatment planning in a multicultural context: Some suggestions for counselors and psychotherapists. In M. M. Leach & J. D. Aten (Eds.), *Culture and the therapeutic process: A guide for mental health professionals* (pp. 117–156). Routledge.

Kaslow, F. W. (2001). Families and family psychology at the millennium. Intersecting crossroads. *American Psychologist, 56*(1), 37–46. https://doi.org/10.1037/0003-066X.56.1.37

Landis, D., & Albert, R. D. (Eds.). (2012). *Handbook of ethnic conflict: International perspectives.* Springer. https://doi.org/10.1007/978-1-4614-0448-4

Malley-Morrison, K., Daskalopoulos, M., & You, H. S. (2006, Winter). International perspectives on governmental aggression. *International Psychology Reporter, 10,* 19–20.

Marsella, A. J. (2007). Education and training for a global psychology: Foundations, issues and action. In M. Stevens & U. Gielen (Eds.), *Toward a global psychology: Theory, research, intervention, and pedagogy* (pp. 333–361). Lawrence Erlbaum Associates.

Moodley, R., Gielen, U. P., & Wu, R. (Eds.). (2013). *Handbook of counseling and psychotherapy in an international context.* Routledge/Taylor & Francis. https://doi.org/10.4324/9780203864906

Nayar, U. (Ed.). (2013). *Child and adolescent mental health.* Sage Publications.

Olenik, C. (2019). The evolution of positive youth development as a key international development approach. *Global Social Welfare: Research, Policy & Practice, 6*(1), 5–15. https://doi.org/10.1007/s40609-018-0120-1

Olweus, D., & Limber, S. P. (2010). Bullying in school: Evaluation and dissemination of the Olweus Bullying Prevention Program. *American Journal of Orthopsychiatry, 80*(1), 124–134. https://doi.org/10.1111/j.1939-0025.2010.01015.x

Ovuga, E., Boardman, J., & Wasserman, D. (2005). The prevalence of depression in two districts of Uganda. *Social Psychiatry and Psychiatric Epidemiology, 40*(6), 439–445. https://doi.org/10.1007/s00127-005-0915-0

Patel, V., Weiss, H. A., Chowdhary, N., Naik, S., Pednekar, S., Chatterjee, S., Bhat, B., Araya, R., King, M., Simon, G., Verdeli, H., & Kirkwood, B. R. (2011). Lay health worker led intervention for depressive and anxiety disorders in India: Impact on clinical and disability outcomes over 12 months. *The British Journal of Psychiatry, 199*(6), 459–466. https://doi.org/10.1192/bjp.bp.111.092155

Pedersen, P. B. (2004). The multicultural context of mental health. In T. B. Smith (Ed.), *Practicing multiculturalism* (pp. 17–32). Allyn & Bacon.

Pick, S., & Sirkin, J. T. (2010). *Breaking the poverty cycle: The human basis for sustainable development.* Oxford University Press. https://doi.org/10.1093/acprof:oso/9780195383164.001.0001

Prilleltensky, I. (2012). Wellness as fairness. *American Journal of Community Psychology, 49*(1–2), 1–21. https://doi.org/10.1007/s10464-011-9448-8

Reyes, G., & Jacobs, G. A. (Eds.). (2006). *Handbook of international disaster psychology* (Vols. 1–4). Praeger.

Sandhu, D. S. (2021). Mental health problems in India: An immediate and urgent call for action. *IAR Journal of Humanities and Social Science, 2*(3), 78–84. https://doi.org/10.47310/iarjhss.2021.v02i03.010

Semugoma, P., Beyrer, C., & Baral, S. (2012). Assessing the effects of anti-homosexuality legislation in Uganda on HIV prevention, treatment, and care services. *SAHARA-J: Journal of Social Aspects of HIV/AIDS, 9*(3), 173–176. https://doi.org/10.1080/17290376.2012.744177

Stevens, M. J., & Gielen, U. P. (2007). *Toward a global psychology: Theory, research, intervention, and pedagogy.* Lawrence Erlbaum Associates.

Sue, D. W., & Sue, D. (2008). *Counseling the culturally diverse* (5th ed.). Wiley.

Suicides Rise Across India. (2011, January 12). *Vietnam News.* https://myvietnamnews.com/2011/01/12/suicides-rise-across-india/

Takagi, E., Silverstein, M., & Crimmins, E. (2007). Intergenerational coresidence of older adults in Japan: Conditions for cultural plasticity. *Journal of Gerontology, 62*(5), S330–S339. https://doi.org/10.1093/geronb/62.5.S330

Thalmayer, A. G., Toscanelli, C., & Arnett, J. J. (2021). The neglected 95% revisited: Is American psychology becoming less American? *American Psychologist, 76*(1), 116–129. https://doi.org/10.1037/amp0000622

UNICEF. (2014). *International Day of the Girl Child: UNICEF fact sheet.* https://www.unicef.org/mena/sites/unicef.org.mena/files/press-releases/mena-media-10-08-2014_DOTG_fact_sheet.pdf

UNICEF. (2017). *The state of the world's children.* https://data.unicef.org/wp-content/uploads/2018/03/SOWC-2017-statistical-tables.pdf

United Nations. (n.d.). *The 17 goals.* https://sdgs.un.org/goals

United Nations. (1989). Convention on the Rights of the Child. G.A. Res. 44/25, U.N. GAOR Supp. 49 at 165. *U.N. Doc. A, 44,* 736.

United Nations. (2021). *The sustainable development goals report 2020.* https://unstats.un.org/sdgs/report/2020/

van Eeuwijk, P. (2014). The elderly providing care for the elderly in Tanzania and Indonesia: Making 'Elder to Elder' care visible. *Sociologus, 64*(1), 29–52. https://doi.org/10.3790/soc.64.1.29

van Mierlo, B. (2012). Community systems strengthening in Afghanistan: A way to reduce domestic violence and to reinforce women's agency. *Intervention (Amstelveen, Netherlands), 10*(2), 134–145. https://www.interventionjournal.com/sites/default/files/VanMierlo_2012_Intervention_10-2.pdf

Verdeli, H., Clougherty, K., Bolton, P., Speelman, L., Lincoln, N., Bass, J., Neugebauer, R., & Weissman, M. M. (2003). Adapting group interpersonal psychotherapy for a developing country: Experience in rural Uganda. *World Psychiatry, 2*(2), 114–120.

Wachtel, P. L. (2008). Psychotherapy from an international perspective. *Journal of Psychotherapy Integration, 18*(1), 66–69. https://doi.org/10.1037/1053-0479.18.1.66

Waldorf, L. (2009). Revisiting Hotel Rwanda: Genocide ideology, reconciliation, and rescuers. *Journal of Genocide Research, 11*(1), 101–125. https://doi.org/10.1080/14623520802703673

Wedding, D., & Stevens, M. J. (2004). *Handbook of international psychology.* Brunner-Routledge.

Wessells, M., & Edgerton, A. (2008). What is child protection? Concepts and practices to support war-affected children. *The Journal of Developmental Processes, 3*(2), 2–12.

Wilson, K. G. (1997). Science and treatment development: Lessons from the history of behavior therapy. *Behavior Therapy, 28*(4), 547–558. https://doi.org/10.1016/S0005-7894(97)80011-1

Wilson, K. G., Whiteman, K., & Bordieri, M. J. (2013). The pragmatic truth criterion and values in contextual behavioral science. In S. Dymond & B. Roche (Eds.), *Advances in relational frame theory & contextual behavioral science: Research & application* (pp. 27–49). New Harbinger.

World Health Organization. (2008). *Integrating mental health into primary care: A global perspective.* https://www.who.int/publications/i/item/9789241563680

World Health Organization. (2013). *Draft comprehensive mental health action plan 2013–2020.* http://apps.who.int/gb/ebwha/pdf_files/EB132/B132_8-en.pdf

World Health Organization. (2022). *Mental health gap action programme (mhGAP).* https://www.who.int/teams/mental-health-and-substance-use/treatment-care/mental-health-gap-action-programme

5

Leadership

How Psychology and Psychologists Develop Global Leaders and Leadership

Sandra L. Shullman, Randall P. White, Lindy Brewster, Steven E. Grande, and Devi Bhuyan

There has never been a more active time to be involved in the study and practice of leadership development and education in global settings. Now, more than ever, organizations and nations are increasingly globally interdependent. Issues such as COVID-19 and climate change alone require global and virtual solutions for all. With continuing technology development, very few organizations are not operating in a global environment (e.g., international dispersion of employee teams, small businesses selling through online platforms with international scope, higher education institutions opening campuses abroad and retaining international students on home campuses, ethical business schemes such as fair trade, participation in the global supply chain). Effective and competent leadership is critical to success in virtually every type and size of institution or organization worldwide (Dyjak-LeBlanc et al., 2016). Psychology has a long and distinguished history of scholarship and practice in the field of leadership (McGiboney, 2017), which can be applied in environments where there are significant cultural, language, and ideological differences.

In this chapter, we focus on leadership development and leadership education in global contexts, addressing how psychological knowledge and psychologists can enhance the capacity, skills, and competencies of individuals and organizations working for positive change (Shullman, 2018). We begin with definitional and conceptual perspectives, and we summarize literature across eight key themes relevant to the development of global leaders and leadership. We next describe four requisites for this work before, during, and after

https://doi.org/10.1037/0000311-006

Going Global: How Psychologists Can Meet a World of Need, C. Shealy, M. Bullock, and S. Kapadia (Editors)

leadership development interventions in global settings: attending to values and ethics, clarifying processes and goals, learning to navigate dualities, and mastering the leadership literature. Using this background, we then discuss kinds of interventions (both in person and virtually) that may be applied in global leadership education and development (e.g., leadership through specialized coursework, in-house education, nonprofit consultation, team and individual coaching) and provide perspectives and resources for psychologists interested in leadership development, concluding with suggestions for behavioral and professional approaches that are relevant to psychologists who intend to practice in the global leadership field.

GLOBAL LEADERS AND LEADERSHIP: DEFINITIONAL AND CONCEPTUAL CHALLENGES

Although there is little disagreement that leaders are working more frequently in global and multicultural contexts, there is no unified theory of "global leader" or "global leadership." However, there are promising developments in this regard. For example, there is continuing and considerable interest in exploring the nature of activities, requirements, and competencies of effective global leaders (e.g., Chhokar et al., 2007; Gundling et al., 2011; Hewlett, 2016; Mendenhall et al., 2019; Mobley et al., 2011). In particular, the ambitious Global Leadership and Organizational Behavior Effectiveness Research Project (GLOBE)—an ongoing, multiyear (20 years) initiative involving more than 150 social science/business scholars—studied 17,000 managers from 62 different cultures (e.g., Bird et al., 2010; Campbell, 2006; House et al., 2004; House et al., 2014; Javidan & Teagarden, 2011). This study resulted in nine cultural attributes that reveal "an integrated theory of the relationship between culture and societal, organizational, and leadership effectiveness" (Javidan et al., 2006, p. 69). At the same time, this work also illustrates a consistent tension in finding a balance between universal aspects of leadership development and aspects that vary with culture and contexts (Javidan et al., 2006; McCall & Hollenbeck, 2002; Mendenhall et al., 2008). As Javidan et al. (2006) cautioned, "it is insufficient for a manager . . . to assume . . . that being open-minded in Atlanta, Helsinki, and Beijing will be perceived identically, or that walking in someone else's shoes will feel the same in Houston, Jakarta, and Madrid" (p. 68). The contention that "a leader is a leader is a leader" may inappropriately encourage leaders trained in one geography, culture, or approach to assume that their skill set for leadership development will be sufficient when exported to other geographies, cultures, or national social structures. Rather, it is essential for leaders to acquire the capacity to adapt existing frameworks to new contexts and navigate the complexities of different cultures (e.g., Chin & Trimble, 2015; Christopher et al., 2014; Dyjak-LeBlanc et al., 2016; Glover & Friedman, 2015; House et al., 2014).

For psychologists interested in global leadership work, it is important to be trained in leadership constructs, such as cross-situational complexity, to understand underlying cognitive and motivational processes and to integrate educational design into cross-cultural interventions (Avolio et al., 2009; Chin & Trimble, 2015; Gardner et al., 2011). Such training can help leaders develop greater capacity to manage ambiguity, demonstrate empathy, and work with competing demands while leading the operational and strategic work essential for an effective global organization (Hodgson & White, 2020). Global leadership development provides growing opportunities in business, government, education, and nonprofit sectors.

Not long ago, global executive leaders were drawn from employees in the "home office" who simply aspired to an offshore assignment through a promotion. Being sent overseas, particularly to choice locations, was an indication of fast-track career status. In the past 2 decades, many organizations have changed this approach dramatically. Now, there is greater understanding that leadership has to include local and contextually grounded processes to succeed. Globally dispersed executives are no longer viewed as simply staffing local branches of an international company. The global COVID-19 pandemic and the proliferation of software meeting platforms have accelerated the need and ability for global leaders to integrate the organizational expectations, values, and practices of the home office in ways that are culturally resonant with the new country and context. For example, General Electric chief learning officer Susan Peters emphasized consistencies among staff in Munich, New Delhi, and elsewhere: "The essence of leadership, we believe, is the same around the world, so we don't change the fundamentals or the content," but she also acknowledged the critical need to incorporate cultural and regional differences: "Course content is taught . . . with the appropriate cultural overtone . . . and those local leaders ensure that it is embedded in the course" (Knowledge@ Wharton, 2012, para. 19).

Ultimately, then, to be successful, global leadership training must help leaders better balance the demands of local contexts and cultures with internationally recognized best practices at home and abroad. As such, development of global leaders' skills, attitudes and knowledge must be based on the literature regarding what we have learned about effective—or ineffective—global leaders and leadership. Psychologists can bring their skill sets of assessment, knowledge of cognitive, motivational, emotional and behavioral change, and reflection on cultural complexity to the facilitation of leadership and organizational development. Such processes challenge leaders to examine their beliefs and values at multiple levels, including their concept of a leader as an individual with singular duties and responsibilities as opposed to organizations within societies where cultural beliefs are grounded in more collective and communal norms and expectations (e.g., Hofstede, 2001).

GLOBAL LEADERS AND LEADERSHIP: A THEMATIC ANALYSIS

For psychologists to engage in global leadership development, it is important to examine prevailing expectations, cultures, challenges, and opportunities within a given organizational setting or context. In this chapter, we take a broad-based approach to the literature, recognizing that there is no "one" literature on leaders and leadership. Building on the important findings from initiatives such as GLOBE, noted earlier, and other scholarly efforts that focus explicitly on "global leadership" (e.g., Gundling et al., 2011), we use a recent innovative and international initiative that culminated in the equilintegration or EI Leadership Model (Dyjak-LeBlanc et al., 2016) as our organizing framework. In the development of this global leadership model over a 2-year period, the competencies of exemplary leaders around the world were systematically examined through a job analysis methodology that was informed by scholarly and applied literature on leaders and leadership development across the eight themes outlined in Table 5.1.

Because these themes were integral to this 2-year job analysis of global organizational leaders (Dyjak-LeBlanc et al., 2016), it may be helpful to review each theme in more detail, a process that also demonstrates the deep importance of psychological knowledge and expertise to global leaders and leadership. Likewise and as noted earlier, one of the problems with the leadership literature more broadly is that it is all over the place. As such, when organized thematically, scholarly and applied literature should become part of any leadership model—in this case, the EI Leadership Model—and juxtaposed with the model itself to illustrate why various leadership components or dimensions are or are not emphasized.[1]

Awareness

Psychologists can help leaders develop awareness of cognitive, emotional, and motivational factors in judgment and decision making that affects their and their employees' behavior, a process aligned with Burke's (2008) emphasis on "leader self-examination." This is especially important under increasingly ambiguous conditions that are ubiquitous within larger global organizational contexts (White & Shullman, 2010). Likewise, psychologists can use the rich research base on cognitive biases and judgment heuristics to help leaders be aware of their own and others' sources of systematic error in attributions and decision making. For example, the availability heuristic (in which people tend to assess the relative importance of issues by the ease with which they are retrieved from memory) may bias assessment of risks and outcomes (Tversky & Kahneman, 1974). Similarly, emotionally charged "intuitive" judgments

---

[1] In other words, to bring greater coherence and directionality to research in the field of leadership and organizational development, we suggest that proposed leadership "models" be accompanied by a review of relevant literature as well as whatever methods were used to develop, evaluate, and refine the model over time. In this way, educators, scholars, and practitioners have a better basis for understanding why a particular leadership model has assumed a particular form and use that understanding for furtherance of the discipline and profession over time. For a more detailed treatment of the EI Leadership Model, and its underlying job analysis methodology and application, see Dyjak-LeBlanc et al. (2016).

TABLE 5.1. Literature-Based Themes Informing a Job Analysis of Global Leaders and Leadership

Theme	Description
Awareness	Demonstrates high emotional intelligence; understanding the impact of self on others; awareness of one's own thoughts and feelings; values the same in others and in the organization's culture
Depth	Has the capacity and inclination to perceive underlying dynamics, both personally and professionally; comprehends how such processes drive organizational decisions and systems, for better or worse; open to basic needs in self and others (e.g., motivations, defenses, insecurities)
Culture	Open to and interested in one's own culture and the beliefs, values, and practices of different cultures; has the ability and willingness to learn, change, and grow in relation to cultural differences
Care	Genuinely empathizes with others and cares for their well-being and advancement; engages them in ongoing processes of growth and development; builds and supports environments where everyone has the opportunity to thrive and achieve their potential
Complexity	Able to make sense of complexity, helping others do the same, preferring "gray" to black-and-white thinking and action; understands interactions among internal processes within people and how those dynamics influence individual and group behavior; able to take into account multiple factors that may simultaneously affect the pursuit of organizational goals
Assessment	Embraces informal and formal models and methods of assessment, recognizing that without appropriate information and feedback, there is no way to understand where an organization and its people are, much less how to make things better going forward; uses assessment data appropriately, to support learning, growth, development, and the pursuit of legitimate goals
Transformation	Creates and sustains work environments where change, innovation, and possibility are valued, by valuing the people and their contributions deeply; models and facilitates an organizational culture in which all members feel, see, and hear that they have a stake in processes and outcomes; provides open communication and support, encouraging thoughtful risk taking
Vision	Shares their vision of what the organization can be, how it got there, and why vision matters; engages others in the cocreation and enactment of this vision; is able to modify their approach by acknowledging the contributions and perspectives of others; takes into account how trends and dynamics may impact their vision and modifies accordingly

may create blind spots regarding what information to attend to or to disregard (Aronson, 2012).

In addition, work on emotional intelligence (Goleman, 1995, 2005; Goleman et al., 2002) suggests the importance of self-regulation, motivation, empathy, and social skills to good leadership. These awareness-based aspects of emotional intelligence, such as self-knowledge and empathy for others, ultimately facilitate trust and fairness in the larger organization. Successful global leaders are able to integrate different perspectives, respond proactively to others' needs, and tolerate uncertainty and tension (e.g., Henson & Rossouw, 2013; Mendenhall et al., 2001; Trompenaars & Hampden-Turner, 2010). The ability to manage affectively mediated aspects of ambiguity and uncertainty are increasingly important as the business environment becomes more complex, global, and hypercompetitive (Hodgson & White, 2001; White & Shullman, 2010). Leaders need to adapt and change quickly as technologies, opportunities, and threats change more rapidly and competitive options proliferate. Listening and questioning empathically are key components of managing the associated ambiguity and uncertainty (Hodgson & White, 2020; Marquardt, 2014). This ability requires an inclination to engage in perspective taking, feeling/sensing "what is going on in the other," and genuinely wanting to help (i.e., "empathic concern"). Without sufficient awareness of self, others, and the larger world, leaders may continue to operate within models that are both ineffective and inflexible, leading to consistent errors of judgment and decision-making.

Depth

Depth refers to unconscious dynamics that may exert a profound impact on decisions and policies in organizational life and that provide "meaning" or a sense of agency (e.g., Kets de Vries, 2019; Wheatley, 2006). For example, leaders may not understand how their own resistance and defense mechanisms, which might seem natural to them, may be experienced as irrational, concerning, and confusing to others and/or deleterious to the functioning of an organization. Helping leaders come to terms with how their "inner theater" (Terry, 2001, p. 8) influences cognition, emotion, and behavior can shed light on a wide range of actions such as hiring and firing decisions as well as preferences for particular organizational priorities or goals. Because these dynamics may affect all aspects of leadership, it is essential that leaders understand and acknowledge that their leadership style or approach may emanate from deep and problematic aspects of *their own self* rather problems with "the other." Some have noted that this awareness, along with the courage to act upon it in the service of the organization and its people, may be the sine qua non of effective leadership (e.g., Dyjak-LeBlanc et al., 2016; Kets de Vries & Balazs, 2005).

Culture

The GLOBE Project defines *culture* broadly as "shared motives, values, beliefs, identities and interpretations or meanings of significant events that result from common experiences of members of collectives that are transmitted across generations" (House et al., 2004, p. 15). Artifacts, stories, symbols, and customs shared and adopted by members of a group or society also are integral to the "culture" construct (Chhokar et al., 2007), which influences how people work to address and solve problems. At the most basic level, psychologists need to assist leaders in developing the capacity to move beyond their unexamined assumption of the "right way to do things" and cultivate openness to the potential effectiveness of different beliefs, perceptions, and behaviors.

In this regard, GLOBE research indicates that an important leadership attribute is understanding of and an ability to articulate (for self and others) local expectations regarding what constitutes a good leader, even more than understanding local cultural values. Likewise, a global mindset is necessary for effective leadership across culturally different settings (Beechler & Javidan, 2007; Levy et al., 2007). Aycan (2001) contended that a global mindset allows leaders to have the big picture in mind, enabling them to balance seeming contradictions or discordances, while trusting process over structure (e.g., they value difference and approach new situations from the standpoint of what needs to be learned rather than what already is known).

In addition to broad cultural context, leaders must understand the "organized disposition" of a given cultural milieu (Schmitz, 2012). This goal may be particularly challenging when beliefs, values, and expected behaviors within an organizational context are unknown or not explicit. To take but one illustration, Trompenaars and Hampden-Turner (1997) observed that attitudes toward time may differentially impact approaches to planning, strategy, and investment as well as strategies for *growing*, rather than recruiting, talent. Individualism in organizations is another example of Western expectations and can be a blind spot for leaders finding themselves in societies where collectivism is the norm. This can not only lead just to misunderstandings of expectations but result in perceived failure to comply or judgments about ability. For example, attributions may be made, such as "They don't make clear, self-driven decisions" or "I wish they would respond with sufficient urgency to crises." Such dynamics can be personally challenging for leaders who are imported into these situations. If they are to lead well, it is essential that they first engage people and the culture at the level of its underlying beliefs and values first, not to change them but to understand and negotiate new ways of reaching desired ends (e.g., Chin & Trimble, 2015).

The role of culture is also illustrated by Lorde's (1995) concept of the "mythical norm." In many Western, industrialized contexts, "this norm is usually defined as white, thin, male, young, heterosexual, Christian, and financially secure. It is with this mythical norm that the trappings of power reside" (Lorde, 1995, pp. 533–534). Such norms can also distort our understanding of difference. As Banaji and Greenwald (2013) suggested, internalizing the dominant culture may lead to underlying biases, outside of our conscious intentions or verbalizations, that contribute to inaccurate perceptions, poor decision-making, and an inability to appreciate cultural difference. Argyris and Schön (1974) described such phenomena as "espoused theories" and "theories in use," wherein verbal commitments may not predict actual behavior (p. 194; see also Aronson, 2012). These theories have tangible consequences because cultural proximity (i.e., the closer one's own fundamental beliefs, values, and behaviors resemble or manifest those of the culture) often translates into greater privileges and fewer obstacles within the organization. Therefore, from a best practice standpoint, Fouad and Arredondo (2007, Chapter 7) recommended that psychologists as organizational change agents be aware of the multicultural characteristics of an organization and cultivate the skills necessary for leaders to translate such awareness into sensitive and effective action. They noted that psychologists as trainers are also "cultural beings, making it necessary for us to engage in awareness building about our worldview and experiences that bias, both positively and negatively, our beliefs about ourselves" (pp. 101–102).

The complex and interacting nature of cultural norms and organizational structure means that bias in one cultural domain may override cultural congruence in another. The role of gender vis-à-vis culture provides a good illustration (e.g., Eisler & Corral, 2009; Pendleton & Furnham, 2016). In some organizational contexts, women must balance not being taken seriously if they present as "feminine" and being considered too aggressive if they present as "manly" (Morrison et al., 1994; Unger, 2001). The intersection of dimensions (e.g., gender and ethnicity or religion) increases the complexity of leadership within culture, particularly in a cross-cultural organizational context (e.g., Chin & Trimble, 2015; Dyjak-LeBlanc et al., 2016; Glover & Friedman, 2015).

Care

Another quality essential for good leadership is care. Followers ultimately are the arbiters of a leader's effectiveness and the degree to which leaders exert influence over them (Kail, 2011). Leaders are encouraged to show care—through empathy in listening and focused attention on what makes each individual unique (e.g., Dyjak-LeBlanc et al., 2016). Kouzes and Posner (2012) observed "how powerful listening and empathy can be in building trust. . . . When people believe that you have their interests at heart—that you care about them—they're more likely to have your interests at heart as well" (pp. 225–226). The "leadership challenge," as Kouzes and Posner described it, requires leaders to "model the way, inspire a shared vision, challenge the process, enable others to act, and encourage the heart" (p. 3). Ultimately, as Kail (2011) observed, "powerful leaders value their followers as individuals. They are also tolerant, willing to investigate the perceptions and positions of others objectively. Empathetic leaders leverage diversity because of individual differences, not in spite of them" (para. 7; see also Chin & Trimble, 2015).

In addition, Bass and Riggio (2006) suggested that caring is a powerful and effective force for change. In Western cultures, caring has been associated with a feminine style of leadership. As such, this approach has been valued less than a more "masculine" style, which eschews "care" in favor of "power," "domination," and "control," all of which are assumed to be integral to the "strength" of the leader. As Hofstede (2001) noted, however, such a gender-based attribution for a caring style is not necessarily found in other cultures (see also Eisler & Corral, 2009). The GLOBE research suggests that respected leaders around the world reflexively care about the feelings, needs, and experiences of those who are led and seek to understand how their approach to leadership is experienced by others (Chhokar et al., 2007). Ultimately, care facilitates trust, which is fundamental to the effective pursuit of shared organizational goals.

Complexity

Given the challenges and opportunities of a globally interconnected and rapidly changing world, and the acceleration of challenges such as pandemics and climate change, even seemingly routine decisions today are subject to change at a moment's notice. As Kouzes and Posner (2012) quipped, effective leaders of today "understand that the command and control techniques of the Industrial Revolution no longer apply" (p. 18; see also Wheatley, 2006). To take just one example, during the global COVID-19 pandemic, leaders came to understand that not everything in their world can be anticipated, much less controlled, and that they need to be able to tolerate increasing ambiguity (Hodgson & White, 2020). Leaders demonstrating complexity appreciate the value of empowerment and partnership approaches where groups or teams come together as "learning organizations" to address challenges and problems (Eisler & Corral, 2009; White & Shullman, 2010). Adaptive leaders (Heifetz et al., 2009), therefore, are systems-level thinkers who observe and raise questions; frame issues; interpret context; and, as needed, challenge norms before intervening. Such leaders must be able and willing to contain and integrate opposing or contradictory thoughts rather than seek to minimize or deny such complexities (Dyjak-LeBlanc et al., 2016; Martin, 2009).

Assessment

Effective leaders in global environments require a toolbox of assessment approaches to understand and interpret (a) their own and others' personal values, beliefs, attitudes, and traits relevant to leadership impact and personal growth and development and (b) cultural and organizational contexts. Leaders finding themselves in cultures and contexts different from that to which they are accustomed need to move beyond simple sensitivity to differences, going deeper into an assessment of underlying beliefs and values—in self and others—with accuracy, depth, and breadth and need to use this information to enhance personal growth, development, and effectiveness over the short term and long term. Unawareness and ignorance of such underlying processes are often at the core of cultural misunderstandings, which can lead to mistrust, failed relationships, and the undermining of partnerships. A lack of clarification regarding beliefs and values places the global leader at risk of behaving in ways that are experienced as antithetical to the local culture (e.g., Dyjak-LeBlanc et al., 2016). Scholarship that has rigorously assessed attitudes and leadership processes within specific cultural milieus illustrates the depth of the challenges faced by individuals who serve in leadership roles across multiple countries and cultures and suggests the dynamics that may be implicit but still have a major impact on work effectiveness. Psychologists can help global leaders identify significant issues that leaders will face and provide solutions such as key cultural "guides" who can serve to help leaders prepare for and successfully enter global assignments.

For example, classic work by Hofstede and colleagues from the 1960s through the 1990s—which compared attitude surveys for IBM across 50 countries (Hofstede, 2001)—revealed cultural differences in attitudes toward the importance of organizational hierarchy (power distance) as well as ambiguity and uncertainty (uncertainty avoidance). Conflicts tended to arise when leaders' assumptions about power distance did not match that of their employees. Similarly, organizations with leaders who are averse to uncertainty may avoid risk taking when a more entrepreneurial approach is needed (e.g., White & Shullman, 2010). More recent work (e.g., Appreciative Inquiry) uses anthropological approaches to develop procedures to involve employees in defining those qualities or attributes that may help their organization achieve its highest potential (House et al., 2004). In short, psychologists can use their skills in assessment methodology and interpretation to assist leaders in illuminating and grappling with these underlying factors: They understand what is meant by psychometrically sound measurement, including relevant constructs and standards (e.g., definitional clarity, ecological validity, theoretical depth), and they know how to translate assessment theory and data into applied form to facilitate leadership development, team functioning, and the pursuit of organizational goals across cultures (Dyjak-LeBlanc et al., 2016; see also Chapter 2, this volume, on assessment).

Transformation

James MacGregor Burns (1978), a Pulitzer Prize–winning historian, used the term *transforming leadership* to describe leaders who use charisma and role-modeling to inspire and transform followers to be intrinsically motivated leaders. Transformational leadership deliberately focuses on enhancing the "motivation, understanding, maturity, and sense of self-worth" of those who are led (Bass, 1997, p. 130) by working to "deal with others as individuals; consider their individual needs, abilities, and aspirations; listen attentively; further their development; advise; teach; and coach" (Bass, 1997, p. 133). Similarly, Keys (2013) observed that transformational leadership is change oriented and that transformational leaders are open to innovation and creativity and will take risks and adapt to uncertainty and ambiguity. From a global standpoint, a transformational leader understands and takes account of cultural expectations of engagement and motivation (e.g., Dyjak-LeBlanc et al., 2016; Morton, 2013).

In contrast to transactional leadership, which views the relationship between managers and their teams as an exchange of rewards for good performance, and reprimands for poor performance, transformational leaders influence others on the basis of interpersonal processes of caring and trust while facilitating personal growth and development. Not surprisingly, leadership effectiveness has been linked to transformational approaches. For example, leaders who were rated by their teams as transformational were experienced as more satisfying, experienced as more motivating, more likely to be associated with people who expressed commitment to their organizations, and more likely to be rated by more senior leadership as effective leaders (Judge & Bono, 2000). Dweck's (2008) notion of a growth mindset illustrates this core aspect of the transformational approach, which believes in the inherent capacity of others, passionately calling upon them to strive for something greater.

Some authors (e.g., Quinn & Quinn, 2009) prefer the term *transformational change agent* over *leader* to emphasize that stakeholders throughout an organization may enact agency in their respective roles. Quinn and Quinn (2009) contended that transformational individuals are inner directed and other oriented, valuing "deep change" over incremental change (p. 69). Such deep change requires a shift of fundamental values, and challenges "productive equilibrium" along with the norms that emerge from a tendency repeatedly to confirm that normative beliefs are correct (Quinn & Quinn, 2009, p. 69; see also Gostick & Elton, 2012; Morton, 2013). Quinn and Quinn also distinguished "change leaders" from "normal managers," suggesting "change leaders get outside the hierarchical box" (p. 58) and not be defined or delimited by their position within an organization.

Vision

A final theme of particular relevance to global leadership is the nature and role of vision (vision also is a core component of the GLOBE definition of charismatic leadership behavior; Chhokar et al., 2007). According to Snyder et al. (1994), vision is "more than just a plan or goal" (p. 18). It emerges from a thoughtful conceptualization of what the future of the organization could be. In articulating vision, it is necessary for leaders to exemplify and communicate a shared understanding of beliefs and values, which is essential for maintaining unity throughout an organization (Dyjak-LeBlanc et al., 2016; Gostick & Elton, 2012; Morton, 2013). As Kouzes and Posner (2012) observed, "Leaders envision the future by imagining exciting and ennobling possibilities" (p. 22). Too often, leaders are led to believe that they need to develop and articulate a vision entirely on their own. In fact, the role of the leader is to facilitate the emergence of a vision by effectively listening to individuals within and outside the organization and by attending to trends and environmental changes.

Griffin et al. (2010) examined how leadership vision has the capacity to influence change over time. Among other findings, openness to role change and role self-efficacy are both associated with the capacity of a leader to articulate a compelling vision. Moreover, the perception and experience of a leader's vision appears directly related to how individual employees experience themselves as effective and relevant, or not (Griffin et al., 2007). Overall, findings suggest that vision is essential for setting organizational direction but should be expressed and modeled in a manner that is explicitly supportive and empowering of all organizational members regardless of position or status.

GLOBAL LEADERSHIP DEVELOPMENT

On the basis of our collective experience engaging international leaders and organizations, these eight themes have considerable applied value in the real world. Three such applications, which are expanded upon next, have proved useful in practice: attend to values and ethics, clarify processes and goals, and learn to navigate paradoxes.

Practice 1: Attend to Values and Ethics

It is incumbent upon psychologists doing global leadership development work to appreciate the central role of ethical guidelines for professional work, such as the American Psychological Association (APA, 2017) *Ethical Principles of Psychologists and Code of Conduct* (APA Ethics Code), as well as the ethics and codes of practice established in the society in which the leader is working (e.g., psychologists interested in global leadership work should consult additional ethical guides, such as those of the United Nations Ethics Office [https://www.un.org/en/ethics/]). Mindfulness of ethical guidelines is important in global leadership education and consulting because it is likely that consultants will be entering contexts that are ill-defined or for which they do not possess previous experience (see Chapter 3, this volume, on consulting). There are countless examples of the harmful effects of misunderstanding local and religious customs or insisting on use of approaches not relevant to the local culture (e.g., Christopher et al., 2014). In this regard, a crucial ethical mandate is to act within one's own area of expertise, which includes careful reflection on the extent to which one does not know local norms, rules, expectations, histories, and customs.

Consider, for example, the challenges two of the authors (Shullman and White) faced upon leading the first executive MBA (EMBA) program in Qatar. Some of the planned activities, common in Western classrooms—such as filming or taking photographs of students, especially female students, or collecting personal data—were received as controversial because they contradicted local cultural prohibitions in photographing female students and/or sharing what would appear as private information. Complicating matters, the lead faculty for the Qatar EMBA were two women, making the course itself a groundbreaking event, which led to substantial scrutiny. From an ethical standpoint, the obligation to "first do no harm" required finding a balance between maintaining consistency in the curriculum and course goals and respecting local prohibitions and norms. The solution, in part, was to deliberate, consult, self-correct, and practice an essential skill of respecting, and even embracing, that which is unknown (White & Shullman, 2010). This led to a real-time reformulation of the leadership consultation in order to resonate more directly with the local values and norms.

At the same time, some ethical issues represent a "bright line" not to be crossed, regardless of country or culture. For example, accepting work that might be detrimental to human rights or harm individuals, communities, corporations, or governments would contradict Principle A: Beneficence and Nonmaleficence from the APA Ethics Code: "Because psychologists' scientific and professional judgments and actions may affect the lives of others, they are alert to and guard against personal, financial, social, organizational, or political factors that might lead to misuse of their influence." Likewise, Principle E: Respect for People's Rights and Dignity from the APA Ethics Code contends that "psychologists respect the dignity and worth of all people, and the rights of individuals to privacy, confidentiality, and self-determination. Psychologists are aware that special safeguards may be necessary to protect the rights and welfare of persons or communities whose vulnerabilities impair autonomous decision making." If there is any doubt in this regard, psychologists are encouraged to consult with the APA and with local psychologist colleagues or organizations for additional guidance. In fact, the current APA Ethics Code is undergoing a revision process to incorporate more of the challenges that emerge in organizational, multicultural, global, and virtual work (APA, 2019). In addition, reviewing international documents such as the *Universal Declaration of Ethical Principles for Psychologists* (International Union of Psychological Science, 2008) may also be useful. In short, ethical principles regarding beneficence and respect for persons require special consideration when working in an international context, sometimes with leaders who have different role expectations or value systems, such as how organizational members are to be regarded and treated.

In addition to the eight global themes discussed previously, at a complementary level, psychologists acting as or working with leaders/organizations internationally should expect ambiguity, paradox, conflict, and compromise to be integral to their work, even as they strive to stay true to the fundamental principles of their own culture and context (e.g., White & Shullman, 2010). This is because positional leaders at a host organization may want to introduce their own perspectives, frame leadership issues, and restrict the inclusion of certain topics or data related to their organization, all of which invite conflict between what the leadership consultant initially was asked to do and what he or she may be able to accomplish. Such situations must be decided and negotiated individually through a careful balance between the organization's legitimate right to protect its own interests and the fidelity we must ensure to the ethics of our own field.

Practice 2: Clarify Processes and Goals

Obtaining an international assignment to engage in leadership or leadership consulting/organizational development typically does not come easily and may be costly. Thus, it is important to understand what psychologists can offer and the role they will play relative to cultural expectations, costs, and outcomes. For example, the role of facilitator is more likely to result in culturally appropriate and successful engagements than the role of expert because it allows the leadership/organizational consultant a wider variety of culturally sensitive roles. The entrance of a consultant trained in one set of models to a new context may make visible differences in individuals' beliefs and values about leadership as well as a host of countertransference reactions and other processes (Chin & Trimble, 2015; Dyjak-LeBlanc et al., 2016; see also Chapter 3, this volume, on consulting). In a leadership and organizational context, Kets de Vries and Balazs (2005) explained such processes by observing that (a) much of mental life lies outside conscious awareness, (b) nothing is more central to who a person is than the way that person expresses and regulates emotions, and (c) human development is an inter- and intrapersonal process (pp. 9–10). For instance, the understanding in many countries that leadership can be learned—a contention based on the idea that leaders are "made" and not "born"—may not be universally accepted depending on the dispositional attributions that prevail within a given society (i.e., why leaders become leaders in the first place; see also Kets de Vries, 2019).

Psychologists must seek to communicate in ways that recognize that, although it may not be possible to step outside of one's own culture, it is important to identify and see beyond the cultural lenses through which each person perceives (Azar, 2009; Chin & Trimble, 2015; Glover & Friedman, 2015; Greenbaum, 2019). The challenges of trying to move beyond a specific cultural lens can be addressed at multiple levels, by (a) creating a learning culture that stresses collaboration, trust, and mutual respect; (b) reinforcing the dignity of each human being with cultural sensitivity and respect for each person's place and opinions in the training site; and (c) protecting the confidentiality of any collected data, striving to put all participants at ease by encouraging honesty and facilitating an environment that supports valid assessment.

It is important to appreciate that leadership development may or may not be consistent with the values of the culture in which the work takes place because there may be differing ideas regarding the nature and form of effective leadership. Thus, leaders, educators, and consultants who focus on leadership need to understand and create expectations that conflicting perspectives will exist and make room to constructively address them. Acknowledging the dynamics of conflicting beliefs, values, and worldviews may attenuate the possibility for judgmental attributions and interpersonal conflict. Harkening back to the previous eight themes, a well-developed capacity to care is necessary for the facilitation of these kinds of discussions (e.g., Gostick & Elton, 2012; Kets de Vries & Balazs, 2005; Quinn & Quinn, 2009). At a metacognitive level, beginning a leadership assignment or intervention with a discussion of expectations from self and others can be a helpful experience because participants are then primed to work with, rather than avoid, intrapsychic and interpersonal conflict (Dyjak-LeBlanc et al., 2016).

By virtue of their role and purpose, psychologists who function as leadership consultants have access to unique opportunities and experience specific challenges because of their outsider status. Not being fully accepted into a group with whom you are engaged in an unfamiliar place, even as you simultaneously are perceived to be an authority, may be uncomfortable as well as inevitable when assuming consultation roles (White & Shullman, 2010). Thus, international leadership consultation requires an intrepid mind and heart because the psychologist must suspend expectations of the familiar and intentionally be open to new insights and learning. At the same time, such outsider status is an important opportunity; it allows the consultant to observe and translate dynamics in an accessible manner to those who are embedded within the organization and the larger cultural milieu and likely may not notice their existence or consequences.

Practice 3: Learn to Navigate Paradoxes

Being an effective leader and consultant in global organizational environments cannot be reduced to a set of techniques or cookie-cutter approaches. Complex challenges such as assessing the degree of alignment between organizational culture and societal culture or determining how power manifests and operates in various contexts such as governmental, organizational, community, faith, and family, are demanding and require a way of thinking, not simply a set of practices. Navigating paradoxes means embracing the dissonance and ambiguity inherent in a global context. At a concrete level, this involves resisting the impulse to eliminate contradictions and reducing complex phenomena to dichotomous variables. Instead, we recommend employing diunital reasoning that "emphasizes both/and thinking, where seemingly contradictory or incompatible ideas exist simultaneously" (Pope et al., 2019, p. 660). An individual's perception of culture is at least partly a reflection of their own worldview and life experiences (Chin & Trimble, 2015; Glover & Friedman, 2015; House et al., 2014; White & Shullman, 2012). An openness to contradiction coupled with substantive reflection on one's own cultural biases not only sharpens a psychologist's self-awareness but positions them to identify and address differences; spotlight cognitive, motivational, and emotional processes; and facilitate growth and development (Dyjak-LeBlanc et al., 2016).

One of the more nuanced and difficult challenges for the leader–consultant is mastering the organizational culture of the sponsor and interpreting responses of leaders-in-training (White & Shullman, 2012). For example, it may be difficult to distinguish whether a high level of engagement among executives undergoing training indicates their own appraisals or their support for the global corporate/organizational mission. That is, overt receptivity to leadership development interventions may be a "public" presentation of self (Aronson, 2012). The consultant therefore needs to encourage views and opinions that may in fact be deeply conflictual while "reading" forms of expression and body language to assess what corporate actors really think and feel. As global leadership consultants, psychologists need to balance attention to organizational goals (e.g., facilitating more effective leadership behaviors) with processes that may be countervailing, such as encouraging leaders to change and become more aware of self and others, even as they remain embedded in their organization's cultures and contexts. Various forms of assessment (e.g., qualitative, quantitative, longitudinal, 360-degree, pre/post, course evaluation) may play a helpful role in facilitating, teaching, and coaching such competencies as long as consultants are aware of the potential for cultural bias through all levels of the assessment process, from the selection of assessment approaches to their eventual usage and interpretation (see Chapter 2, this volume, on assessment).

In the final analysis, it is important to identify and understand cultural, organizational, interpersonal, and intraindividual complexities because rules and protocols may supersede the individual cultures represented among the learners. Thus, leaders and leadership consultants need to be observant of potential conflicts and issues and strive for empathic responses to individual affronts or discomforts that may occur when well-intentioned learning activities are not a good fit with local customs (e.g., religious, cultural, class based, gender based). Ultimately, if a learner is deeply uncomfortable (e.g., with feedback; speaking freely in a classroom; revealing issues that may question the leadership of superiors within the organization), learning engagement may be compromised. The astute leader or leadership consultant leads by example, modeling discretion and good judgment in the course of each intervention (e.g., by treating cultural conflicts within the classroom as learning opportunities). After all, a core competency of international leadership psychologists is showing clients how to be most effective in working with diverse groups, and psychologists must strive to exemplify these competencies as consultants (Chin & Trimble, 2015). Last, an objective of this learning partnership approach is striving to create an environment in which there is respect for everyone's dignity and point of view (e.g., Eisler & Corral, 2009). Each person has a narrative, and their story is based on the individual as a member of cultures, organizations, groups, and memberships that may or may not be aligned.

HOW TO GET INVOLVED IN GLOBAL LEADERSHIP DEVELOPMENT

An initial question for engagement in leadership education or consultation is how to start. Our first suggestion is to become aware of the lay of the land. Within psychology, a number of APA Divisions are relevant to international leadership development and consultancy such as Division 9, Society for the Psychological Study of Social Issues (https://www.apa.org/about/division/div9.aspx); Division 13, Society of Consulting Psychology (https://www.apa.org/about/division/div13.aspx); Division 14, Society for Industrial and Organizational Psychology (https://www.apa.org/about/division/div14.aspx); and Division 52, International Psychology (https://www.apa.org/about/division/div52.aspx). These divisions all offer excellent guidance and perspectives regarding the opportunities and competencies that may be of particular relevance to individuals who aspire to global leadership consultation and education work, and they offer a window into allied organizations, initiatives, and opportunities. Consider joining divisions as a student, early career psychologist, or established professional. Other organizations may be particularly relevant: the

International Association of Applied Psychology (https://iaapsy.org/) and the International Council of Psychologists (https://www.icpweb.org).

A second strategy for becoming more involved in global leadership development is to immerse oneself in the relevant leadership literature, including the eight themes noted earlier, as well as multicultural psychology, organizational development, and consulting education, scholarship, and practice. Although there is no substitute for interacting with different cultures, exploring new geographic regions and simply feeling like an outsider are learning experiences that can enhance one's ability to make linkages to relevant scholarship and literature. Being effective globally requires the ability to interpret complex and oftentimes contradictory experiences. Lacking such cognitive complexity not only will lead to confusion but also can be perilous. There can be no substitute for learning from those who have gone before, and for thinking—deeply and persistently—about relevant models and methods that are integral to this work. In addition, there are competence guidelines for psychologists working outside their country of origin/residence (e.g., Morgan-Consoli et al., 2018).

As a third strategy for getting started in leadership development work, it helps to understand the differences between, and opportunities within, the corporate and nonprofit sectors. On the global corporate side, the demand for consultants and educators is increasingly locally derived because the main market for products and services is not in the home office, or in the country of origin, but in that corporation's international office or offices. In fact, many of the professional activities described in this chapter would not have happened had the authors not partnered with international business schools or international consulting firms that have a larger presence than any single consultant or small firm could hope to achieve. As such, it may be advisable for those considering a career in a global leadership context—particularly in the corporate/business realm—to seek relationships with larger organizations. At the same time, it should be noted that the bar is set high for qualification and experience. Despite these caveats, there is much work to be done, and the opportunity to improve executive education, leadership development, and the effectiveness of nongovernmental organizations is vast, even as this field is rapidly evolving.

Psychologists can also serve as teacher or coach, thanks to a growing recognition of the importance of human development and change processes. Services such as open enrollment curricula, private leadership development programs, nonprofit leadership institutes, organizational development consulting, and individual coaching are in high demand. Such work may be experienced as emotionally intense, so assessing one's own strengths, commitments, values, and weaknesses prior to committing to such a career path is advisable, as is the need to be strategic (e.g., entering such a field via business schools or international consulting firms). Because global corporations are increasingly "going local," we also recommend first working with firms that are developing their global leaders at the local or regional level before seeking to venture further abroad.

Conducting leadership development work for nonprofits merits special discussion. The need is substantive, and the opportunities are abundant, but finding ways to make a living doing this work represents an additional challenge, as many nonprofits do not have the means to compensate a consultant or educator at the rate of their corporate counterparts. We recommend that aspiring global leadership consultants gain experience by identifying nonprofits that may benefit from the particular skill set a psychologist may bring to bear, such as needs assessment, strategic planning, the assessment of organizational functioning, or facilitation of leadership development. Involvement is these activities may well entail some remuneration or could be provided as "pro bono" service in a valued organization, which allows for the acquisition of relevant experience.

There are a number of paths into nonprofit leadership consulting, including (a) investigating opportunities for paid and unpaid internships or actual positions within nonprofits (e.g., sites such as Idealist [https://www.idealist.org/] and the Career Center at The NonProfit Times [https://www.thenonprofittimes.com/]); (b) consulting with more established colleagues who have engaged in nonprofit work and join relevant organizations (e.g., the APA divisions noted previously); (c) investigating the possibility of grant-based/external funding for leadership development in nonprofits (e.g., educational institutions and nonprofits often are aware of such opportunities); (d) if enrolled in an academic program (undergraduate or graduate), determining whether such a project may be organized under the auspices of a course (e.g., an independent study) or whether such goals may best be pursued through more formal study (e.g., nongovernmental organization/regional/global studies); (e) finding a champion (e.g., faculty member; center/institute director) who may be interested in partnering on an organizational development/leadership project, either locally or globally; and (f) contacting relevant nonprofits directly to see whether they may be interested in dialogue about their particular needs/interests. As noted previously, an existing nonprofit may be seeking the very skill set that psychologists can offer. In the end, getting a foot in the door to secure relevant experience is the sort of currency that demonstrates effectiveness and efficacy not only in the nonprofit world but also in corporate/business contexts.

SUMMARY AND CONCLUSION: DEVELOPING GLOBAL LEADERS AND LEADERSHIP IN PSYCHOLOGY

Whether the focus is consulting, coaching, or educating, most potential employers are looking for credibility derived from the knowledge, skills, and experience of psychologists who have expertise in leadership and organizational development. At the same time, although competencies in areas such as assessment and leadership development are necessary, they are not sufficient for global leadership work. As emphasized throughout this chapter, psychologists who aspire to international leadership development work must be committed to the personal and professional cultivation of emotional, social, and cultural intelligence (i.e., understanding personal impact and acknowledging the limits of the intervention, listening empathetically and adapting one's approach to ensure an intervention is meaningful and developmental attuned, being open to concerns and encouraging feedback as well as cultivating confidence in providing it to others, and being willing to learn along the way). At the same time, knowing when to say no to an engagement also is critical. Ethically, psychologists begin with a mandate to do no harm and to work within their areas of competence. Defining competence, as noted earlier, goes beyond content matter knowledge and skills to include an ability to see beyond one's own cultural perspective (e.g., Chin & Trimble, 2015; Dyjak-LeBlanc et al., 2016; Glover & Friedman, 2015; Morgan-Consoli et al., 2018; see also Chapter 3, this volume). In the final analysis, whatever the context, culture, or country, global leadership development work can be deeply fulfilling, affording a unique opportunity to apply our knowledge, skills, and values to individuals, groups, organizations, and societies around the world that are seeking better, wiser, and more effective leaders and leadership.

REFERENCES

American Psychological Association. (2017). *Ethical principles of psychologists and code of conduct* (2002, Amended June 1, 2010, and January 1, 2017). https://www.apa.org/ethics/code/index.aspx

American Psychological Association. (2019, December 12). *Update of the APA Ethics Revision Task Force to the APA Board of Directors.*

Argyris, C., & Schön, D. A. (1974). *Theory in practice: Increasing professional effectiveness.* Jossey-Bass.

Aronson, E. (2012). *The social animal* (11th ed.). W. H. Freeman.

Avolio, B. J., Walumbwa, F. O., & Weber, T. J. (2009). Leadership: Current theories, research, and future directions. *Annual Review of Psychology, 60*(1), 421–449. https://doi.org/10.1146/annurev.psych.60.110707.163621

Aycan, Z. (2001). Expatriation: A critical step toward developing global leaders. In M. Mendenhall, T. Kuhlmann, & G. Stahl (Eds.), *Developing global business leaders: Policies, processes and innovations* (pp. 119–136). Quorum Books.

Azar, B. (2009, January). American culture sets us up for the economic fall, psychologists say. *Monitor on Psychology, 40*(1), 30.

Banaji, M. R., & Greenwald, A. G. (2013). *Blindspot: Hidden biases of good people.* Delacorte Press.

Bass, B. M. (1997). Does the transactional–transformational leadership paradigm transcend organizational and national boundaries? *American Psychologist, 52*(2), 130–139. https://doi.org/10.1037/0003-066X.52.2.130

Bass, B. M., & Riggio, R. E. (2006). *Transformational leadership* (2nd ed.). Lawrence Erlbaum Associates. https://doi.org/10.4324/9781410617095

Beechler, S., & Javidan, M. (2007). Leading with a global mindset. In M. Javidan, R. M. Steers, & M. A. Hitt (Eds.), *The global mindset (advances in international management)* (Vol. 19, pp. 131–169). Emerald Group.

Bird, A., Mendenhall, M., Stevens, M. J., & Oddou, G. (2010). Defining the content domain of intercultural competence for global leaders. *Journal of Managerial Psychology, 25*(8), 810–828. https://doi.org/10.1108/02683941011089107

Burke, W. B. (2008). *Organization change: Theory and practice.* Sage Publications.

Burns, J. M. (1978). *Leadership.* Harper & Row.

Campbell, D. P. (2006). Globalization: The basic principles of leadership are universal and timeless. In W. H. Mobley & E. Wheldon (Eds.), *Advances in global leadership* (Vol. 4, pp. 143–158). JAI Press/Elsevier. https://doi.org/10.1016/S1535-1203(06)04010-X

Chhokar, J. S., Brodbeck, F. C., & House, R. J. (Eds.). (2007). *Culture and leadership across the world: The globe book of in-depth studies of 25 societies.* Lawrence Erlbaum Associates. https://doi.org/10.4324/9780203936665

Chin, J. L., & Trimble, J. E. (2015). *Diversity and leadership.* Sage.

Christopher, J. C., Wendt, D. C., Marecek, J., & Goodman, D. M. (2014). Critical cultural awareness: Contributions to a globalizing psychology. *American Psychologist, 69*(7), 645–655. https://doi.org/10.1037/a0036851

Dweck, C. (2008). *Mindset: The new psychology of success.* Ballantine Books.

Dyjak-LeBlanc, K., Brewster, L., Grande, S., White, R. P., & Shullman, S. L. (2016). The EI Leadership Model: From theory and research to real world application. In C. N. Shealy (Ed.), *Making sense of beliefs and values: Theory, research, and practice* (pp. 531–574). Springer Publishing.

Eisler, R., & Corral, T. (2009). Leaders forging values-based change: Partnership power for the 21st century. *Beliefs and Values, 1*(1), 31–44. https://doi.org/10.1891/1942-0617.1.1.31

Fouad, N. A., & Arredondo, P. (2007). *Becoming culturally oriented: Practical advice for psychologists and educators.* American Psychological Association. https://doi.org/10.1037/11483-000

Gardner, W. L., Cogliser, C. C., Davis, K. M., & Dickens, M. P. (2011). Authentic leadership: A review of the literature and research agenda. *The Leadership Quarterly, 22*(6), 1120–1145. https://doi.org/10.1016/j.leaqua.2011.09.007

Glover, J., & Friedman, H. L. (2015). *Transcultural competence: Navigating cultural differences in the global community.* American Psychological Association. https://doi.org/10.1037/14596-000

Goleman, D. (1995). *Emotional intelligence.* Bantam Books.

Goleman, D. (2005). *Emotional intelligence: Tenth anniversary edition.* Random House.

Goleman, D., Boyatzis, R., & McKee, A. (2002). *Primal leadership: Learning to lead with emotional intelligence.* Harvard Business Review.

Gostick, A., & Elton, C. (2012). *All in: How the best managers create a culture of belief and drive big results.* Free Press.

Greenbaum, Z. (2019, March). Overturning long-term biases. *Monitor on Psychology, 50*(3), 20.

Griffin, M. A., Neal, A., & Parker, S. K. (2007). A new model of work role performance: Positive behavior in uncertain and interdependent contexts. *Academy of Management Journal, 50*(2), 327–347. https://doi.org/10.5465/AMJ.2007.24634438

Griffin, M. A., Parker, S. K., & Mason, C. M. (2010). Leader vision and the development of adaptive and proactive performance: A longitudinal study. *Journal of Applied Psychology, 95*(1), 174–182. https://doi.org/10.1037/a0017263

Gundling, E., Hogan, T., & Cvitkovitch, K. (2011). *What is global leadership: 10 key behaviors that define great global leaders.* Nicholas Brealey.

Heifetz, R., Grashow, A., & Linsky, M. (2009). *The practice of adaptive leadership: Tools and tactics for changing your organization and the world.* Harvard Business Press.

Henson, C., & Rossouw, P. (2013). *Brainwise leadership.* Learning Quest.

Hewlett, S. A. (2016, October 13). The attributes of an effective global leader. *Harvard Business Review.* https://hbr.org/2016/10/the-attributes-of-an-effective-global-leader

Hodgson, P., & White, R. P. (2001). *Relax, it's only uncertainty: How to lead the way when the way is changing.* Prentice Hall.

Hodgson, P., & White, R. P. (2020). *Relax, it's only uncertainty: How to lead the way when the way is changing* (2nd ed.). RPW Executive Development.

Hofstede, G. H. (2001). *Culture's consequences: Comparing values, behaviors, institutions, and organizations across nations.* Sage Publications.

House, R. J., Dorfman, P. W., Javidan, M., Hanges, P. J., & Sully de Luque, M. F. (2014). *Strategic leadership across cultures: The GLOBE study of CEO leadership behavior and effectiveness in 24 countries.* Sage Publications.

House, R. J., Hanges, P. J., Javidan, M., Dorfman, P. W., & Gupta, V. (Eds.). (2004). *Culture, leadership, and organizations: The GLOBE study of 62 societies.* Sage Publications.

International Union of Psychological Science. (2008). *Universal declaration of ethical principles for psychologists.* http://www.iupsys.net/about/governance/universal-declaration-of-ethical-principles-for-psychologists.html

Javidan, M., Dorfman, P. W., De Luque, M. S., & House, R. J. (2006). In the eye of the beholder: Cross cultural lessons in leadership from Project GLOBE. *The Academy of Management Perspectives, 20*(1), 67–90. https://doi.org/10.5465/amp.2006.19873410

Javidan, M., & Teagarden, M. B. (2011). Conceptualizing and measuring global mindset. In W. H. Mobley, M. Li, & Y. Wang (Eds.), *Advances in global leadership* (Vol. 6, pp. 13–39). Emerald Group. https://doi.org/10.1108/S1535-1203(2011)0000006005

Judge, T. A., & Bono, J. E. (2000). Five-factor model of personality and transformational leadership. *Journal of Applied Psychology, 85*(5), 751–765. https://doi.org/10.1037/0021-9010.85.5.751

Kail, E. (2011, October 28). Leadership character: The role of empathy. *The Washington Post.* https://www.washingtonpost.com/blogs/guest-insights/post/leadership-character-the-role-of-empathy/2011/04/04/gIQAQXVGQM_blog.html

Kets de Vries, M. (2019). *Down the rabbit hole of leadership: Leadership pathology of everyday life.* Palgrave Macmillan. https://doi.org/10.1007/978-3-319-92462-5

Kets de Vries, M., & Balazs, K. (2005). Organizations as optical illusions: A clinical perspective on organizational consultation. *Organizational Dynamics, 34*(1), 1–17. https://doi.org/10.1016/j.orgdyn.2004.11.006

Keys, T. (2013). *Leading transformational change: Leadership practices for the 21st century.* Trinity Leadership Products.

Knowledge@Wharton. (2012, May). *How GE builds global leaders: A conversation with chief learning officer Susan Peters.* https://knowledge.wharton.upenn.edu/article/how-ge-builds-global-leaders-a-conversation-with-chief-learning-officer-susan-peters/

Kouzes, J. M., & Posner, B. Z. (2012). *The leadership challenge: How to make extraordinary things happen in organizations.* Jossey-Bass.

Levy, O., Beechler, S., Taylor, S., & Boyacigiller, N. A. (2007). What we talk about when we talk about 'global mindset': Managerial cognition in multinational corporations. *Journal of International Business Studies, 38*(2), 231–258. https://doi.org/10.1057/palgrave.jibs.8400265

Lorde, A. (1995). Age, race, class and sex: Women redefining difference. In M. L. Anderson & P. H. Collins (Eds.), *Race, class and gender: An anthology* (2nd ed., pp. 532–540). Wadsworth.

Marquardt, M. J. (2014). *Leading with questions: How leaders find the right solution by knowing what to ask.* Jossey-Bass.

Martin, R. (2009). *Opposable mind: Winning through integrative thinking.* Harvard Business School Publishing.

McCall, M. W., Jr., & Hollenbeck, G. P. (2002). *Developing global executives: The lessons of experience.* Lexington Books.

McGiboney, G. W. (2017). *The psychology of leadership: Principles, practices and priorities.* Reveltree Group.

Mendenhall, M. E., Kühlmann, T. M., & Stahl, G. K. (2001). *Developing global business leaders: Policies, processes, and innovations.* Quorum Books.

Mendenhall, M. E., Osland, J. S., Bird, A., Oddou, G. R., & Maznevski, M. L. (2008). *Global leadership: Research, practice, and development.* Routledge.

Mendenhall, M. E., Weber, T. J., Arnandottir, A. A., & Oddou, G. R. (2019). Developing global leadership competencies: A process model. In J. S. Osland, B. S. Reiche, B. Szkudlarek, & M. E. Mendenhall (Eds.), *Advances in global leadership* (pp. 117–146). Emerald Publishing.

Mobley, W. H., Li, M., & Wang, Y. (Eds.). (2011). *Advances in global leadership* (Vol. 6). Emerald Group. https://doi.org/10.1108/S1535-1203(2011)6

Morgan-Consoli, M. L., Inman, A. G., Bullock, M., & Nolan, S. A. (2018). Framework for competencies for U.S. psychologists engaging internationally. *International Perspectives in Psychology: Research, Practice, Consultation, 7*(3), 174–188. https://doi.org/10.1037/ipp0000090

Morrison, A. M., White, R. P., & Van Velsor, E. (1994). *Breaking the glass ceiling: Can women reach the top of America's largest corporations?* Addison Wesley.

Morton, R. (2013, June). The theory of belief-based leadership. *Public Sector Digest,* pp. 1–5. http://www.publicsectordigest.com/articles/view/1150

Pendleton, D., & Furnham, A. F. (2016). *Leadership: All you need to know* (2nd ed.). Springer Publishing.

Pope, R. L., Reynolds, A. L., & Mueller, J. A. (2019). "A change is gonna come": Paradigm shifts to dismantle oppressive structures. *Journal of College Student Development, 60*(6), 659–673. https://doi.org/10.1353/csd.2019.0061

Quinn, R. E., & Quinn, R. W. (2009). *Lift: Becoming a positive force in any situation.* Berrett-Koehler Publishers.

Schmitz, P. (2012). *Everyone leads: Building leadership from the community up.* Jossey-Bass.

Shullman, S. L. (2018). Leadership at the .05 level: Reflections on psychologists and leadership. *The Counseling Psychologist, 46*(4), 530–543. https://doi.org/10.1177/0011000018776930

Snyder, N. H., Dowd, J. J., Jr., & Houghton, M. (1994). *Vision, values and courage: Leadership for quality management.* The Free Press.

Terry, R. W. (2001). *Seven zones for leadership: Acting authentically in stability and chaos.* Davies-Black.

Trompenaars, F., & Hampden-Turner, C. (1997). *Riding the waves of culture: Understanding diversity in global business* (2nd ed.). McGraw-Hill.

Trompenaars, F., & Hampden-Turner, C. (2010). *Riding the waves of innovation.* McGraw-Hill.

Tversky, A., & Kahneman, D. (1974). Judgment under uncertainty: Heuristics and biases. *Science, 185*(4157), 1124–1131. https://doi.org/10.1126/science.185.4157.1124

Unger, R. K. (2001). *Handbook of the psychology of women and gender.* Wiley & Sons.

Wheatley, M. J. (2006). *Leadership and the new science: Discovering order in a chaotic world.* Berrett-Koehler.

White, R. P., & Shullman, S. L. (2010). Acceptance of uncertainty as an indicator of effective leadership. *Consulting Psychology Journal, 62*(2), 94–104. https://doi.org/10.1037/a0019991

White, R. P., & Shullman, S. L. (2012). Thirty years of global leadership training: A cross-cultural odyssey. *Consulting Psychology Journal, 64*(4), 268–278. https://doi.org/10.1037/a0031654

6

Policy

Why and How to Become Engaged as an International Policy Psychologist

Merry Bullock, Tor Levin Hofgaard, Ezequiel Benito, Pamela Flattau, Amanda Clinton, Craig Shealy, and Shagufa Kapadia

We commonly hear that the world has "become global" (e.g., Friedman, 2005). This process refers to several interrelated dynamics, such as the broad interchange of worldviews, ideas, and cultures; the development of a world economy; the proliferation of service, industry, and educational sectors that span national and geographical regions; and a perspective that attends to global patterns in health, migration, development, and sustainability. Most products we use have a global history before ending up in our hands. Decisions about educational systems are often based on broad international comparisons of student performance, societal needs, and teaching processes. Knowledge is shared faster than ever, as are news events. Humans are more "on the move" (through displacement, migration, and immigration) than ever before. At the same time, long-standing inequalities across race, gender, education, income, and life outcomes are more starkly visible.

Our human experience of self, others, and the larger world takes place within this new globalization and raises questions that are psychological in nature: How do communities adjust to rapid changes in population or depopulation, to large movements of industry to the global east and south? How do we integrate massive human migrations around the world? How do we manage worldwide health threats, a challenge made all too salient by the COVID-19 pandemic? How do we live side by side with people with varying backgrounds, histories, and worldviews? How do we marshal our expertise to address the challenges that globalization has made even more visible, such as environmental

https://doi.org/10.1037/0000311-007
Going Global: How Psychologists Can Meet a World of Need, C. Shealy, M. Bullock, and S. Kapadia (Editors)

sustainability, inequity, poverty, and violence—the global and local issues we collectively face (Alford & Head, 2017)?

This chapter addresses how psychology and psychologists can contribute to these and other global challenges by helping societies and governments develop and implement policies that foster well-being. Psychology can make important contributions to global policy by translating our knowledge, skills, models, and methods into actionable proposals for policy content, delivery, and communication. To address how psychology and psychologists can be involved in policy at the global level, the material is divided into three complementary sections: (a) policy and psychology, (b) international psychology and policy, and (c) becoming engaged as an international policy psychologist.

POLICY AND PSYCHOLOGY

Psychology has much to offer to policy makers. Psychologists provide robust models, tools, and practices for gathering, organizing, and understanding information; for describing and assessing populations; for promoting sustainable and community-based solutions; and for improving decision-making processes. Understanding that much of our data come from studies in relatively wealthy, well-educated, Western societies, which may limit generalization—and that behavior is powerfully influenced by culture, identity, and history—psychological science and practice can offer empirically grounded and field-tested advice to national, regional, and global organizations and governments regarding how they may approach a globalizing world undergoing rapid change.

In an ideal world, policy makers would welcome psychologists to the loftiest of policy discussions to provide expertise about the human dimensions of the issues they confront and to use psychological expertise as they weigh evidence, articulate and reconcile different values, and make choices. Psychology has a lot to contribute to the goals of evidence-based policy making (e.g., Nishitani, 2020; Parkhurst, 2017). Our discipline and profession provide empirically supported insights and approaches for facilitating a more tolerant citizenry with greater capacity and inclination to embrace different cultures and identities (e.g., Christie & Dawes, 2001) and can facilitate adaptation to change and uncertainty (e.g., Anderson et al., 2019), processes that bear directly on how policies and programs are designed, delivered, evaluated, and experienced. Addressing these and other questions related to policy development, implementation, and evaluation is an important aspect of "going global" and "meeting a world of need" for the 21st century and beyond (e.g., Allen & Dodd, 2018; Arfken & Yen, 2014; Miller, 1969).

Yet, there is a paradox. Although understanding the dynamics of human behavior is central to addressing many of the largest challenges of our time, psychology is rarely at the policy table. In part, this is because policy makers do not understand how psychology is integral to the challenges they are trying to address. But it is also because psychology has not adapted its delivery of scientific output and applied expertise to meet the needs of policy makers. If you ask policy makers, "What is psychology?" common answers focus on the provision of therapy or the examination of mental illness. Almost no one outside of psychology is aware of how our discipline and profession can offer conceptually robust and empirically grounded guidance on the most pressing issues of our day, such as education, health, poverty, violence, the environment, disasters, migration, or a myriad of other problems that will require psychological expertise if credible policies are to be crafted, delivered, evaluated, and refined in an effective and sustainable manner (e.g., Alford & Head, 2017; Antonucci et al., 2019; Schmuck & Schultz, 2002).

Psychology professor Daniel Kahneman elaborated on policy makers' understanding of psychology in an interview conducted after he received the Nobel Memorial Prize in Economic Sciences:

> Policy makers, like most people, normally feel that they already know all the psychology and all the sociology they are likely to need for their decisions. I don't think they are right, but that's the way it is. . . . Something else has happened in recent years that is amusing, but also frustrating for psychologists. When it comes to policy making, applications of social or cognitive psychology are now routinely labeled behavioral economics. . . . The consequence is that psychologists applying their field to policy issues are now seen as doing behavioral economics. (Singal, 2017, paras. 13–14)

Our experience is congruent with Kahneman's observations. Although psychological issues are often front and center in discussions of problems and solutions, psychological scientists or practitioners are rarely included in policy-based conferences, review boards, and advisory councils. Anecdotally at least, expert advice is solicited from colleagues in education, economics, political science, sociology, social work, and anthropology but rarely psychologists, even when psychological expertise is transparently relevant to the issues at hand.

To have a voice, to be heard, and to have an impact, psychology and psychologists need to become engaged in the policy process. We need to understand the goals and motivations of policy makers and their constituents; highlight the utility of our research and expertise; and provide knowledge, data, tools, and strategies for action in a way that is relevant and transparent (e.g., Antonucci et al., 2019; Ruggieri, 2017; Schmuck & Schultz, 2002). To do so, we also need to cultivate skills for translating psychological science and practice into accessible and actionable form and to design our research to provide information on feasibility, cost, measurement, and outcomes that policy decisions require. Finally, we need to recognize that the voice of psychologists will always be one of many that must be heard by policy makers, no matter how prominent we might become over time (e.g., Parkhurst, 2017; Ruggieri, 2017).

Despite these challenges, there are visible and explicit calls for psychology and psychologists to engage in policy development, implementation, and evaluation (e.g., the Psychology Day at the United Nations website at https://www.unpsychologyday.com/). One reason is rooted in our deep commitment to improving the human condition and the well-being of societies. This commitment is reflected in the organizing principles or mission statements of many psychology organizations or universities and academies where psychologists learn, teach, and conduct research. Given the blatantly obvious psychological dimension to some of the most vexing problems we face as a species, many also call for individual psychologists—as professionals and citizens—to accept a moral, ethical, and humanistic obligation to be more engaged in the world around them and to bring their expertise to bear on societal issues that impact us all (e.g., Alford & Head, 2017; Allen & Dodd, 2018; Arfken & Yen, 2014).

A frequently cited call for engagement in policy making is the 1969 address by American Psychological Association (APA) president George Miller, who coined the phrase "giving psychology away." He said, "The most urgent problems of our world today are the problems we have made for ourselves" (p. 1063). Importantly, however, in terms of "going global" and "meeting a world of need," he also observed that

> our scientific results will have to be instilled in the public consciousness in a practical and usable form so that what we know can be applied by ordinary people . . . (p. 1070). Our responsibility is less to assume the role of experts and try to apply psychology ourselves, than to give it away to the people who really need it—and that includes everyone. . . . I am keenly aware that giving psychology away will be no simple task (p. 1071) . . . [but for] . . . myself, I can imagine nothing we could do that would be more relevant to human welfare, and nothing that could pose a greater challenge to the next generation of psychologists, than to discover how best to give psychology away. (Miller, 1969, p. 1074)

Miller's fundamental points are as salient today as they were decades ago, and his perspective serves as both inspiration and guidance to any who also aspire to be engaged as an international policy psychologist.

INTERNATIONAL POLICY AND PSYCHOLOGY

Merriam-Webster's dictionary defines *policy* as "a definite course or method of action selected from among alternatives . . . to guide and determine present and future decisions" (Merriam-Webster, n.d.). Relatedly, Bardach (2012, as cited in MacLachlan, 2014, p. 853) defined *policy* as "a set of principles which guide the prioritization of actions and the allocation of resources." In this chapter, we adopt a broad definition to capture activities that help shape the decisions, directions, or programmatic activities of organizations, communities, systems, societies, and governments.

Putting Psychology Into International Policy

We define international policy psychology in terms of two types of policy activities and three levels of policy analysis. Policy activities comprise (a) programs and practices (e.g., interventions, systems, or guidelines designed to prevent or ameliorate any number of phenomena and/or enhance the public good on the basis of theoretically robust frameworks and ecologically valid data) and (b) models and methods (e.g., guidance on how policies might best be developed, implemented, and evaluated; assessing policy-relevant knowledge, attitudes, or behaviors; enhancing decision-making or predicting processes and outcomes). These activities may be addressed at three levels of analysis: (a) individual action (e.g., using individual expertise to offer knowledge, experience, and recommendations as a psychologist, locally, nationally, regionally, and/or globally, often through consortia or multidisciplinary teams), (b) organizational action (e.g., developing and delivering demonstrably effective models, methods, programs, and practices through organizational networks, therefore becoming "stakeholders" in policy endeavors), and (c) governmental action (e.g., collaborating with local, national, regional, or international decision makers in the development, implementation, evaluation, and refinement of policies and their attendant programs and practices).

Implications and Applications

As may be clear, we interpret the term *international policy psychology* broadly. For example, psychologists might address policies in their own workplace or organization with global implications (e.g., policies on human rights orientation, accessibility, global equity). They might engage in policy work based upon a comparison of how other countries or regions approach issues of common concern (e.g., justice systems, sex education, drug treatment, economic disparities) to advance policies or programs and practices in their own country (e.g., Antonucci et al., 2019; Parkhurst, 2017; Reiter et al., 2016). Similarly, psychologists might provide input to a government, agency, or funder concerning their international activities or priorities (e.g., advising the U.S. Centers for Disease Control and Prevention on health measures for programs in other continents or advising the U.S. Justice Department on global drug prevention programs). Such consultation might take place at home or in another country that has asked for expertise in building systems or developing measures or evaluations (e.g., decision makers in international health, education, trade, transportation, or diplomacy). It might occur with regional agencies or governing structures (e.g., European Union, Pan American Health Organization, or Pan-African agencies), global agencies (e.g., the United Nations [UN]; World Health Organization [WHO]; UNICEF; United Nations Educational, Scientific and Cultural Organization [UNESCO]), governance bodies (e.g., North Atlantic Treaty Organization, Organization for Economic Co-operation and Development [OECD]), or international organizations and agencies (e.g., the Red Cross/ Red Crescent, Doctors Without Borders).

Although issues in international policy may be addressed through a variety of outlets, from global to regional to national to local, global agendas often may be understood by reviewing the purview of global systems, such as the UN and its specialized agencies. Although there are many other exemplars, international policy psychologists should be cognizant of these sorts of organizations.

The UN Family and Other Global Organizations: Relevance to Psychology

In 2015, the UN (2021) formally introduced a global agenda, the Sustainable Development Goals (SDGs) that outlined a "plan of action for people, planet and prosperity . . . and universal peace in larger freedom" (Preamble; UN, 2015). Building upon the Millennium Developmental Goals and other antecedent initiatives, the SDGs set out 17 broad agendas to end poverty and hunger; protect the planet; and foster prosperity, peace, and partnership. The UN members (governments) pledged to promote inclusive policies and programs addressing a range of topics within the purview of psychological expertise, such as ending poverty and hunger, improving health and well-being, ensuring quality education, improving gender equality, providing decent work, reducing inequality, building peace, addressing climate change, and building partnerships to work to achieve these goals. Each of these areas may be meaningfully addressed by psychological science and practice. To date, within psychology a range of articles have discussed how psychology is relevant to these policy areas, including several journal special issues (e.g., Antonucci et al., 2019; Jaipal, 2014; Verma et al., 2019).

Beyond the SDGs, within the UN system, 15 specialized agencies develop policies and programs, including several of interest to psychology. Among the better known, we highlight WHO, UNESCO, and the International Labour Organization (ILO).

WHO (2022) is a UN specialized organization responsible for international public health, setting policy for global health and mental health initiatives. WHO works directly with local governments to address a range of mental health treatment and prevention issues and with other intergovernmental agencies on developing policies and programs for humanitarian emergencies. UNESCO (https://en.unesco.org) focuses on education, cultural rights, and science. Its policies and programs include curriculum development, initiatives to promote gender equality, healthy child development, scientific exchange, and the celebration of cultural heritage. ILO (2022) strives to advance social and economic justice through an overarching goal to "to set labour standards, develop policies and devise programmes promoting decent work for all women and men." Each of these agencies promotes international- and country-level policies and programs.

Of course, international policy making also takes place outside the UN. To present just a few examples, the International Standardization Organization (https://www.iso.org) sets guidelines for all manner of goods and services, including psychological services. OECD (n.d.-d), "an international organisation [its members are countries] that works to build better policies for better lives" (Who We Are section, para. 1), releases more than 500 reports and many policy briefs each year, focusing on economic, environmental, and social change. In addition, OECD uses its convening power to bring governments and civil society representatives together to engage in policy development. The mission of the World Bank (https://www.worldbank.org) is to end extreme poverty and promote shared prosperity. It does so by partnering with its 189 member countries to develop social and economic policies. In 2019, the World Bank established a "behavioral insights" program to "improve how we approach policy and program design to be more realistic, efficient and effective" (Sánchez-Páramo et al., 2019). As a final example, the International Red Cross/ Red Crescent Movement helps those facing disaster, conflict, and health and social problems and engages policy debates on humanitarian issues (International Committee of the Red Cross, n.d.-a).

In addition to these global organizations, several "high-level" gatherings that are also platforms for policy development occur annually. Regular forums include UN Commissions (e.g., on the Status of Women, for Social Development, on Population and Development, on Sustainable Development), which meet yearly (United Nations, 2022), the Davos Forum on Economic Affairs (World Economic Forum, 2022), the OECD (n.d.-c) Forum, and the G7 Summit (BBC News, 2021). These gatherings are important because they provide information regarding lessons learned across governments, help set priorities for action, and offer a global forum for scholarly and applied input and exchange (e.g., Lee, 2009).

Key Points and Perspectives

In his APA Humanitarian Award address, Malcolm MacLachlan (2014; see also MacLachlan & McVeigh, 2021) set out a model of global policy making that, he argued, must include "macropsychology." Macropsychology, like macroeconomics, is concerned with the broader contextual, structural, and cultural determinants of human behavior. It is, noted MacLachlan,

> more concerned with 'understanding up,' or how individuals or groups influence the settings and conditions of the society in which they live. Micropsychology is more interested in 'understanding down,' that is, with the influence of individuals or groups on other groups, individuals, or indeed intrapsychic and biological processes within individuals, such as emotional regulation, or immune functioning. (p. 853)

Using this perspective, he called on psychology to use its traditional base to expand to encompass a "big data" mindset to explore behavior at national and global levels and to address questions about how psychology can influence, not merely explain or react to, settings and conditions. Psychology has been used in this "macro" way in the establishment of a Behavioural Insights Team in 2010 in the United Kingdom. A function of this team was to advise the government on how to effect societal-level change in behavior (e.g., increasing savings levels, or tax compliance, or organ donors, or adopting energy efficient strategies) by changing the framing for messaging and incentives. Since then, according to a World Bank report (Sánchez-Páramo et al., 2019), this use has spread broadly across governments. Today, the original Behavioral Insights Team has been incorporated in a global organization—Nesta—that advises governments worldwide on a range of topics, including education, health, and energy efficiency (see Nesta at https://www.nesta.org.uk/). In this context, psychology is seen as a tool to improve performance or adherence to socially desirable programs.

To adopt this more "macro" approach (MacLachlan & McVeigh, 2021), psychological research must be translated and applied in large real-world settings to communicate the importance and value of including a psychological perspective, and psychologists must consider societal-level explanatory systems (e.g., mental health status as an outcome of power imbalance). Over the years, many activities have had the goal of developing these strategies, from initiatives of national association presidents to journal special issues to curriculum development. But moving into the policy arena also requires a change in attitude. The path from research to policy application is not direct and occurs in complex political and politicized contexts. As Walker et al. (2018) noted,

> this requires psychologists, as a professional group, to give serious discussion and debate to what they are doing in a broader social political, economic, and cultural context. It requires psychologists to raise questions about how they should (or should not) contribute to policy. (p. 108)

In addition, as MacLachlan (2014) added, "Policy has not been attractive to many psychologists. It is generally messy and inexact" (p. 853). We return to the implications of these features of policy for building skill sets of those who aspire to be engaged as international policy psychologists.

Where Are Psychologists Active?

Although psychologists are actively involved in policy venues in various ways, by far the most common is to indirectly influence international policy through research. No one road map shows the areas of research that will be relevant to specific global policy concerns. Overall, policy makers are interested in research that will help them understand what to do, how to do it, and "what works," for whom, and in what contexts. In other words, policy makers need assurance that the research they use to back their decisions is valid and is generalizable to their specific contexts and concerns. In practice, this means that psychology research needs to be conveyed in a form that makes clear how specific policies and their attendant practices will address particular needs. The breadth of such implications and applications are wide and diverse, including but not limited to health and well-being; educational goals or social programs; the impact of various economic models on work behavior; factors and forces that are associated with healthy family functioning or childhood outcomes; risk and ameliorative factors for vulnerable groups or populations; the causes and consequences of social inequality; best practices for conflict resolution, negotiation, or decision making; and cross-cultural comparisons that yield nuanced recommendations for development and implementation.

One way that research enters the policy pipeline is through policy reports, white papers, green papers, and the like, which are designed to help people make action-oriented policy decisions (see Stanford Law School, n.d., for a useful glossary). National Academies, think tanks, and policy institutes are often commissioned to provide expert-based, authoritative reports. For example, the U.S. National Academies of Sciences, Engineering and Medicine gives "authoritative, independent advice on important matters in science and health policy" (National Academies of Sciences, Engineering, and Medicine, 2022, National Academies Press section). Many of these reports include psychologist authors and psychology research. For example, the U.S. Institute of Medicine published a multidisciplinary call for governments to invest in child development (Huebner et al., 2016), showing the economic, social, health, peace, and security benefits of attending to such matters. This multiauthored report (including many psychologists) was intended to "close the gap between what is known and what is done" (Huebner et al., 2016, p. 1). Numerous independent research institutes produce reports from a cadre of affiliated experts, such as RTI International (https://www.rti.org/practice-areas), which provides programs and expert advice on a range of psychosocial issues, or the International Institute for Applied Systems Analysis (2021), which "conducts policy-oriented research into issues that are too large or complex to be solved by a single country or academic discipline" (para. 1).

In short, through their research, psychologists provide models and methods to facilitate informed policy decisions, actions, and evaluation of outcomes. Psychologists have a special skill in the development of measures for behavioral outcomes and processes that may be applied to each aspect of the policy process. The following examples of data gathering, decision making, and outcome evaluation illustrate some of psychology's contributions.

Gathering Policy-Related Data

Governments often are interested in assessing their own programs in health, education, or public services—compared with those of other countries—as a benchmarking process to understand factors important to good outcomes, to map the range of variation, to see trends over time, or to chart the outcomes of reform processes. International comparative studies aid in this process by providing a systematic look at behaviors and outcomes across countries. Although these studies take many forms, from descriptive compilation of data to testing of explanatory models, they share the need to develop both solid measures that can yield comparable, valid cross-country data and rigorous methodologies that are workable across countries of administration. Psychologists have long been involved in the development of such measures—for example, in cross-national studies of educational outcomes, such as Trends in International Mathematics and Science Study (TIMSS; https://www.iea.nl/studies/iea/timss) and the Program for International Student Assessment (PISA; https://www.oecd.org/pisa/), as well as in comparative studies of specific topics such as adolescent social and political attitudes (Malak-Minkiewicz & Torney-Purta, 2021), bullying (Menesini & Salmivalli, 2017), street children (Koller & Hultz, 2001), and child development (White & Sabharwal, 2014). Psychologists' roles include defining constructs, specifying psychometric criteria for measures, checking construct validity, and exploring cross-cultural generalizability through a multimethod approach to construct validation across cultures and contexts (e.g., Marsh et al., 2006; see also Chapter 2, this volume, on assessment).

Another example is the development of subjective well-being measures. Until relatively recently, country-level well-being and social progress were measured in terms of economic terms (gross domestic product) and vital statistics (life expectancy, health status). However, studies showing that subjective well-being influences a number of outcomes—including productivity, employment, earnings, longevity, cardiovascular risk, criminality, drug and alcohol use, and prosocial behavior (e.g., volunteering; OECD, 2013; Stone & Mackie, 2013; Winefield et al., 2012)—have increased interest in the development of robust and reliable measures of subjective well-being for cross-country comparisons. The purpose of these comparisons is to help monitor national progress and potential areas of policy intervention, such as social services for special populations (e.g., youth, elderly; Stone & Mackie, 2013), gender equality, poverty reduction, or life satisfaction (e.g., OECD, 2011b). A number of well-being measures developed by psychologists are now used globally, including the Cantril Ladder (also referred to as the Self-Anchoring Striving Scale), which asks people to rate how they value their life in terms of the *best possible life* (10) through to the *worst possible life* (0).[1] This measure has been used in the World Gallup Poll since 2005, which has been the source for such indices as the World Happiness Index, and used to develop models of how wealth, life circumstances, and social conditions impact well-being. The promise of including subjective well-being is that policy makers will be able to fine-tune the anticipated and unanticipated effects of policy decisions and implementation.

Helping Governments Make Decisions

Government leaders engage in the formulation of policies and programs by considering a set of options for action presented in the form of briefings, white papers, expert counsel, and the like. Psychologists have played an important role by facilitating an understanding of options through risk analysis and leadership development. For example, projects from the International Institute for Applied Systems Analysis, led by mathematic psychologist Detlof von Winterfeldt, integrated statistics, decision, risk analyses, and behavioral decision research to develop a statistical basis for negotiating trade-offs in emission reductions across neighboring countries (Kryazhimskiy & von Winterfeldt, 2009), calculating the world energy outlook (Cofala et al., 2011), and estimating the relationship between education and employment workforce projections in Germany (Loichinger, 2010).

Assessing Outcomes

Psychologists have actively engaged in the design of the evaluation of numerous policy and program outcomes. As one example, the Belgian Red Cross of Flanders examined the "lessons learned" from the 2004 Sri Lanka Tsunami that took more than 30,000 lives in less than an hour, "injured more than

---

[1]The score for each country is calculated as the mean value of responses to the Cantril Ladder for that country (OECD, 2011a).

15,000 people and displaced more than 800,000 destroying all they possessed" (Vaes & Goddeeris, 2012, p. 4). Based on a series of carefully crafted interviews, the Red Cross ultimately joined other humanitarian agencies in assessing the pros and cons of owner-driven construction (including subsidized vs. participatory housing approaches) and donor-driven construction (including contractor-driven housing "in place" vs. contractor-driven relocation services). Any number of studies, of course, demonstrate the role of behavioral scientists in anticipating and/or measuring the outcome and impacts of programs and policies in international disaster relief (e.g., International Federation of Red Cross and Red Crescent Societies, 2009; see also Chapter 2, this volume, on assessment).

The Role of Psychology Organizations

National, regional, and international professional organizations of psychology can serve as important catalysts for the application of psychology to policy. These organizations represent the breadth of psychology from psychological science and research to practicing psychologists at all levels of activity, from education, training, and licensure through research and teaching careers. Many national organizations are actively involved in policy setting in a broad range of topics within their own countries, and some have joined regional and international organizations in addressing global policy issues.

One example of an innovative effort to advance policy efforts in psychology on an international scale is the Global Psychology Alliance (GPA). In November 2019, the APA and the Portuguese Order of Psychologists convened the International Summit on Psychology and Global Health in Lisbon, Portugal. This 2½-day working meeting brought together high-level leaders in psychological organizations from across the world to join forces and detail a plan for how psychology—as represented by national, regional, and international associations across the world—could address important global challenges. The SDGs provided a basis for prioritizing shared efforts, which were initially focused on climate change. During 2020, this group expanded its membership and changed focus to the COVID-19 pandemic, meeting once to twice per week to develop materials to address pandemic-related needs. The expanded group returned to its original focus on climate change in 2021. As the group worked to develop and publicize its outputs, it identified itself as the GPA (APA, n.d.), which now includes representatives from approximately 60 distinct organizations from every continent of the world and continues to meet on a regular basis.

Those who participate in the GPA (each a representative from a national, regional, or international psychology association) do so as part of a horizontal leadership group focused on enhancing psychology's presence in the global policy arena. All voices are incorporated into the work of the GPA with the aim of sharing resources (i.e., across associations, from publications to experts on specific topics); working together to design tools of use to the members and/or residents of each respective country (i.e., an information sheet about the increase in home-based violence created from an international perspective, adaptable to each country, translated, and distributed widely; see APA, 2020a); and supporting advances in regulation, training, and recognition of the profession (i.e., shared statement on the role of psychologists in addressing the global mental health crisis). In its current focus on climate change, the GPA is preparing to take an active role in promoting evidence-based policy incorporating psychological dimensions to upcoming global climate change summits.

The two major international psychology organizations—the International Association of Applied Psychologists (https://iaapsy.org) and the International Union of Psychological Science (https://www.iupsys.net)—also address policy issues. IAAP, whose members are individual psychologists, encourages its members to apply their research to policy issues and sponsors special projects on climate change, gender equality, immigrants, quality education, and promoting decent work for all. The International Union of Psychological Science (whose members are national psychology associations) has promulgated a number of statements about the conduct of research and application (International Union of Psychological Science, n.d.) and participates to represent psychology in major international organizations, including the International Science Council, UNESCO, WHO, and the UN.

Psychology as a field and profession also has a standing presence within the UN through recognition of individual associations as nongovernmental organizations (NGOs) with representation to the Economic and Social Council and the Department of Global Communication and through their collective grouping, the Psychology Coalition at the United Nations (PCUN). Individual organizations and the PCUN regularly showcase the work of psychology to UN diplomats and policy makers, and the PCUN organizes the annual Psychology Day at the United Nations around a particular relevant theme. The day

> is a celebration of psychology in the context of the United Nations. It provides an opportunity for psychology to share with U.N. Permanent Missions, U.N. agencies, NGOs and the private sector the activities of psychologists at the U.N. and the role of psychology in addressing concerns of global importance. Psychology Day also introduces psychologists and psychology students to psychology's current and potential involvement in U.N. activities and issues. (PCUN, n.d.)

Each of these efforts illustrates how the world of organized psychology can actively advance the application of psychological knowledge and skill to create change for problems that all people, and their governments, face.

International policy psychology can also take place at home. A synergistic relation exists across local, national, regional, and global levels of policy development, implementation, and evaluation. Psychologists can address international policy locally (i.e., in their own community, region, nation, and society) by exploring how policy in other countries and cultures is envisioned, enacted, and evaluated. To take just one example, policy makers in the United States could learn a great deal from research on how the criminal justice system is conceptualized and delivered in other countries, particularly because the United States presently incarcerates a greater proportion of its citizens than any other country in the world. International comparative studies (e.g., Maghan, 1997) or reports on practices elsewhere (e.g., Reiter et al., 2016) illustrate how fruitful this exchange can be. Many organizations and systems in the United States—and around the world—grapple actively with policy-related matters such as these. Within the APA (2021b), many of its organizational divisions address policy directly and, in so doing, both learn from and contribute to policy-related work by other psychologists, interdisciplinary colleagues, and policy makers around the world.

BECOMING ENGAGED AS AN INTERNATIONAL POLICY PSYCHOLOGIST

Most of us are not ready to plunge into areas of professional activity when we feel unprepared. This is especially true for engagement in international policy activities. Researchers may feel that involvement in policy activities will detract from their publications and impact factor; applied psychologists may not see a connection between what they do in their everyday work and international policy. However, like any other endeavor, preparedness is critical for effective action. Effective involvement in international policy activities does not necessarily require extensive additional training, but it does require a set of skills that are not part of the usual psychology curriculum. The purpose of this section is to describe those skills and how you can acquire them.

Adopting a Policy Perspective

When psychologists enter the policy arena, whether local, national, regional, or international, they are engaging a new environment where the goals of communication are to provide information, expertise, and technical assistance that is perceived as useful and relevant to policy makers. The work required in this realm may fall outside the comfort zone for many psychologists; this is not surprising, as there are several ways in which meeting the needs of policy makers are different from the usual discourse in psychology about theories, data, and phenomena.

Information that is useful to policy makers often is characterized by its direct relevance to current issues and by its perceived role in helping policy makers make decisions about specific courses of action. Psychologists, however, do not usually receive training in international, national, regional, or even local issues, or in applying their research to these often very applied and specific contexts. For example, the focus in research training is typically on methodology and statistics, addressing issues of internal validity and statistical power but not on the application to "real-world" questions or needs or on translating significant results to applicable recommendations for policy. Thus, to "go global," psychologists need to broaden their focus to include a deliberate emphasis on providing information relevant to policy decisions, including economic, political, and social implications. At the same time, certain inherent complexities must also be addressed as part of any policy-related toolbox. As Walker et al. (2018) noted, many psychologists may assume that the path from research to policy is direct, without sufficiently appreciating the political and politicized contexts in which policy is developed and deliberated. Legislative bodies are strewn with the wreckage of policy proposals that not only make excellent sense but also are empirically supportable through robust research. At the same time, all manner of policy that has no research backing at all—or research indicating serious flaws—is promulgated but is implemented nonetheless. That is because politics often trumps policy.

Although psychologists certainly can learn through experiencing the political process, the path from knowledge to policy could be included in our education and training systems, including questions about the reliability of policy-relevant evidence, the economic impact of proposed policies, and political expediency. Expanding psychology education in this manner can encourage increased engagement, comfort, and competency in the policy arena, whereas highlighting how international policy work can provide excellent opportunities for scholarly collaboration and output (e.g., publications, presentations, grants, consulting), both individually and in collaboration with other colleagues.

How to Get Started

In this final section, we address how current and future internationally minded psychologists may begin to address policy issues. These suggestions are focused on complementing psychologists' substantive skill sets. In other words, here we present a range of dynamic opportunities that build upon competencies most psychologists acquire through their education and training.

- **Review and read policy-oriented journals, reports, and databases.** It is important to become familiar with the wider context of policy making, which is multidisciplinary and multifaceted and may use models or constructs outside the psychology purview. You can find these journals in a number of ways. For example, it may help to review reference lists in policy-related articles and search large databases. Users of EBSCO databases can search for lists of journals using keyword searches (e.g., *health policy; education policy*). Specific journals focused exclusively on policy studies also offer excellent materials and points of reference (e.g., the *Policy Studies* home page at https://www.tandfonline.com/journals/cpos20; the *Policy Studies Journal* home page at https://onlinelibrary.wiley.com/journal/15410072). A new field of "science diplomacy" also features a journal *Science Diplomacy* published by the AAAS (https://www.sciencediplomacy.org/). In addition, national advisory bodies (e.g., U.S. National Academies of Science, Medicine and Engineering) regularly publish authoritative policy guidance (e.g., https://www.nap.edu).

- **Search for articles that discuss the role of psychology in local, national, regional, and global policy.** It is not always easy to find the most efficient search terms for these articles. One way is to look for specific authors (e.g., Fischhoff, 1990; Ruggieri, 2017; Walker et al., 2018). Another way is to search for journals or journal special issues that specifically mention the term *policy* (e.g., *Psychology, Policy and Law* at https://www.apa.org/pubs/journals/law; *Frontiers in Psychology*, the special issue on policy and psychology at https://www.frontiersin.org/research-topics/3543/psychology-and-policy; or *Analyses of Social Issues and Public Policy* from the Society for the Psychological Study of Social Issues at https://spssi.onlinelibrary.wiley.com/journal/15302415). In addition, *International Perspectives in Psychology: Research, Practice and Consultation*, the journal of APA's Division 52 (international), regularly features "policy briefs" in which authors are asked to specifically draw out the implications of their research for policy with an emphasis on work that is relevant to the UN Sustainable Development Goals (see https://issuu.com/hogrefegroup/docs/ipp_flyer).

- **Seek information on "big picture" organizations and institutes that are involved in policy.** Several of these organizations have been mentioned in this chapter (e.g., WHO, PAHO, ILO, UNICEF), but there are many others (e.g., United for Global Mental Health, n.d.; the Interagency Standing Committee). These organizations publish reports on major global issues. Read the reports and follow up with the listed citations that seem particularly relevant to your specific interests or goals.

- **Review webpages of policy-oriented "think tanks" and research institutes.** These are "public policy research, analysis, and engagement organizations that generate policy-oriented research, analysis, and advice on domestic and international issues that enable policy makers and the public to make informed decisions about public policy issues" (University of Pennsylvania, n.d.).

- **Search out psychology organizations that serve as knowledge brokers and are directly involved in policy.** Example organizations include the Psychology Coalition at the UN, a grouping of a dozen psychology associations involved with the UN NGO Community (https://www.psychologycoalitionun.org), Psychologists for Social Responsibility (https://www.psysr.net), and the Global Network of Psychologists for Human Rights, which provides information and discusses issues related to social justice and human rights issues (https://www.humanrightspsychology.org)

- **Seek out and attend conferences addressing global policy issues.** In addition to live and virtual conferences, many organizations offer webinars and training sessions. Although we encourage you to become familiar with venues outside of psychology, most national psychology organizations offer conferences with sessions devoted to policy issues (see APA, 2020b, for examples of internationally focused policy-oriented sessions at the 2020 Virtual APA Convention).

- **Explore educational programs or certificates that emphasize policy.** There is no explicit compendium of programs with an international and policy focus, but areas to search include *psychology/policy*, which yields information on graduate programs in psychology and policy such as the McCourt School of Public Policy (Georgetown University, n.d.) Policy and Human Development program, the Kroc Institute for International Peace Studies (https://kroc.nd.edu/), or global studies programs (e.g., Duke University, n.d.; the Global Studies Consortium website [https://globalstudiesconsortium. org/]; International Beliefs and Values Institute, n.d.). The Association of professional Schools of International Affairs (n.d.) offers a list of graduate programs in international affairs, which is another entry point. The UN system also offers training at a general level through its Science Technology and Innovation Policy programs (UNESCO, n.d.-b).

- **Explore opportunities to work directly in policy settings.** Psychologists at a variety of experience/educational levels are eligible for certain fellowships, internships, and assistantships in policy-related settings, both nationally and internationally. Exhibit 6.1 is a sample list of organizations. In addition to specific programs, many professional organizations offer opportunities to serve as a representative to policy-related advisory boards, governmental and quasi-governmental organizations, funding agencies, and consortia, or to nominate their members for such roles. Relatedly, you can seek opportunities to apply your interests and expertise through international bodies. For example, the UN (n.d.-a) runs a Consultant Registry for expert consultants and technical assistance, and UNESCO (n.d.-a) highlights policy-related opportunities on its Science Technology and Innovation Policy platform.

- **Forge alliances with policy makers and their constituents.** Throughout this chapter, we have iterated the importance of knowing what policy makers need and how to communicate in a way to address those needs. Engaging in the policy process through a broader involvement with those who ultimately can benefit from psychological expertise facilitates this process. For example, your own government representatives often grapple with local, national, and global matters that are relevant to the goals and emphases of international policy psychology. The World Federation for Mental Health (https://wfmh.global/), an international multidisciplinary advocacy and education organization, brings together researchers, scholars, patient advocates, caregivers, and service users and regularly engages with policy makers.

CONCLUSION: BRINGING PSYCHOLOGY TO THE INTERNATIONAL POLICY TABLE

For psychologists—trained in careful analysis, cautious interpretation of data, and multidimensional thinking—entering the policy arena may seem daunting. Policy makers often want rapid answers, surefire solutions, and simple models. Yet the clear relevance of psychology to the global challenges of our time can

EXHIBIT 6.1

International Fellowship and Internship Opportunities

Fellowships and Internships Specifically for Psychologists

- **APA–IUPsyS Global Mental Health Fellowship:** Yearly selection of one Fellow to work with the WHO Department of Mental Health and Substance Abuse. The Fellow develops a work plan with WHO staff (APA, 2022).

- **APA Congressional Fellowship:** This unique program provides psychologists "with an invaluable public policy learning experience, to contribute to the more effective use of psychological knowledge in government, and to broaden awareness about the value of psychology-government interaction among psychologists and within the federal government" (APA, 2021a, para. 1; see also American Association for the Advancement of Science, n.d.).

Fellowships, Internships, and Programs not Specifically for Psychologists

- **Fulbright Program:** "Led by the United States government in partnership with more than 160 countries worldwide, the Fulbright Program offers international educational and cultural exchange programs for passionate and accomplished students, scholars, artists, teachers, and professionals of all backgrounds to study, teach, or pursue important research and professional projects" (U.S. Department of State, n.d., para. 1).

- **Jefferson Science Fellows:** The Jefferson Science Fellows program is open to tenured, or similarly ranked, faculty from U.S. institutions of higher learning who are U.S. citizens. Jefferson Science Fellows spend 1 year on assignment at the U.S. Department of State or United States Agency for International Development serving as advisers on issues of foreign policy or international development (National Academies of Sciences, Engineering, and Medicine, n.d.).

- **Centre for Science and Policy, University of Cambridge, UK, Policy Fellowships Programme:** This program connects academics "with the policy world, and across Government as a uniquely powerful opportunity for problem-solving, professional development, network building and access to expertise" (University of Cambridge, 2022, para. 3). Fellows are generally senior administrative officials in governments or in NGOs.

- **German Chancellor Fellowship:** This program is targeted to university graduates from Brazil, China, India, Russia, South Africa, and the United States who have an international outlook and initial leadership experience. It is intended to promote new solutions to the global issues of our times. Fellows pursue self-developed, research-based projects that are societally relevant and have the potential for long-term, publicly visible impact (Humboldt Foundation, 2021).

- **ICRC Traineeships:** The International Committee of the Red Cross (n.d.-b) offers a variety of internships, apprenticeships, and trainee programs focused on their mission to protect the lives and dignity of victims of armed conflict and other situations of violence and to provide them with assistance.

(continues)

EXHIBIT 6.1

International Fellowship and Internship Opportunities (*Continued*)

- **OECD Internship Program:** The mission of the OECD is to provide high-quality policy advice, drawing on multidisciplinary perspectives and peer-learning approaches. Its work "promotes policies to improve the economic and social well-being of people around the world. The OECD brings together governments, members of parliament, businesses, community leaders, civil organisations and academics to seek solutions to common problems, develop global standards, share experiences and identify best practices in a collaborative effort towards—**better policies for better lives**" (OECD, n.d.-b, What Brings Us Together section; emphasis in original). Students enrolled in a fully accredited degree programme (bachelor's, master's, PhD) can apply (OECD, n.d.-a).

- **UN Internship Program:** The objective of the UN internship is to provide a firsthand impression of the day-to-day working environment of the UN. Interns work directly with career professionals and senior management; they are exposed to high-profile conferences and meetings and contribute to analytical work and organizational policy of the UN. Students enrolled in or who are within 1 year of graduation from bachelor's, master's, or PhD programs are eligible to apply (UN, n.d.-b).

Note. OECD = Organization for Economic Co-operation and Development; UN = United Nations.

encourage us to develop effective ways to sit at the policy table. To capture this reality, we close with some sage and sobering comments from Baruch Fischhoff (1990) on what happens when science and politics meet, which seem as salient today as when they appeared in the *American Psychologist* decades ago:

> (a) Expect to make slow progress in understanding the underpinnings of one's own field; (b) expect to fulfill non-psychological roles; (c) expect one's empirical results to be distorted, both deliberately and inadvertently; (d) expect 'amateurs' to try to usurp the need for psychological expertise, replacing our research with their self-serving speculations; (e) expect to stick with a problem long after any financial support has been exhausted; (f) expect conflicts of conscience (and charges of bias) when balancing science and politics; (g) expect to be misdirected by the presenting symptoms described by clients; and (h) expect the temptation to overshoot one's competence. The final analysis for such involvements might include three questions: Is it good for society? Is it good for psychology? Is it good for oneself? (p. 652)

For all of us who aspire to see psychology fulfill its potential as a source of important policy advice, such admonitions require reflection. At the same time, the most pressing issues of our day—exemplified by the SDGs and the "wicked problems" we collectively face (e.g., climate change, racial conflict, gender relations, conflict resolution)—require our serious and sustained attention as psychologists, because they focus on human action directed toward local and global well-being. We hope that current and emerging international psychologists will be inspired to address policy needs locally and globally. If we do so diligently and responsibly—engaging with policy makers, adopting a "macro" perspective, reflecting on our input, and finding ways to translate our science and practice into relevant guidance—there is every reason to believe that psychology and psychologists can finally take their place at the global policy table.

REFERENCES

Alford, J., & Head, B. W. (2017). Wicked and less wicked problems: A typology and a contingency framework. *Policy and Society, 36*(3), 397–413. https://doi.org/10.1080/14494035.2017.1361634

Allen, L., & Dodd, C. (2018). Psychologists' responsibility to society: Public policy and the ethics of political action. *Journal of Theoretical and Philosophical Psychology, 38*(1), 42–53. https://doi.org/10.1037/teo0000077

American Association for the Advancement of Science. (n.d.). *Science and technology policy fellowships.* https://www.aaas.org/programs/science-technology-policy-fellowships

American Psychological Association. (n.d.). *The Global Psychology Alliance.* https://www.apa.org/international/networks/global-psychology-alliance

American Psychological Association. (2020a, June). World's psychological associations unite against home-based violence during COVID-19. *Global Insights Newsletter.* https://www.apa.org/international/global-insights/home-based-violence

American Psychological Association. (2020b, August 26). *Global sessions at the 2020 Virtual APA Convention.* https://www.apa.org/international/global-insights/global-sessions-virtual-convention

American Psychological Association. (2021a, October). *APA Congressional Fellowship.* https://www.apa.org/about/awards/congress-fellow

American Psychological Association. (2021b, October). *APA Divisions.* https://www.apa.org/about/division

American Psychological Association. (2022, January). *APA-IUPSYS Global Mental Health Fellowship.* https://www.apa.org/about/awards/mental-health-fellowship

Anderson, C., Carleton, R. N., Diefenbach, M. & Han, P. (2019). The relationship between uncertainty and affect. *Frontiers in Psychology, 12.* https://doi.org/10.3389/fpsyg.2019.02504

Antonucci, T. C., Bial, M., Cox, C., Finkelstein, R., & Marchado, L. (2019). The role of psychology in addressing worldwide challenges of poverty and gender inequality. *Zeitschrift fur Psychologie mit Zeitschrift fur Angewandte Psychologie, 227*(2), 95–104. https://doi.org/10.1027/2151-2604/a000360

Arfken, M., & Yen, J. (2014). Psychology and social justice: Theoretical and philosophical engagements. *Journal of Theoretical and Philosophical Psychology, 34*(1), 1–13. https://doi.org/10.1037/a0033578

Association of Professional Schools of International Affairs. (n.d.). *Graduate schools and programs.* https://apsia.org/graduate-schools-programs/

BBC News. (2021, June 11). *G7 summit: What is it and why is it in Cornwall?* https://www.bbc.com/news/world-49434667

Christie, D., & Dawes, A. (2001). Tolerance and solidarity. *Peace and Conflict, 7*(2), 131–142. https://doi.org/10.1207/S15327949PAC0702_04

Cofala, J., Borken-Kleefeld, J., Heyes, C., Klimont, Z., Rafaj, P., Sander, R., Schopp, W., & Amann, M. (2011, September). *Emissions of air pollutant for the World Energy Outlook 2011 energy scenarios* (Final report to the International Energy Agency).

Duke University. (n.d.). *Alumni.* https://internationalcomparative.duke.edu/alumni

Fischhoff, B. (1990). Psychology and public policy: Tool or toolmaker? *American Psychologist, 45*(5), 647–653. https://doi.org/10.1037/h0091626

Friedman, T. L. (2005). *The world is flat: A brief history of the twenty-first century.* Farrar, Straus and Giroux.

Georgetown University. (n.d.). *MPP/PhD in psychology.* https://mccourt.georgetown.edu/programs/dual-degree-programs/mpp-phd-in-psychology/

Huebner, G., Boothby, N., Aber, J. L., Darmstadt, G. L., Diaz, A., Masten, A. S., Yoshikawa, H., Redlener, I., Emmel, A., Pitt, M., Arnold, L., Barber, B., Berman, B., Blum, R., Canavera, M., Eckerle, J., Fox, N. A., Gibbons, J. L., Hargarten, S. W., . . . Zeanah, C. H. (2016). Beyond survival: The case for investing in young children globally. *NAM Perspectives* [Discussion paper]. National Academy of Medicine. https://doi.org/10.31478/201606b

Humboldt Foundation. (2021). *German Chancellor Fellowship*. https://www.humboldt-foundation.de/en/apply/sponsorship-programmes/german-chancellor-fellowship#h12003

International Beliefs and Values Institute. (n.d.). *Applied global studies: Preparing agents of change to meet a world of need*. http://www.ibavi.org/content/applied-global-studies.php

International Committee of the Red Cross. (n.d.-a). *International Red Cross/Red Crescent movement*. https://www.icrc.org/en/who-we-are/movement

International Committee of the Red Cross. (n.d.-b). *Students, graduates and civilists*. https://careers.icrc.org/content/Graduates/?locale=en_GB

International Federation of Red Cross and Red Crescent Societies. (2009, June 1). *World Disasters Report 2009: Focus on early warning, early action*.

International Institute for Applied Systems Analysis. (2021, July 12). *IIAA in brief*. https://iiasa.ac.at/web/home/about/whatisiiasa/informationkit/brief.html

International Labour Organization. (2022). *About the ILO*. https://www.ilo.org/global/about-the-ilo/lang—en/index.htm

International Union of Psychological Science. (n.d.). *Declarations*. https://www.iupsys.net/about/declarations/

Jaipal, R. (2014, June). Psychological contributions to sustainable development. *Psychology International, 25*(2). https://doi.org/10.1037/e520362014-002

Koller, S. H., & Hultz, C. S. (2001). Street children: Psychological perspectives. In N. J. Smelser & P. B. Baltes (Series Eds.), *International encyclopedia of the social and behavioral sciences* (pp. 15157–15160). Elsevier. https://doi.org/10.1016/B0-08-043076-7/01817-9

Kryazhimskiy, A., & von Winterfeldt, D. (2009, June). *On a boundary rational pareto-optimal trade in emission reduction*. IIASA interim report.

Lee, Y. (2009, October 27–30). *Child rights and child well-being* [Paper presentation]. Third OECD World Forum, Busan, Korea. https://www.oecd.org/site/progresskorea/44137252.pdf

Loichinger, E. (2010). *Exploring the role of education in projecting future employment in Germany* [IIASA presentation]. Austrian Academy of Sciences, Vienna.

MacLachlan, M. (2014). Macropsychology, policy, and global health. *American Psychologist, 69*(8), 851–863. https://doi.org/10.1037/a0037852

MacLachlan, M., & McVeigh, J. (Eds.). (2021). *Macropsychology: A population science for sustainable development goals*. Springer. https://doi.org/10.1007/978-3-030-50176-1

Maghan, J. (1997). Review of the book *Prisons 2000: An international perspective on the current state and future of imprisonment* [Review of the book *Prisons 2000: An international perspective on the current state and future of imprisonment*, by R. Matthews & P. Francis, Eds.]. *Journal of Criminal Justice, 25*(6), 541–544. https://doi.org/10.1016/S0047-2352(97)00038-X

Malak-Minkiewicz, B., & Torney-Purta, J. (Eds.). (2021). *Influences of the IEA civic and citizenship studies*. Springer. https://doi.org/10.1007/978-3-030-71102-3

Marsh, H. W., Hau, K. T., Artlett, C., Baumert, J., & Peschar, J. L. (2006). OECD's brief self-report measure of educational psychology's most useful affective constructs: Cross-cultural, psychometric comparisons across 25 countries. *International Journal of Testing, 6*(4), 311–360. https://doi.org/10.1207/s15327574ijt0604_1

Menesini, E., & Salmivalli, C. (2017). Bullying in schools: The state of knowledge and effective interventions. *Psychology, Health & Medicine, 22*(Suppl. 1), 240–253. https://doi.org/10.1080/13548506.2017.1279740

Merriam-Webster. (n.d.). Policy. In *Merriam-Webster.com dictionary*. https://www.merriam-webster.com/dictionary/policy

Miller, G. A. (1969). Psychology as a means of promoting human welfare. *American Psychologist, 24*(12), 1063–1075. https://doi.org/10.1037/h0028988

National Academies of Sciences, Engineering, and Medicine. (n.d.). *Jefferson Science Fellows program.* https://sites.nationalacademies.org/PGA/Jefferson/index.htm

National Academies of Sciences, Engineering, and Medicine. (2022). *Publications.* https://www.nationalacademies.org/publications

Nishitani, H. (2020). *English education reform-based on EBPM* [Evidence-Based Policy Making]. https://www.openaccessgovernment.org/english-education-reform/79823/

Organization for Economic Co-operation and Development. (n.d.-a). *Internship programme.* https://www.oecd.org/careers/internship-programme

Organization for Economic Co-operation and Development. (n.d.-b). *OECD careers.* https://www.oecd.org/careers/

Organization for Economic Co-operation and Development. (n.d.-c). *OECD forum.* https://www.oecd.org/forum/

Organization for Economic Co-operation and Development. (n.d.-d). *Who we are.* https://www.oecd.org/about

Organization for Economic Co-operation and Development. (2011a). *Compendium of OECD well-being indicators.* https://www.oecd.org/general/compendiumofoecdwell-beingindicators.htm

Organization for Economic Co-operation and Development. (2011b). *Society at a glance 2011—OECD social indicators.* https://www.oecd.org/els/social/indicators/SAG

Organization for Economic Co-operation and Development. (2013). *OECD guidelines on measuring subjective well-being.* https://doi.org/10.1787/9789264191655-en.

Parkhurst, J. (2017). *The politics of evidence: From evidence-based policy to the good governance of evidence.* Routledge.

Psychology Coalition at the United Nations. (n.d.). Mission. *Psychology Day at the United Nations.* https://www.unpsychologyday.com/

Reiter, K., Sexton, L., & Sumner, J. (2016, February 2). Denmark doesn't treat its prisoners like prisoners—And it's good for everyone. *The Washington Post.* https://www.washingtonpost.com/posteverything/wp/2016/02/02/denmark-doesnt-treat-its-prisoners-like-prisoners-and-its-good-for-everyone/?utm_term=.a0b3e590e99a

Ruggieri, K. (2017). Psychology and policy [Editorial]. *Frontiers in Psychology, 8.* https://doi.org/10.3389/fpsyg.2017.00497

Sánchez-Páramo, C., Vakis, R., & Afif, Z. (2019). *Behavioral science in public policy: Future of government?* https://blogs.worldbank.org/developmenttalk/behavioral-science-public-policy-future-government

Schmuck, P., & Schultz, W. (Eds.). (2002). *Psychology of sustainable development.* Springer. https://doi.org/10.1007/978-1-4615-0995-0

Singal, J. (2017, July 11). Daniel Kahneman's gripe with behavioral economics. *The Daily Beast.* https://www.thedailybeast.com/articles/2013/04/26/daniel-kahneman-s-gripe-with-behavioral-economics.html

Stanford Law School. (n.d.). *Policy papers and policy analysis.* https://www-cdn.law.stanford.edu/wp-content/uploads/2015/04/Definitions-of-White-Papers-Briefing-Books-Memos-2.pdf

Stone, A. A., & Mackie, C. (Eds.). (2013, December 18). *Panel on Measuring Subjective Well-Being in a Policy-Relevant Framework; Committee on National Statistics; Division on Behavioral and Social Sciences and Education; National Research Council.* National Academies Press.

United for Global Mental Health. (n.d.). *UN agencies and mental health: A review.* http://unitedgmh.org/sites/default/files/2020-09/UN%2BAgencies%2Band%2BMental%2BHealth%2BFINAL.pdf

United Nations. (n.d.-a). *Consultants.* https://careers.un.org/lbw/home.aspx?viewtype=CON

United Nations. (n.d.-b). *Internship programme.* https://careers.un.org/lbw/home.aspx?viewtype=ip

United Nations. (2015). *Transforming our world: The 2030 agenda for sustainable development.* https://sdgs.un.org/2030agenda

United Nations. (2021). *The sustainable development goals report 2020.* https://unstats. un.org/sdgs/report/2020/

United Nations. (2022). *ECOSOC subsidiary bodies.* https://www.un.org/ecosoc/en/ content/ecosoc-subsidiary-bodies

United Nations Educational, Scientific and Cultural Organization. (n.d.-a). *Science, technology and innovation policy.* http://www.unesco.org/new/en/natural-sciences/ science-technology/sti-systems-and-governance/capacity-development-in-sti-policy/ training-and-workshops-in-sti-policy/

United Nations Educational, Scientific and Cultural Organization. (n.d.-b). *Training and Workshops in Science, Technology and Innovation Policy.* http://www.unesco.org/ new/en/natural-sciences/science-technology/sti-systems-and-governance/capacity-development-in-sti-policy/training-and-workshops-in-sti-policy/

University of Cambridge. (2022). *Policy fellows.* https://www.csap.cam.ac.uk/policy-fellowships/policy-fellows/

University of Pennsylvania. (n.d.). *Global go to think tank index reports.* https://www. gotothinktank.com/global-goto-think-tank-index

U.S. Department of State. (n.d.). *The Fulbright Program.* https://eca.state.gov/fulbright? page=1

Vaes, B., & Goddeeris, M. (2012, March 16). A donor and own driven reconstruction approach to construction delegates. *Sri Lanka tsunami 2004: Lessons learned.* Belgian Red Cross Flanders. https://reliefweb.int/sites/reliefweb.int/files/resources/SLtsunami ReconstructionLessons.BelgianRCF12.pdf

Verma, S., Petersen, A. C., & Lansford, J. E. (Eds.). (2019, April). Sustainable human development: Challenges and solutions for implementing the United Nations' goals [Topical issue]. *Zeitschrift für Psychologie, 227*(2).

Walker, C., Speed, E., & Taggert, D. (2018). Turning psychology in to policy: A case of square pegs and round holes? *Palgrave Communications, 4*(1), Article 108. https:// doi.org/10.1057/s41599-018-0159-8

White, H., & Sabharwal, S. (2014). Quasi-experimental design and methods: Method-ological briefs—Impact evaluation. *Methodological Briefs, 8.*

Winefield, H., Gill, T., Taylor, A., & Pilkington, R. (2012). *Psychological well-being and psychological distress: Is it necessary to measure both?* https://www.researchgate.net/ publication/257885640_Psychological_well-being_and_psychological_distress_Is_ it_necessary_to_measure_both

World Economic Forum. (2022). *The Davos agenda.* https://www.weforum.org/events/ the-davos-agenda-2021

World Health Organization. (2022). *Who we are.* https://www.who.int/about/who-we-are

7

Research

International Possibilities and Partnerships for Psychologists

Shagufa Kapadia, Chandra M. Mehrotra, Bonnie Kaul Nastasi, and
Melanie M. Domenech Rodríguez

The world is becoming increasingly global with cross-border connections on the rise. Evidence for this trend is apparent at multiple levels, including the use of search and publication terms such as "international," "cross-cultural," "collaboration," and "partnership" and the eagerness of psychology research scholars across the world to venture outside of their familiar territory to share, discuss, debate, and create novel knowledge that has wider social relevance for humankind (Kliegl & Bates, 2011). How has this situation emerged? Why is international collaboration in research valuable? What does it entail? How does one go about it? This chapter addresses these questions with the goals of demystifying the process of international research and describing how scholars at all levels can engage in such work. Through a pragmatic look at how early and established scholars may join or create international research projects, this chapter seeks to address (a) ways that current and future psychologists and allied colleagues may learn about and participate in small and large multinational and interdisciplinary research projects and (b) what resources, processes, and considerations are advisable in developing and implementing an international research project.

Before venturing into the how-to of international research, we explore the need for international research vis-à-vis changing global dynamics and opportunities that are increasingly conducive to cross-cultural dialogue and partnership. The next section discusses a range of methodological issues that should be considered before, during, and after engagement in an international

https://doi.org/10.1037/0000311-008
Going Global: How Psychologists Can Meet a World of Need, C. Shealy, M. Bullock, and
S. Kapadia (Editors)

research initiative. We then focus on cross-cultural or international research collaborations that set the stage for our penultimate section, which provides practical guides for, or the "nuts and bolts" of, engaging in international research. By way of conclusion, we offer some broad reflections on the fascinating enterprise that is international research.

THE NEED FOR INTERNATIONAL AND CROSS-CULTURAL RESEARCH IN PSYCHOLOGY

Contemporary global scenarios of intersecting geographical boundaries and increasing movement across the globe—accompanied by growing cross-cultural encounters, easier access to cross-border information, wide ranging and overlapping social challenges, and a recognition that comparisons across cultures and countries offer valuable scientific insights—are rapidly prodding psychology toward greater international research collaboration.

One Psychology? Many Psychologies?

At the outset, it is important to recognize that psychology is not culture free, value neutral, or ahistorical. Researchers are cultural beings shaped by the beliefs, values, and paradigms of their cultural communities, life experiences, and sociodemographic factors such as race, caste, class, gender, religion, region, and age (Wandschneider et al., 2015). Researchers' perspectives are thus refracted through their disciplinary and cultural contexts. Acknowledgment of such realities is particularly significant within the social sciences because the subjects of inquiry—behavior, development, affect, and cognition—are embedded in and defined by these context variables.

In recent decades, the assumed claim of the universal applicability of Western psychology, which refers to theory and research paradigms rooted in Western European and American contexts, has been questioned as a result of significant developments in the field. These include findings that show important cultural variation in constructs thought to be universal; a growing tendency to explore alternate worldviews to better understand human development within a cultural context; and the evolution of new areas, such as global psychology (Stevens & Gielen, 2007). The identification of different cultural perspectives and needs is likely to result in a better balance between "the universal" and "the local" in explaining human behavior (Bullock, 2012). Ultimately, exploring multiple worldviews or multiple psychologies allows for critical reflection about psychological perspectives and approaches from Western and other contexts, supports culturally sensitive adaptation, and promotes new ways of thinking about and doing research in psychology that is more responsive to rapidly evolving global needs and dynamics.

Changing Global Scenario: A Springboard for International Dialogue and Collaboration

Through increasingly porous geographical boundaries, global change is infiltrating all societies of the world, creating an interaction of the "local and global" with immense potential to impact cross-cultural relations. For example, the global push for internationalization has enhanced interactions among psychologists through participation in international conferences and seminars, fellowship residencies in universities abroad, student and faculty exchange programs, and cross-national faculty mobility. Social media, the internet, and electronic communication allow international discussion and affordable, rapid collaboration. In many countries, growing numbers of immigrants from all over the world are necessitating interaction with people who are "different" from themselves (Shweder et al., 2002), thereby compelling academic scholars and practitioners to focus greater attention on the history, culture, and perceptions of different ethnic groups. For these and other reasons, the zeitgeist is right for understanding, sharing, and exchanging knowledge across cultures, countries, and contexts.

A significant parallel occurrence is growing attention in psychology to its usefulness and value for society, and its role in addressing underserved populations and real-world problems. Psychologists are realizing the need to respond to the many global challenges such as the COVID-19 pandemic, climate change, poverty, violence, discrimination, substance abuse, terrorism, infant mortality, gender equity, and HIV/AIDS, among other issues faced by nations across the world (https://www.un.org/sustainabledevelopment/ sustainable-development-goals/). The following section discusses some central epistemological and methodological considerations in initiating and fostering international collaborations.

Epistemological and Methodological Considerations

Cross-cultural or international research involves simultaneously navigating two major dimensions: epistemological and methodological. In entering the realm of international research, scholars need to be cognizant of the long-prevalent tendency to regard Western concepts and methods as psychological universals. Indigenous cultural concepts and approaches have been mostly disregarded or exoticized, thereby presenting misconstrued realities of non-Western people and societies (Gergen et al., 1996).

Issues of concepts and methods are critical in cross-cultural research. Concepts are culturally embedded and may not assume the same identity or functional equivalence in different contexts (Anandalakshmy, 2008). Broad labels or classifications of cultures (e.g., independent–interdependent, tight–loose, hierarchy–egalitarianism) may be appealing. However, scholars need to be cautious in using such classifications to generalize findings from a study with a particular cultural group on a particular issue to other cultural groups if it precludes recognition of distinctive, more nuanced cultural outlooks that characterize specific populations. This was demonstrated in a recent study on social support exchange involving three cultural groups, Americans, Indians, and Japanese. Despite being classified as interdependent, Japanese and Indians differed in communal norms in social support. For instance, whereas Indians treated both siblings and friends as ingroup members, the Japanese tended to distinguish between the two and clearly relied on communal norms only in the case of siblings. It is, therefore, important to recognize that, while global contrasts between individualism and collectivism may hold, all cultural differences cannot be explained in terms of this simple dichotomous classification (Miller et al., 2017). In the same vein, as researchers, we need to be cautious in interpreting "cross-national" research as "cross-cultural" research, especially in studies that recruit international students as participants, since such students may or may not be broadly representative of their culture of origin (Matsumoto & Hwang, 2017).

Similarly, methodological approaches are also culturally rooted. A key issue in any cross-cultural research is to strive for "equivalence" of meaning (Matsumoto & Yoo, 2006) regarding sampling methods and characteristics, language, data collection procedures, theoretical framework, and relevance of hypotheses. Differences in ways of knowing and attributing meaning (epistemology) have crucial implications for psychological research. At the same time, even as we strive to ensure appropriate equivalence of models and methods between cultures, core aspects of research design and measurement remain essential across cultures (Geisinger, 2013). For example, meticulous procedures of reliability and validity in quantitative research and trustworthiness in qualitative research (Seale, 1999) are of special consequence. In general, when working internationally, multidisciplinary perspectives and multimethod approaches to research design and measurement—which strive for epistemological equivalence and methodological rigor—are necessary to address questions of variability and universality across context and to appropriately characterize psychological processes within a country. In this regard, the guidelines developed by various groups such as the International Test Commission and the Comparative Survey Design and Implementation Guidelines (Survey Research Center, 2016) are likely to be useful, as they accommodate universal as well as culture-specific aspects of assessment (see Chapter 2, this volume, on assessment).

A key aspect of establishing equivalence of measures is translation. The recommended procedure of translation or back-translation is useful; however, it does not always ensure equivalence of meaning. A more collaborative approach involving steps such as generating equivalent concepts, translation by two independent translators, and then pretesting would generate better equivalence (Douglas & Craig, 2007). Ideally, all instruments should be administered in the local language of a culture, even if the research involves English-speaking participants. A best practice would be to provide an instrument in both English and the local language. Scholars also advocate for a "decentering" process in which the research instrument is simultaneously developed in multiple languages or cultures at the initiation of the study. This precludes privileging any single cultural frame of reference or even source language (Baumgartner & Weijters, 2017; see also Chapter 2, this volume).

Benefits of Engaging in International Collaborative Research

Across the world, scholars increasingly are recognizing the value of cross-cultural and international collaboration across all stages of research, from conception to dissemination. Although such collaboration is challenging—and requires overcoming multiple substantive, financial, and logistical barriers—the benefits go beyond the research itself (Thompson, 2006). Several such benefits are described next.

Academic, Intellectual, and Scholarly Gains

Researchers who have been predominantly trained in "traditional" or "mainstream" psychology—often equated with Western psychology—may approach other perspectives as binary contrasts in constructs (e.g., marginal–mainstream, local relevance–international stature, common knowledge–expert knowledge) and methodologies (e.g., subjective–objective, conversations–interviews). Involvement in cross-border collaborations introduces the researcher to models that challenge this framework while illuminating pluralistic conceptualizations (Bakker, 2009). International collaborations facilitate encounters with new areas of research, challenge untested assumptions about psychological processes, increase understanding of different cultural practices, and introduce the possibility of complementary and, sometimes, "better" practices in other cultures (Goodnow, 2008).

Broaden Horizons and Enhance Personal Growth

Involvement in international research collaboration opens the doors to new places, people, languages, and diverse ways of living and thinking, thereby making one mindful of the limitations of one's own beliefs, assumptions, values, and paradigms, or "cultural baggage" (Thomas et al., 2009). Such experiences not only expand perspectives but may also contribute to personal growth (e.g., enhanced empathy, critical thinking, self-reflection). Perhaps most significant, such collaborations often result in social networks that go beyond the research project, earning long-term friendships (Freshwater et al., 2006).

Capacity Building

Working with partners from other cultures builds one's capacity and professional repertoire (e.g., learning a new method of data analysis) and affects faculty and students who engage in such work. For example, students interact with senior researchers and peers from other countries, thereby enhancing their own scholarly development over time (Cordery et al., 2002).

Advancement of Career and Institution

Experience with international projects offers opportunities for academic advancement outside of one's own country by adding value to one's academic profile through increased diversity and flexibility within the broader job market. International research also offers an opportunity for department colleagues to interact with scholars from other cultures, which, in turn, augments the capacity and status of the department and university. In general, such engagements enhance the transnational competence of faculty and students alike (Koehn et al., 2011).

Overall, then, international collaboration contributes to the development of international scholarship and vice versa, thereby forming a mutually enriching feedback loop. Such collaboration may assume several forms, each offering a unique contribution to the development and career of the global researcher. These aspects are discussed next via the processes through which international and intercultural partnerships are established and maintained.

ISSUES IN INTERNATIONAL AND INTERCULTURAL PARTNERSHIPS

Inclination toward and engagement with other cultures is a good harbinger of successful international research collaboration. From a definitional standpoint, *collaboration* is understood as all forms of interaction between "two or more scientists in a project with a specific goal or objective attained by sharing knowledge, skills or resources" (Ynalvez & Shrum, 2009, p. 872), from short- to long-term, small- to large-scale, and funded to nonfunded. A second important and aspirational dimension of collaboration is the development of "partnerships" to reflect active involvement and negotiation among researchers across cultures and disciplines (Serrano-García, 1990). Engagement in such participatory endeavors involves sharing of resources and expertise and requires a commitment to developing shared meanings and perspectives to guide the collaboration. Successful international research partnerships involve negotiating across cultural boundaries (e.g., languages, vocabulary, worldviews, values, norms), which often necessitates building consensus regarding terminology, constructs, methodology, goals, and approaches to interpersonal communication, as well as vigilant attention to issues related to establishing and maintaining relationships across cultures and over time.

Forms of International Scholarship

Involvement in international scholarship may occur in a myriad of ways among students and early career, mid-career, and senior scholars. For example, a scholar may conduct research on international topics individually or in association with another scholar or groups of scholars. Such work could be conducted within a single cultural context or across cultural contexts. The scope of research may also range from small-scale individual projects to large-scale collaborative projects involving teams of scholars from different cultural contexts. For example, one might conduct research during a study abroad or international exchange program or choose to pursue research with an international focus (e.g., in another country). In addition, a scholar might collaborate with a colleague already engaged in international work or make use of archival international data sets;[1] these options require minimal resources, facilitate initial formative research in a specific area of study, and enable connections with colleagues elsewhere and development of cross-cultural projects. All forms of international scholarship are likely to further the cultural competence of individual researchers, which is the topic of the next section.

Intercultural Competence

The importance of intercultural competence in psychology is confirmed by its inclusion in professional ethics (e.g., American Psychological Association [APA], 2017) and discussion in the larger psychology literature (Morgan-Consoli et al., 2018; Nastasi, 2017; Nastasi & Varjas, 2011). The process of becoming a culturally competent researcher includes personal reflection; intercultural learning through experiencing the culture; resolution of cognitive dissonance reflected in cultural beliefs, values, language, and behavioral norms; and a shared understanding of the meaning of intercultural competence.

Although many terms are used to describe such competence, including cross-cultural, cultural, multicultural, and international, we prefer the terms "intercultural" and "transcultural" to reflect the importance of developing a shared cultural and disciplinary framework through exchange and negotiation. Whereas *cross-cultural* refers to comparison and contrast of different cultures (usually with reference to one's culture of origin), *intercultural* refers to interactions across cultures (e.g., between individuals of different cultural backgrounds, Lucas, 2003). Similarly, *cultural competence* has been defined as "the ability to generate appropriate strategies of action unconsciously [e.g., as one might do in a familiar culture] . . . [whereas] *inter*cultural competence is the ability to explore one's repertoire and actively construct an appropriate strategy" (Friedman & Antal, 2005, pp. 74–75). Thus, "intercultural competence involves overcoming the constraints embedded in an individual's culturally shaped repertoire, creating new responses, and thereby expanding the repertoire of potential interpretations and behaviors available in future intercultural interactions" (p. 75). At a complementary level, the term *transcultural competence* refers to the ability to consider both the culturally familiar and unfamiliar and achieve a shared understanding (Koehn, 2004).

At the individual level, intercultural or transcultural competence requires transcending one's own culture to consider alternative ways of thinking and acting within different cultural contexts. At the dyadic or group level, this requires articulation of cultural perspectives and negotiation to achieve a

---

[1]It is also possible to study cross-cultural issues using data sets such as those available from the Human Relations Area Files (https://hraf.yale.edu/), the Leibnitz Institute for Psychology Information (https://zpid.de/index.php?wahl=products&uwahl=frei&uuwahl=psychdatainfo&lang=EN), or via other archival data sets with international data.

shared understanding that guides subsequent exchange and action. Likewise, processes of reflection, learning, and negotiation are critical at both individual and collective levels. Allan (2003), for example, referred to *intercultural learning* that stems from cultural dissonance experienced as one crosses cultural boundaries, overcomes ethnocentricity, and transcends one's cultural boundaries. It results in a capacity to enter the worldview of others, with the attendant development of a "multicultural" (intercultural) personality or identity. Drawing upon the work of Friedman and Antal (2005) and others (e.g., Allan, 2003), we propose four processes for achieving intercultural competence with particular implications for scholarly activities (see also Morgan-Consoli et al., 2018).

1. **Examine identity.** Become cognizant of your own personal identity, which is formed by multiple cultural influences, and how that cultural identity influences self-definition, perceptions of reality, interpretation of experiences, perceived norms, underlying assumptions, and the inclination toward specific actions, both personally and professionally.

2. **Challenge worldview.** Engage in experiences that challenge your cultural identity and work toward resolution of dissonance through integration of disparate cultural interpretations. For example, B. K. Nastasi recently engaged in collaborative work with colleagues in Saudi Arabia. The culture norms, particularly around gender roles and segregation in all aspects of society, challenged this researcher to think about her own values and beliefs while respectfully following local customs.

3. **Encounter culture.** Participate in intercultural interactions that require you to negotiate discrepant cultural realities and expand your cultural repertoire. The outcomes of this process may provide the opportunity to appreciate others' perceptions and actions and lead to a deeper and shared understanding regarding why things are the way they are.

4. **Persistently reflect.** For each individual, intercultural competence requires a continuing process of contemplation and integration vis-à-vis cultural experiences in order to develop an intercultural identity that is consistent with the gestalt of perspectives and actions that characterize intercultural competence generally, and particularly as an international researcher.

Developing International Research Partnerships

The process of establishing and maintaining effective international partnerships requires the intercultural competencies described earlier, as well as an intent to devote the time and personal energy to finding and sustaining a research relationship. In this section, we describe a participatory process for engaging in intercultural or international research and development based on the work of Nastasi and colleagues (e.g., Nastasi & Varjas, 2011). We use the term *participatory* rather than *collaborative* to reflect active involvement and negotiation among researchers across cultures and disciplines. This perspective is consistent with our conceptualization of competence as intercultural and transcultural.

Identifying Potential Partners

All collaborative activities begin by identifying potential partners who possess relevant expertise and an established or promising record of scholarship and publications. Of course, the choice of partner(s) depends upon one's interests regarding the research topic, academic discipline, and region of the world. Researchers may find it helpful to contemplate the following questions: What is unique about the country and the partner that will allow the two (or more) of you to accomplish together what you cannot do separately? What will each of you contribute to the whole? How will you work together? What scholarly impact might you make together via this project? As may be evident, the underlying premise here is that individuals, especially from different countries, can accomplish more working together than separately. Partners in any research team must come to a common understanding of the nature and goals of the research questions and methodology. In entering cross-cultural collaborations, researchers from both high- and low-income countries need to be particularly mindful to guard against what is called "parachute research," wherein the role of low-income countries is essentially to provide the data, with little real collaboration or coauthorship in ensuing publications (Urassa et al., 2021). Issues of equity in research partnerships must be addressed at the outset, and all efforts must be made to ensure that it is upheld throughout the research process.

We next describe the range of potential partners from psychology or other disciplines, community providers, and cultural brokers.

Intradisciplinary and Interdisciplinary Research Partners

Depending on the nature and scope of research questions, effective research teams may include a wide range of expertise that can cross disciplinary and subdisciplinary lines. When relevant, such collaborations draw upon the experiences and knowledge bases of different backgrounds, work settings, and specialty areas within and outside of psychology. The integration of intra- or interdisciplinary colleagues should occur early in the research collaboration process to ensure that all members of the team (e.g., research psychologists, health care providers, social workers, economists, statisticians) contribute to decisions about research questions, hypotheses, and methods.

Community Providers

Efforts to seek partners from other countries do not need to be limited to academic departments and programs located in colleges and universities. Especially if research involves the development, application, or evaluation of international or within-country programs, it is important to include relevant stakeholders in such work (e.g., community providers, treatment consumers, policy advisors). Community-based groups, including nongovernmental organizations (NGOs), bring complementary knowledge, understanding, and skills to research projects, which may contribute to the successful conceptualization, implementation, analysis, and dissemination of results. For example, Schensul et al. (2006) involved community-based groups (e.g., private nonallopathic doctors, Hindu and Muslim religious leaders), leaders of local political groups, and members of community-based organizations as partners to enhance the feasibility and sustainability of program efforts.

Cultural Brokers

In addition to research partners from other countries, a cultural broker is critical, especially for community-based applied research. Cultural brokers are local individuals who may facilitate access to local communities, interpret cultural norms, and negotiate across cultural boundaries (Nastasi et al., 2004). A broker may be a professional colleague or local resident who is knowledge-able about the culture and possesses sufficient intercultural competence to bridge the cultural gaps for one or more guest researchers. Once partners are identified, the process of establishing and maintaining effective relation-ships begins.

Establishing and Maintaining International Relationships

Consistent with the development of intercultural competence, establishing relationships across cultural boundaries involves a process of learning, inquiry, and negotiation in order to achieve culturally constructed perspectives, goals, and actions. Such research relationships require negotiation across cultural boundaries at personal, professional, and institutional levels Although face-to-face contact is ideal, with the increased use of electronic communication technology, many cross-cultural interactions can occur without personal visits to research sites. However, to the extent possible, and subject to availability of resources, it is necessary to plan personal visits to the research site to observe and understand the context and lived realities of the research participants. The process of intercultural learning and negotiation continues throughout the life of a research project or program. Ongoing attention to discrepancies in language, thinking, and norms is essential and requires formal and informal opportunities for review of culturally negotiated details of the project and oppor-tunities for revision when appropriate.

Building Interpersonal Competencies and Effective Group Functioning

Specific interpersonal competencies are essential at both the dyadic and group levels. These include empathy, perspective taking, flexibility in communication style (verbal and nonverbal), willingness to engage in dialogue, appreciating differences in perspective, consensus building, problem solving, and conflict resolution. Successful team functioning in this context also means that the roles and responsibilities of team members are determined via consensus-based dialogue and are then communicated clearly to the larger group. Finally, it is important to establish a system by which team functioning may be evaluated in an appropriate manner to monitor group processes and make adjustments as needed. This process should be constructive, recurrent, and agreed to in advance by all team members (e.g., Nastasi et al., 2004).

Conceptualizing International Research

Engaging in international research requires a process of reflection, intercultural learning, negotiation, and construction of shared academic perspectives about the "nature of reality," what subject matter is worthy of inquiry, and how our methodologies may be directed toward answering the research questions (Nastasi & Varjas, 2011). Research priorities among high- and low-income countries may be different in that "'Blue sky' research questions about human behavioral variation, sometimes prioritized by HIC (high income) scholars, may appear trivial to LMIC (low and middle income) researchers often more engaged with topics concerning human wellbeing" (Urassa et al., 2021, p. 669). Sorting out priority topics is the first step in initiating international research partnerships. To provide guidance, we first discuss key considerations for individual researchers as they prepare to engage in projects across cultural boundaries within or across professional disciplines.

Reflection on Personal Theories Relevant to Research Interests

A critical step for each participant in an international research endeavor is to engage in a substantive and sustained examination of the theories that guide not only their personal beliefs and actions but also the disciplinary foundations that guide their research and practice (e.g., the psychological theories, research-based knowledge, evidence-based practices, and research methodologies that are informed by their own training, cultural identity, and perspective). *Self-awareness* involves "actively examining our personal biases, beliefs, values, and worldview and how they influence our perceptions and interactions with others" (Trimble et al., 2012, p. 52). *Other-awareness* involves authentic interest in learning about the beliefs, biases, values, and worldview of others and the prejudices we may inadvertently have inherited during our own education and training. The differences experienced should serve as a fascinating and indispensable prompt for dialogue and engagement with colleagues with alternative points of view (Wandschneider et al., 2015). The resulting synergistic process is a wellspring for creativity and engagement that may fundamentally shape the nature and form of the research questions that are pursued.

Exploring Research Foundations and Knowledge in the Host Culture or Context

The culture of psychological research can be learned through dialogue with research partners and cultural brokers, reading professional literature conducted in the host culture, and engaging in formative research. Consistent with the goal of intercultural learning, formative research might mean engaging in dialogue with colleagues about how research is taught in their institutions, the types of scholarly themes that are prioritized, and the prior experiences and expectations of the local community regarding research. Formative research might also involve collecting ethnographic or phenomenological data about the constructs of interest.

Identifying an Intercultural Research Focus

Through a process of dialogue and negotiation—what may be referred to as *intercultural construction*—partners decide on various aspects of the research enterprise, including purpose, questions, data collection, analysis methods, and procedures for interpretation and dissemination. Throughout this phase, it is crucial to acknowledge cultural influences that might impact intercultural construction of research endeavors.

PRAGMATICS OF INTERNATIONAL RESEARCH PARTNERSHIPS

Building on our discussion of the processes by which intercultural research partnerships may be established and research projects may be conceptualized, we turn now to the how-to of international partnerships. We begin with practical suggestions about how to identify primary international partners and then discuss key questions necessary to guide discussions with partners during international research collaborations.

How to Identify Potential Research Partners

Collaboration can be initiated in almost as many ways as interpersonal communication allows. This discussion assumes that you already have some idea of the content you wish to research or the contexts you wish to explore. It also assumes that you have done some homework by searching the literature for relevant authors and articles and reading broadly about your chosen topic.

Face-to-Face Contact

Undoubtedly, an ideal venue through which potential international partners may be identified is the "old-school" method of a face-to-face meeting. As noted previously, the human dimension of research collaboration should not be underestimated, and it is facilitated by the opportunity to sit down and talk with a prospective partner, thereby gaining a sense of interpersonal and professional compatibility.

Electronic Communications

Internet and email provide an effective and efficient method of initiating contact with international colleagues. Published articles frequently list email addresses for further contact, or you may search for the author's email address directly on their institution's website or by simply searching for "name" or "email." In our experience, the first contact email is important for further collaboration, and you should prepare this message carefully. You might include information about the colleague's materials you have read, any presentations you attended, and what drew your interest to the prospective partner's work. You may further elaborate on how their scholarship relates to yours, as well as your wishes or expectations. Including a sample of your own publications may be an appropriate element of such outreach.

International Centers, Organizations, and Networks

Aside from individual contacts, there are internet-based interest groups that focus on specific approaches or topics, as well as organizational Listservs, professional networks,[2] and centers and organizations that may correspond to your own areas of interest. Web searches and perusing the institutions of relevant authors often provide relevant contacts. To take just a couple of examples, researchers interested in health-related research can review (a) the activities supported by the National Institutes of Health Fogarty International Center, which was created to foster global health research and reduce health disparities; or (b) projects funded by the European Science Foundation's Research Networking Programs (https://www.esf.org/coordinating-research/research-networking-programmes/social-sciences-soc.html). Relatedly, NGOs typically welcome advanced graduate students, as well as early career and senior psychologists who are willing to undertake activities such as creating cultural equivalency among assessment measures (see also Chapter 2, this volume), collecting and analyzing data, conducting impact evaluation studies, carrying out program evaluations, and addressing varied research needs of different stakeholders, especially in developing countries.

International Research: Questions Worth Asking

In addition to important relational, conceptual, and partnership issues in establishing and maintaining international research partnerships, there are pragmatic issues that need to be addressed as one engages in international research. We propose several questions and offer suggestions for consideration before, during, and after initiation of an international research project. Proactive discussion of the following questions with one's partners during planning helps increase the likelihood of successful collaborations.

---

[2]For example, see the American Psychological Association's student Listserv (https://www.apa.org/apags/resources/listservs/), other Listservs, a list of international networks and databases (https://www.apa.org/international/networks/databases/index.aspx), and links to networks around the world across a variety of topics (https://www.iupsys.net/). See also international associations of researchers, such as the International Society of Behavioral Development (https://www.issbd.org/), the International Association of Cross-Cultural Psychology (https://www.iaccp.org), and the International Association of Applied Psychology (https://www.iaapsy.org/). For a complete list of organizations, please see the Directory of International Associations maintained by the APA (https://www.apa.org/international/networks).

How Will Responsibilities Be Shared for Tasks Related to the Proposed Research?

Before beginning the study, partners should explicitly discuss roles, responsibilities, and timelines associated with the project. In particular, collaborators should aim to reach agreement regarding the allocation and timeline of specific tasks, such as developing the research design, identifying and accessing the sample, collecting data in the field or in the laboratory, conducting data analysis, interpreting the results, preparing reports and formal publications, and sharing the results with the host community (Nastasi & Mehrotra, 2014). An important aspect of international collaboration is the need to create opportunities for scholars from non-Western countries to move beyond participation and assume leadership roles in the research process (Urassa et al., 2021).

Who Will Be Responsible for Securing External Funding, if Needed?

In the initial discussions of the research, all members of the team should ideally be involved regarding possible sources of external funding. If the proposed research involves preparing grant applications to secure external funding, all partners will need to be included in the process. However, a record of obtaining external funding can be a deciding factor as to who will be selected to write and submit the grant application. Another factor contributing to this decision could be based on the institution where most of the research activities would be conducted or from where the proposed activities will be coordinated (Northern Illinois University, 2005).

If the proposed research is to be conducted in a community-based setting, service providers may also be part of the grant-writing phase in order to build trust and buy-in and to ensure that the proposed research design is compatible with the context of the agency. This may include, for example, confirming that it will be possible to collect the data needed in community settings. Full involvement of both academics and service providers from the host country is vital for a successful partnership that is mutually beneficial, useful in the given context, and respectfully collaborative.

Who Will "Own" the Data, and How Will Publication Outlets and Priorities Be Determined?

In addition to determining responsibilities for various aspects of the project, it is also important to negotiate how outputs (e.g., measurement instruments, data files) and findings of the proposed research will be shared. This is particularly important in conducting applied research or in contexts where research findings may be informing program improvement, policy development, or other applied goals. Agreement in this regard is also particularly important because empirical research, whether qualitative or quantitative, may include sensitive information, which is subject to restrictions on dissemination and use. In addition, because research often generates data that may be used and analyzed for diverse purposes, including testing additional hypotheses, it is important to decide how decisions are made regarding who will own the data and have continued access to it over time.

How Will Results Be Disseminated?

This topic includes publication submission processes, publication outlets, and the order and scope of authorship that results from international collaboration. Negotiating such matters in advance reduces the likelihood of future disagreements, which may arise from colleagues whose tenure or promotion may be affected by authorship order or who feel pressure from the local community to publish research results locally and rapidly (Nastasi & Mehrotra, 2014). A related matter pertains to the tension between sharing the research results locally with the community versus publishing it in a national or international journal, and ways to accomplish both may need to be worked out. Sharing the results with the participating community before publishing it in professional journals allows the researchers to hear the community's interpretation of the results and allows them to perhaps learn even more from that interpretation (Mehrotra & Wagner, 2019). This practice promotes colearning, an empowering process that attends to social inequalities (Israel et al., 1998).

Who Will Deal With Politics?

While the processes of conducting and disseminating research may have much in common around the world, it will be necessary to address various social and political issues as the project unfolds. Such matters include negotiating with "gatekeepers," identifying the systems that must grant approval for conducting the study, and ensuring community participation in all phases of the study. This also implies a need to allocate time and resources for addressing these issues.

How Will Partners Communicate?

Ongoing communication in all phases of the project is essential to successful research collaboration. Planning the collaborative study should, therefore, include a discussion regarding each other's preferred mode of communication (e.g., telephone, email, Skype, Zoom) and opportunities for interactions at project meetings, conferences, or other venues. In deciding on these aspects, partners from high-income countries need to bear in mind the likelihood of resource constraints in low-income countries, for example, the quality of internet and Wi-Fi services, as well as travel funds to attend conferences and meetings.

How Will Compliance With Human Subject Research Requirements Be Ensured?

All members of the research team are responsible for learning about, and adhering to, the laws, regulations, and procedures regarding research in participating countries. It is essential that researchers at all sites adhere to local institutional or government and federal or national regulations for protecting the welfare of research participants. Written documentation regarding awareness of and adherence to such protocols and research ethics is strongly recommended. Team members must understand that approval of research may be required of *all* institutions involved in research activities. Regulatory bodies inevitably have different criteria for safety and protection of all participants. Clear and open communication across sites may be needed to negotiate competing demands, although some regulations may not be negotiable (see Schwetz, 2006). Collaborators who are not affiliated with an institution that has its own research approval process will need to identify a local regulatory body to oversee approval for the proposed project.

How Will Researchers Navigate the Cultural Dimensions of Ethics?

Western academic contexts typically require psychological research to adhere to the prescribed ethics code of conduct and get it approved by the respective institutional review or research ethics boards. Often, the Western requirements of ethical review are not in harmony with the social and cultural norms of another country. Miller et al. (2015) shared an example from the first author's experience of doing research in India. During her visit to a university, she planned to conduct a study with college students. She requested the class professor's help in recruiting participants. On a specific day, the professor invited the researcher to her class and shared with the students the nature of the research to be conducted. At the same time, she announced that all would take part in the study. The students complied without any hesitation or questions. This exemplifies the students' role-related responsibility to meet the expectations of the professor, the inclination to avoid loss of face for their professor in front of a visitor, and the desire to respect the guest professor. By Western ethical standards, this would probably be considered misuse of authority. Following this incident, the visiting professor took time to convey individually to each student that not participating in the study would be equally acceptable, thereby offering a culturally workable approach to informed consent. It is also relevant to note that, in some cultures, people are not comfortable signing written forms, and, hence, oral consent may be necessary.

Yet another departure from the Western ethical norms involves the issue of paying participants for contributing their time. This may be acceptable in one context but viewed as a form of bribe or even exploitation in another culture, especially if the research involves vulnerable populations. On the other hand, in some cultures, participants from economically well-off contexts may regard any payment as an affront; accepting payment can cast doubts on their intention to help when requested, especially if the person making the request is someone they know. For instance, in a cross-cultural study that involved urban Indian college-going students (Miller et al., 2017), instead of offering payment, the Indian research partner gave each participant a folder and a notepad, items that the students would find useful, and this was readily accepted. Similarly, when working in schools in the low-income country of Sri Lanka, Nastasi and her colleagues (Nastasi et al., 1998, 2011) provided school supplies and snacks to students and nominal donations to schools. Schools, regardless of their resources, routinely provided tea and snacks to the researchers during meetings as a show of hospitality. Insofar as possible, international researchers need to understand and work with such cultural outlooks, while also reflecting deeply upon attendant ethical considerations and seeking consultation as necessary.

Notions of privacy and confidentiality, key matters mandated by ethical committees, tend to be different in different cultures and may often influence data collection, both positively and adversely. For example, a typical Indian house, especially in rural settings and low-resource communities, usually remains open to neighbors, friends, and relatives, and it is not uncommon for people to walk in without knocking on the door. Hence, access may not be very difficult for the researcher, who is likely to be treated with much hospitality, as they are "a guest after all." At the same time, it may be rather difficult to find time alone for an individual interview, especially if the participant is a young girl or a woman. It is a common practice for the elders to sit around out of curiosity, as a mark of protection, or even to monitor what is being asked and answered lest the participant says something that may put the family in a bad light in front of visitors. As Morelli et al. (2018) contended, it is crucial that researchers and practitioners take the time to understand the perspectives and lived realities of a culture and appreciate how factors such as socioeconomic resources, age, and gender intervene in people's everyday lives. Tensions between ethical and social codes need to be discussed and resolved in the best interest of the research and cultural norms. For example, in a research project involving married women in a slum community in India, Maitra et al. (2015) were faced with social norms suggesting that husbands would give consent for their wives to participate. Such dilemmas must be negotiated with attention to both cultural norms and ethical codes.

The ethics question is embedded not only in the research process but also in the perspective of the researcher. Often with the best of intentions, social science change agents from the minority world enter majority-world societies to offer their inputs in advancing aspects of human development, little realizing that the conceptual frames that they carry may not be relevant in other societies. A case in point is parenting interventions, which advocate and teach parenting practices that make little sense in other cultures. Morelli et al. (2018) discussed how a UNICEF Care for Child Development (CCD) parenting intervention largely based on Western child-rearing assumptions that involve regular play and talk between mother and child do not synchronize with many rural subsistence communities. In the latter, the child is generally exposed to multiple caregivers. Most conversations between adults and children address ongoing activities. There is more talk among children than between adults and children, and socialization essentially focuses on developing sensitivity to others' needs and interests. As such, in planning any such interventions, it is critical to attend to cultural beliefs and practices related to child rearing, people's lifestyles, and the social and economic resources of the communities in question. It would behoove international researchers to actively engage in knowing a culture through ethnographic accounts, consulting with local members while initiating the intervention, and being prepared to revise ethical considerations so that any intervention is respectful of the members of the community.

How Will Research Operations Abroad Be Established and Maintained Across Countries?

To establish research operations abroad, it will be necessary to set up plans for communication with all relevant parties and hold discussions to ensure that everyone agrees on the details of the project and that relevant personnel and processes are in place to move the project forward. To address such matters, it may be useful to engage research administrators from participating institutions to complete legal registration, ensure financial stability and sustainability, monitor project expenses, and prepare financial reports.

How Will Program Staff Be Hired?

If a project requires additional staff, such as research assistants, data analysts, or the like, an ideal plan is to hire staff through some or all project institutions to ensure representation of different perspectives during all phases of the project, from planning and implementing the study to reporting the results. Staff members hired from a host institution will have a better understanding of the local context, culturally appropriate approaches, political realities, follow-up activities, and reporting of results to local communities. Exhibit 7.1 is a checklist for establishing such research operations abroad.

How Should International Collaborations Be Concluded?

Completion of research projects involves addressing questions such as the following: (a) Who will be responsible for preparing final financial and project reports and/or publications, presentations, or other scholarly or professional outputs and submitting them to the funding agencies if applicable? (b) How and when will research staff be notified about the completion of the project and their continued employment? (c) Who will protect and store project records, data files, equipment, books, journals, and other materials? (d) Who will complete and document any close-out requirements for project sponsors? In this regard, Urassa et al. (2021) provided practical recommendations for researchers from high income as well as low- and middle-income contexts.

EXHIBIT 7.1

Checklist for Establishing Operations Abroad

1. Establish internal review/approval processes including an explicit definition of roles.

2. Create delegated authorities (e.g., for executing contracts, hiring personnel, financial management, using university trademarks/logos, developing relationships with local officials).

3. Develop administrative processes for addressing unique needs that arise.

4. Consider financial stability (e.g., ability of local partners to provide working capital).

5. Consider financial sustainability (e.g., consistent funding sources; the possibility of unexpected costs).

6. Consider the safety and security of all personnel.

INTERNATIONAL RESEARCH IN PSYCHOLOGY: FUTURE DIRECTIONS AND CONCLUDING REFLECTIONS

> Psychology in the 21st century is on its way to new international synthesis that has no single-country dominance of ideas and where cultural heritages of European, Asian, and American (South, Central, and North) kinds intermingle in the making of a new look at psychology. (Valsiner, 2009, p. 16)

The contents and contours of psychology are becoming increasingly varied and international in scope. To respond proactively, we need to critically review and reflect upon our teaching and training paradigms and their potential to acquaint students with the "real world" in preparation to become global citizens and, within psychology, to address worldwide issues as global psychologists. Initiatives such as Education for Sustainability (EfS) and Education for Sustainable Development (ESD; e.g., https://www.unesco.org/en/education/sustainable-development; https://summitx.org/) offer a rich source of needs and opportunities with which psychologists can engage, including sustainable development, HIV/AIDS, human rights, gender equality, educational access, and teaching quality. Psychologists are well-positioned to research such themes, supporting the APA's mission "to promote the advancement, communication, and application of psychological science and knowledge to benefit society and improve lives" by "utilizing psychology to make a positive impact on critical societal issues" (https://www.apa.org/about/). Likewise, the APA's Division of International Psychology (Division 52) encourages the development of a more international perspective in psychology, supporting a range of activities, including initiatives on human rights, international ethics, immigration, women in developing countries, internationalizing the psychology curriculum, cross-cultural research, assessment and counseling, global trauma and disaster, collaboration with international organizations, and student and early career advancement (https://div52.net/about/).

We also need to examine whether psychology education and research training are optimally equipping us to respond to such big-picture issues. We propose the following series of reflection questions to prod such examination:

- To what extent does research training (in methods, seminars, and reviews of the literature) enable students to engage with global forces, such as climate change, terrorism, sustainable consumption, migration, and global mental health?

- What is the place of culture in the psychology curriculum, especially in the development of conceptual frameworks and methodologies for research? To what extent are debates on concepts such as cultural hegemony, ethnocentrism, pluralism, and diversity integrated into our teaching?

- How does the psychology curriculum—or how should it—promote knowing and appreciating research and research possibilities that fall outside our typical orbit (e.g., the development and implementation work of NGOs around the world who are trying to bring about positive change vis-à-vis a range of social issues)? Do we consider the knowledge that others around the world (e.g., other scholars, practitioners, teachers, NGOs) have developed, and do we incorporate this knowledge in our own theories and studies?

- Where should we find inspiration for the research we do? How and why do we select specific topics to study, and are global issues seen as relevant? Could we imagine, pursue, and support research activities at the undergraduate, graduate, and professional level—both in the private and public sectors—that go far beyond traditional topic areas that already have been well investigated or have little relationship to the sorts of topics, needs, and themes described in this chapter and book? If we made much greater room for such research, how would the field and profession of psychology—and our educators, scholars, students, practitioners, and leaders—be experienced and perceived? Would such emphases not increase our relevance and impact?

- How willing are we to step outside of our disciplinary comfort zones to work in an interdisciplinary and interprofessional manner to address real world challenges, needs, and opportunities?

- How do we structure the theory–research–practice interface in the curriculum or our research? Do we explore methodologies that offer a judicious balance between precision and social relevance? How deeply do we reflect upon the epistemologies that undergird what we call real, true, or worthy of study?

- How do the bodies that regulate the teaching and training of psychology through accreditation or certification support—or impede—an international perspective and attention to the global challenges of our day? How do we open up and reimagine such systems since they are, after all, largely created and managed by us as psychologists?

Psychologists across the world need to actively deliberate and persistently reflect on these and related questions to sharpen the discussion of priorities vis-à-vis teaching, training, practice, and research. Given the historical evolution of the discipline of psychology, partners from the more resourced and developed world need to be particularly sensitive to the dangers of cultural imperialism or providing well-intentioned support that may be culturally inappropriate or antithetical to capacity building (Thompson, 2006). In the same vein, researchers from the majority world need to become more articulate in expressing their worldviews and making their underlying epistemologies and preferred methods explicit, candidly considering what may or may not work in other contexts and making collaboratively informed modifications when appropriate and indicated. Respectful, curious, open, honest, ongoing, and nondogmatic dialogue is needed to engage such matters at the level they must be for us to create and sustain a truly global, culturally sensitive approach to research.

In the final analysis, academic environments across the globe offer fertile ground for rich encounters among apparently dichotomous perspectives of

West–non-West, north–south, urban–rural, women–men, rich–poor, linear–nonlinear, and so on, through increasing engagement with other cultures, perspectives, experiences, and needs. As scholars of psychology and educators of psychologists, we must embrace the unparalleled and extraordinary research opportunities that this changing global scene provides, while actively working to reconstruct and shape psychology as a truly international, inclusive, engaged, and global discipline.

REFERENCES

Allan, M. (2003). Frontier crossings: Cultural dissonance, intercultural learning and the multicultural personality. *Journal of Research in International Education, 2*(1), 83–110. https://doi.org/10.1177/1475240903021005

American Psychological Association. (2017). Guidelines on multicultural education, training, research, practice, and organizational change for psychologists. *American Psychologist, 58*(5), 377–402. https://doi.org/10.1037/0003-066X.58.5.377

Anandalakshmy, S. (2008). How independent is the independent variable? In S. Anandalakshmy, N. Chaudhary, & N. Sharma (Eds.), *Researching children and families. Culturally appropriate methods* (pp. 13–27). Sage.

Bakker, T. M. (2009). Reflections on the local and the global in psychology: Innovation, liberation and testimonio. *Qualitative Report, 14*(2), 201–226.

Baumgartner, H., & Weijters, B. (2017). Methodological issues in cross-cultural research. In H. van Herk & C. Torelli (Eds.), *Cross cultural issues in consumer science and consumer psychology: Current perspectives and future directions* (pp. 169–190). Springer. https://doi.org/10.1007/978-3-319-65091-3_10

Bullock, M. (2012, October). Reaching out internationally—Where are we now? *Psychology International.* https://www.apa.org/international/pi/2012/10/column

Cordery, J., Griffin, M. A., & Kabanoff, B. (2002). Global vision: International collaboration. *The Industrial/Organizational Psychologist, 40,* 71–75.

Douglas, S. P., & Craig, C. S. (2007). Collaborative and iterative translation: An alternative approach to back translation. *Journal of International Marketing, 15*(1), 30–43.

Freshwater, D., Sherwood, G., & Drury, V. (2006). International research collaboration: Issues, benefits and challenges of the global network. *Journal of Research in Nursing, 11*(4), 295–303. https://doi.org/10.1177/1744987106066304

Friedman, V. J., & Antal, A. B. (2005). Negotiating reality: A theory of action approach to intercultural competence. *Management Learning, 36*(1), 69–86. https://doi.org/10.1177/1350507605049904

Geisinger, K. F. (Ed.). (2013). *APA handbook of testing and assessment in psychology: Vol. 1. Test theory and testing and assessments in industrial and organizational psychology.* American Psychological Association.

Gergen, K. J., Gulerce, A., Lock, A., & Misra, G. (1996). Psychological science in cultural context. *American Psychologist, 51*(5), 496–503. https://doi.org/10.1037/0003-066X.51.5.496

Goodnow, J. J. (2008). The benefits of cross-cultural collaboration. In National Research Council, *International Collaborations in Behavioral and Social Sciences Research: Report of a Workshop* (pp. 47–63). National Academies Press.

Israel, B. A., Schulz, A. J., Parker, E. A., & Becker, A. B. (1998). Review of community-based research: Assessing partnership approaches to improve public health. *Annual Review of Public Health, 19*(1), 173–202. https://doi.org/10.1146/annurev.publhealth.19.1.173

Kliegl, R., & Bates, D. (2011). International collaboration in psychology is on the rise. *Scientometrics, 87*(1), 149–158. https://doi.org/10.1007/s11192-010-0299-0

Koehn, P. H. (2004). Global politics and multinational health-care encounters: Assessing the role of transnational competence. *EcoHealth, 1*(1), 69–85. https://doi.org/10.1007/s10393-004-0002-0

Koehn, P. H., Deardorff, D. K., & Bolognese, K. D. (2011). Enhancing international research and development-project activity on university campuses: Insights from U.S. senior international officers. *Journal of Studies in International Education, 15*(4), 332–350. https://doi.org/10.1177/1028315310365540

Lucas, J. S. (2003). Intercultural communication for international programs: An experientially-based course design. *Journal of Research in International Education, 2*(3), 301–314. https://doi.org/10.1177/1475240903002003003

Maitra, S., Brault, M. A., Schensul, S. L., Schensul, J. J., Nastasi, B. K., Verma, R. K., & Burleson, J. A. (2015). An approach to mental health in low-income and middle-income countries: A case example from urban India. *International Journal of Mental Health, 44*(3), 215–230. https://doi.org/10.1080/00207411.2015.1035081

Matsumoto, D., & Hwang, H. C. (2017). Methodological issues regarding cross-cultural studies of judgments of facial expressions. *Emotion Review, 9*(4), 375–382. https://doi.org/10.1177/1754073916679008

Matsumoto, D., & Yoo, S. H. (2006). Toward a new generation of cross-cultural research. *Perspectives on Psychological Science, 1*(3), 234–250. https://doi.org/10.1111/j.1745-6916.2006.00014.x

Mehrotra, C. M., & Wagner, L. S. (2019). *Aging and diversity: An active learning experience.* Routledge.

Miller, J. G., Akiyama, H., & Kapadia, S. (2017). Cultural variation in communal vs. exchange norms: Implications for social support. *Journal of Personality and Social Psychology, 113*(1), 81–94. https://doi.org/10.1037/pspi0000091

Miller, J. G., Goyal, N., & Wice, M. (2015). Ethical considerations in research on human development and culture. In L. A. Jensen (Ed.), *The Oxford handbook of human development and culture: An interdisciplinary perspective* (pp. 14–27). Oxford University Press.

Morelli, G., Quinn, N., Chaudhary, N., Vicedo, M., Rosabal-Coto, M., Keller, H., Murray, M., Gottlieb, A., Scheidecker, G., & Takada, A. (2018). Ethical challenges of parenting interventions in low- to middle-income countries. *Journal of Cross-Cultural Psychology, 49*(1), 5–24. https://doi.org/10.1177/0022022117746241

Morgan-Consoli, M. L., Inman, A. G., Bullock, M., & Nolan, S. A. (2018). Framework for competencies for U.S. psychologists engaging internationally. *International Perspectives in Psychology: Research, Practice, Consultation, 7*(3), 174–188. https://doi.org/10.1037/ipp0000090

Nastasi, B. K. (2017). Cultural competence for global research and development: Implications for school and educational psychology. *International Journal of School & Educational Psychology, 5*(3), 207–210. https://doi.org/10.1080/21683603.2016.1276817

Nastasi, B. K., Jayasena, A., Summerville, M., & Borja, A. (2011). Facilitating long-term recovery from natural disasters: Psychosocial programming in tsunami-affected schools of Sri Lanka. *School Psychology International, 32*, 512–532. https://doi.org/10.1177/0143034311402923

Nastasi, B. K., & Mehrotra, C. M. (2014). *Going international: A practical guide for psychologists, Book 2: Engaging in international collaborative research* [Brochure/Fact Sheet]. https://doi.org/10.1037/e525202015-001

Nastasi, B. K., Moore, R. B., & Varjas, K. M. (2004). *School-based mental health services: Creating comprehensive and culturally specific programs.* American Psychological Association. https://doi.org/10.1037/10724-000

Nastasi, B. K., & Varjas, K. (2011). International development of school psychology. In M. A. Bray & T. J. Kehle (Eds.), *Oxford handbook of school psychology* (pp. 810–828). Oxford University Press.

Nastasi, B. K., Varjas, K., Sarkar, S., & Jayasena, A. (1998). Participatory model of mental health programming: Lessons learned from work in a developing country. *School Psychology Review, 27*(2), 260–276.

Northern Illinois University. (Producer). (2005). *Responsible conduct in collaborative research: Establishing the relationship* [Online course]. https://ori.hhs.gov/education/products/niu_collabresearch/collabresearch/crabout.html

Schensul, S. L., Nastasi, B. K., & Verma, R. K. (2006). Community-based research in India: A case example of international and interdisciplinary collaboration. *American Journal of Community Psychology, 38*(1-2), 95–111. https://doi.org/10.1007/s10464-006-9066-z

Schwetz, B. A. (2006). Protection of human subjects: Interpretation of assurance requirements. *Federal Register, 71*(131), 38645–38646.

Seale, C. (1999). Quality in qualitative research. *Qualitative Inquiry, 5*(4), 465–478. https://doi.org/10.1177/107780049900500402

Serrano-García, I. (1990). Implementing research: Putting our values to work. In P. Tolan, C. Keys, F. Chertok, & L. Jason (Eds.), *Researching community psychology: Issues of theory and methods* (pp. 171–182). American Psychological Association. https://doi.org/10.1037/10073-013

Shweder, R. A., Minow, M., & Markus, H. R. (2002). Engaging cultural differences. In R. A. Shweder, M. Minow, & H. R. Markus (Eds.), *Engaging culture differences: The multicultural challenge in liberal democracies* (pp. 1–15). Russell Sage Foundation.

Stevens, M. J., & Gielen, U. P. (2007). *Toward a global psychology: Theory, research, intervention and pedagogy.* Erlbaum.

Survey Research Center. (2016). *Cross-Cultural Survey Guidelines.* https://ccsg.isr.umich.edu/

Thomas, R., Tienari, J., Davies, A., & Merilainen, S. (2009). Let's talk about "Us": A reflexive account of a cross-cultural research collaboration. *Journal of Management Inquiry, 18*(4), 313–324. https://doi.org/10.1177/1056492608324457

Thompson, D. R. (2006). International collaboration and sharing lessons learned. *Journal of Research in Nursing, 11*(4), 285–287. https://doi.org/10.1177/1744987106066967

Trimble, J. E., Scharrón-del-Río, M. R., & Hill, J. S. (2012). Ethical considerations in the application of cultural adaptation models with ethnocultural populations. In G. Bernal & M. M. Domenech Rodríguez (Eds.), *Cultural adaptations: Tools for evidence-based practice with diverse populations* (pp. 45–67). American Psychological Association. https://doi.org/10.1037/13752-003

Urassa, M., Lawson, D. W., Wamoyi, J., Gurmu, E., Gibson, M. A., Madhivanan, P., & Placek, C. (2021). Cross-cultural research must prioritize equitable collaboration. *Nature Human Behaviour, 5*(6), 668–671. https://doi.org/10.1038/s41562-021-01076-x

Valsiner, J. (2009). Integrating psychology within the globalizing world: A requiem to the post-modernist experiment with Wissenschaft. *Integrative Psychological & Behavioral Science, 43*(1), 1–21. https://doi.org/10.1007/s12124-009-9087-x

Wandschneider, E., Pysarchik, D. T., Sternberger, L. G., Ma, W., Acheson-Clair, K., Baltensperger, B., Good, R. T., Brubaker, B., Baldwin, T., Wang, F., Reisweber, J., & Hart, V. (2015). The Forum BEVI Project: Applications and implications for international, multicultural, and transformative learning. In C. N. Shealy (Ed.), *Making sense of beliefs and values* (pp. 407–484). Springer Publishing. https://doi.org/10.36366/frontiers.v25i1.350

Ynalvez, M. A., & Shrum, W. M. (2009). International graduate science training and scientific collaboration. *International Sociology, 24*(6), 870–901. https://doi.org/10.1177/0268580909343501

Service

Toward a Global Psychology of Collaboration, Counterflow, and Capacity Building

Chris E. Stout, Elaine D. Hanson, and Gwen V. Mitchell

International (or global) psychology is a branch of psychology that has emerged over the past several decades. It focuses on psychology's worldwide practice in terms of networking, communication, scholarship, cross-cultural comparison, pedagogy, and practice (Stevens & Gielen, 2007). In this chapter, we focus on the "service" implications and applications of these important developments. Depending upon the level of analysis, we refer to three interdependent expressions of such "service": (a) "humanitarian service" (referring to the overall field), (b) "global humanitarian service" (referring to humanitarian service in a global context), and (c) "humanitarian service in global psychology" (referring to humanitarian service for global psychologists). As will become clear, all three expressions of service may be fraught with a myriad of ethical, moral, and pragmatic challenges. This chapter addresses such issues vis-à-vis the translation of humanitarian service aspirations into concrete global action. For current and future psychologists interested in making a difference in the world, we begin by considering the scope of humanitarian service, as well as attendant ethical issues, as two "case studies" in disaster psychology and mental health. We then offer guidance for developing skills, identifying partners, and managing the logistics of humanitarian service before, during, and after one's career in psychology. By way of concluding, readers are encouraged to use this information as a starting point—and to conceptualize humanitarian service in terms of collaboration, counterflow, and capacity building—while becoming familiar with exemplary people, programs, organizations, training opportunities, role models, and resources within this compelling domain of inquiry and practice.

https://doi.org/10.1037/0000311-009
Going Global: How Psychologists Can Meet a World of Need, C. Shealy, M. Bullock, and S. Kapadia (Editors)

THE SCOPE OF HUMANITARIAN SERVICE IN GLOBAL PSYCHOLOGY

Civil conflict (Caldwell, 2009), violence (Fitzduff & Stout, 2005), education inequity (Kronenberg & Savaiano, 2009), rights for women and girls (Butterfield et al., 2009), natural disasters (Arole & Arole, 2009), human rights (Caldwell, 2009), social justice (Stout, 2008), and pandemic disease and famine (Stout, 2004) are among the areas of global psychology that position it highly in the public consciousness. The last 20 years have seen a concerted attempt by humanitarian agencies—nongovernmental organizations (NGOs) and inter-governmental bodies (e.g., United Nations)—to develop best professional practice in their fields of operation (Stout, 2009; Zetter, 1999). As the humanitarian service sector has evolved and integrated a deeper understanding of the impact of trauma on individual and societal functioning—as well as the power of service-based interventions more generally—psychologists have gradually begun to devote more of their efforts toward the work of humanitarian agencies.

Until recently, the role of mental health in humanitarian service projects mostly subscribed to a "rubber band" model (Mollica et al., 1998) which assumed that once food, water, shelter, and essential services are provided, individuals would snap back and resume their normal lives (Gewertz, 2005). In recent years, however, humanitarian service interventions have been increasingly informed by greater knowledge about the complex interactions that mediate and moderate real-world outcomes and mental health concerns.

In addition to the integration of biopsychosocial knowledge and principles into service-oriented interventions, humanitarian organizations are now becoming increasingly aware of the need to integrate services that are explicitly designed to ameliorate psychological conditions (e.g., Stout, 1996, 2009). Beyond mental health-oriented services, other initiatives are drawing on psychological expertise in a range of areas in order to further other areas of humanitarian service delivery, including mental health programming, ethnographic research, design and evaluation of programs, and training local service providers (Keyes, 2007). Such trends are augmented by the understanding that mental health is integral to health more generally (World Health Organization, 2001). Finally, even broad-based frameworks—such as sustainable development—recognize the importance of subjective well-being, the value of which goes beyond individual health benefits to include all of society (Friedli, 2002). As psychology becomes more integral to work within the domain of public health, recognition of the role and need for humanitarian service delivery by psychologists is likely to increase.

ETHICAL CONSIDERATIONS FOR HUMANITARIAN SERVICE IN GLOBAL PSYCHOLOGY

The ethical and culturally sensitive application of psychological knowledge and principles is especially important when the target populations have been exposed to disaster, trauma, human rights abuses, or related circumstances.

This raises questions as to whether psychologists working in a humanitarian service situation are able to maintain their ethical obligations (Aubé, 2011). For example, in the Congo, abortion is illegal, and the procedure may be relabeled by medical staff to avoid legal and social risks to women seeking the procedure. Does a psychologist working in that situation have an ethical duty to protect the woman, and is that an ethical violation to avoid duplicity (Aubé, 2011)?

The potential for dual relationships is also heightened when working in humanitarian service settings. For example, a psychologist may be asked to treat multiple members of a single family, maintain a relationship with someone who receives services outside of the office, or provide "counseling" services to members of an organization staff in settings that would be considered informal at best (e.g., coffee shops). One might work alongside team members in a professional context while providing therapeutic support to those same individuals. Psychologists may also be offered gifts or asked to visit or stay at the homes of clients who do not understand the nuances of dual relationships and whose culture may encourage and honor close personal relationships with teachers and healers. Oftentimes, refusing such invitations may be viewed as rude, elitist, or culturally insensitive. Moreover, in humanitarian service settings, especially those in which there are few workers trying to address a large need, psychologists may also be asked to work in areas that are outside of their zone of specific expertise, such as a child psychologist providing consultation about an adult client, raising ethical issues about scope of competence (see also Chapter 4, this volume, on intervention).

Psychologists providing humanitarian service in a global context must learn to navigate these challenges, ever mindful of their "at home" ethical guidelines. These guidelines are still applicable, even though the psychologist is working in a different culture and context (Drogin, 2019). A few codes of ethics or licensing laws explicitly provide guidelines for practice internationally across cultural, national, and linguistic boundaries. The *Universal Declaration of Ethical Principles for Psychologists* (International Union of Psychological Science [IUPsyS], 2008) outlines the principles that should apply, such as "do no harm" and "respect for persons," but it does not specify action guidance in specific instances. In the United States, the American Psychological Association's (APA's; 2017) *Ethical Principles of Psychologists and Code of Conduct* (i.e., APA Ethics Code) guides and informs the practice of psychology, but it does not explicitly address dilemmas that may arise in international contexts. Moreover, clinical practice is largely unregulated in many of the settings where humanitarian psychologists work. Many developing countries do not have licensing laws for mental health workers or training programs for clinical psychologists. Thus, when working internationally, it is imperative to ascertain the status of regulations pertaining to practice in the host country, document that one has done so, and conduct one's work in a manner that is consistent with both the ethics code that is operative in their country of origin, as well as any additional guidelines that are specified by the country in which one works (Azar, 2009).

The preamble to APA's Ethical Principles states: "Psychologists are committed to increasing scientific and professional knowledge of behavior and people's understanding of themselves and others and to the use of such knowledge to improve the condition of individuals, organizations and society." This is followed by a discussion of five principles: Beneficence and Nonmaleficence, Fidelity and Responsibility, Integrity, Justice, and Respect for People's Rights and Dignity (APA, 2017). What implications do such principles have for the work of humanitarian psychologists?

First and foremost, the activities of psychologists working in global humanitarian service settings must be undertaken with knowledge, skills, and values—the competencies necessary to do this work appropriately. Like all psychologists, those working in humanitarian settings must first strive to do no harm. While this commitment sounds simple on the surface, in practice, fidelity to it may be challenging to execute in a cross-cultural context for the aforementioned reasons (Wessells, 2009). These and related ethical considerations are important because secondary trauma may result inadvertently from the very best of intentions, especially when we don't know what we don't know (Jacobs, 2007; Shealy, 2016).

An excellent resource is the task force report of the International Society of Traumatic Stress Studies (Weine et al., 2002), which offers guidelines for working with traumatized populations that are instructive for global humanitarian service. The guidelines emphasize the concepts of multicultural competence: first doing no harm, grounding interventions in scientific knowledge insofar as possible, appreciating contextual challenges, and ongoing assessment of the efficacy of any intervention (Tabit et al., 2016; Weine et al., 2002).

Finally, the APA Ethics Office offers the following clarification regarding these important matters. On the one hand, "the Introduction and Applicability section of *Ethical Principles of Psychologists and Code of Conduct* makes clear that the Ethics Code applies 'only to psychologists' activities that are part of their scientific, educational, or professional roles as psychologists.'" On the other hand,

> the *Ethical Principles of Psychologists and Code of Conduct* states that "Membership in the APA commits members and student affiliates to comply with the standards of the APA Ethics Code . . ." [Introduction and Applicability section]. There is no geographic limitation on this commitment. Therefore, if you are a member of APA acting as a psychologist, you are bound by the *Ethical Principles of Psychologists and Code of Conduct* regardless of where and what you do as a psychologist anywhere in the world. (L. Childress-Beatty, personal communication, May 5, 2015)

Such ethical guidance is especially important in light of the APA Independent Review ("Hoffman Report") of 2015, which concluded (among other findings) that psychologists had been directly and inappropriately involved in the development of interventions designed to torture captives of the U.S. government (APA, 2015).

Case Study 1: Humanitarian Service and Disaster Psychology

The 20th and 21st centuries have witnessed growing cognizance of natural and human-activated disasters in conjunction with concerted ameliorative efforts. Events such as intense political strife and wars, extreme weather events, natural disasters, and worldwide health crises have resulted in catastrophic loss of life and large-scale exposure to trauma. And yet, survivors must find a way to go on with their lives in situations that are challenging, if not overwhelming, often having lost family members while simultaneously lacking basic access to rudimentary assistance, which might help them find a way forward. Disaster psychology is a specialized domain of training, research, and service provision applied to individuals, communities, and nations exposed to a disaster. A key aim of practitioners in this area is to reduce initial distress and foster short- and long-term adaptive functioning following a disaster (see also Chapter 4).

Early attempts to respond to the psychological impact of disasters were often medicalized and characterized by inadequate knowledge and understanding of the culture in question, especially the mental health models. "Traumatic stress and mental health knowledge were applied widely and enthusiastically, but outcomes were not always beneficial, and in many cases may have been hurtful" (Weine et al., 2002, p. 393). These standards include work by the Inter-Agency Standing Committee (IASC, 2007) and the Sphere Project (2018). The IASC Guidelines are seen as a significant accomplishment for humanitarian service in general and for international disaster psychology specifically. These guidelines include a multidisciplinary, multisectoral, interagency framework that enables integrated action encompassing diverse complementary approaches for effective interventions in such situations.

Likewise, the Sphere Project is one of the most widely known and internationally recognized compendiums of common principles and universal minimum standards for the delivery of quality humanitarian response, including best practices in mental health (Sphere Association, 2018). Additionally, the International Federation of Red Cross and Red Crescent Societies (IFRC, 2019) have been providing global humanitarian service for over 100 years in order to prevent and heal emotional wounds caused by natural disasters, health issues, and conflict.

Finally, the work of Jacobs and colleagues (2016) commendably illustrates how psychological principles and practices can be applied to disaster mental health and community-based psychological first aid. These tools include critical incident stress debriefing, self-care for those traumatized, active problem solving, and other psychosocial approaches. These approaches reflect the insights of practitioners from different geographic regions, disciplines, and sectors and suggest an emerging consensus on good practice among practitioners. They should be read by any current or future psychologist who aspires to humanitarian service work.

Case Study 2: Humanitarian Service and Mental Health

Humanitarian service work may well pose risks. For example, recent research suggests that humanitarian service providers face numerous mental health and psychosocial challenges, including increased risk for depression, anxiety, and burnout (Giauque et al., 2019) Although, historically, most staff care services have focused on intervention for acute stressors (e.g., the aftermath of direct exposure to potentially traumatic events such as a bombing or sexual assault), it also has become clear that chronic stress resulting from multiple environmental factors may be just as debilitating. As the Antares Foundation (2006) observed:

> Workers suffering from the effects of stress are likely to be less efficient and less effective in carrying out their assigned tasks. They become poor decision makers and they may behave in ways that place themselves or other members of the team at risk or disrupt the effective functioning of the team. They are more likely to have accidents or to become ill. A consequence for humanitarian agencies is that staff stress and burnout may impede recruitment and retention of qualified staff, increase health care costs, compromise safety and security of staff and create legal liabilities. (p. 6)

Not surprisingly, then, humanitarian service agencies increasingly are concerned about the potential impact of staff stress on the effectiveness and efficiency of service delivery. For example, in the last decade, widely supported guidelines for providing mental health and psychosocial support for humanitarian service staff have been developed, including, but not limited to, the IASC (2007), the Sphere Project (2018), and Welton-Mitchell's (2013) United Nations High Commissioner for Refugees' Mental Health Support. Subsequently, humanitarian service agencies have introduced staff welfare initiatives, with many organizations modifying their historical approach to mental health and psychosocial services. Such initiatives may include debriefing and processing opportunities, stress management and self-care, team support, and establishing a culture of open dialogue on feelings and concerns. Taken together, organizations are realizing that they must be accountable to their aid workers in the same manner they strive for accountability to their target populations.

In addition to their role in supporting, facilitating, evaluating, and improving mental health services to aid agencies, humanitarian service psychologists can also aid organizations in developing screening and selection procedures, implementing critical incident and reentry debriefings, and establishing processes for ongoing psychological monitoring and support for workers in high-intensity environments. Additional interventions include the incorporation of psychological assessment; psychosocial rehabilitation as appropriate in the context of the family, community, and workplace; and psychoeducational sessions for both the aid worker and their family in order to help make sense of the range of responses to trauma exposure. Such interventions may emphasize the humanitarian service provider's need for a sense of belonging, control, social support, and meaning making, each of which may be experienced as tenuous upon returning home (McCormack et al., 2009). The advent of secure, internet-based technologies may be instrumental in providing regular support to aid workers in the field (e.g., web-based "check-in" sessions with qualified mental health staff). Thus, another role for humanitarian service psychologists is to develop interventions designed to care for caregivers. This will become more common and necessary as international humanitarian service aid activities increase.

HUMANITARIAN SERVICE IN GLOBAL PSYCHOLOGY: RESOURCES FOR PSYCHOLOGISTS

Those interested in humanitarian service in global psychology may find benefit in learning about the numerous organizational resources that are available. Some of these derive from the work of professional associations, such as APA, which provides links to health and mental health-related initiatives, activities, and organizations. For example, APA's (2020c) Office of International Affairs provides a list of educational resources and humanitarian service organizations and training. Many of APA's (2020a) 54 Divisions or submembership groups focused on substantive content areas have an international focus and provide links to resources. The IUPsyS (https://www.iupsys.net/about/) also provides a range of publications and resources related to psychology around the world; materials on psychology teaching, research, testing, and practice; and a set of standards comprising a compendium of codes of ethics and responsible conduct of research. The final resource, the annual roundtables at APA's annual convention—"Internationalizing Your Psychology Life"—provide information and inspiration for aspiring or established humanitarian service psychologists. It should be noted that the resources offer some examples of humanitarian service work, but they typically do not provide specific guidance on how to get started. So, we suggest outreach to and engagement with people who are involved in humanitarian service psychology in order to receive necessary support and consultation.

EDUCATION AND TRAINING FOR HUMANITARIAN SERVICE IN GLOBAL PSYCHOLOGY

A number of U.S. universities, professional schools of psychology, and NGOs have developed degree and certificate programs for those seeking training in the area of humanitarian service in global psychology, broadly defined. Programs offer a variety of degrees or certificates in more focused content training. Universities that have substantial commitment to global humanitarian service include the University of Denver's International Disaster Psychology Program in Trauma and Global Mental Health, The Chicago School of Professional Psychology's International Psychology track, Lehigh University's International Counseling Psychology program, and Brandeis University's Conflict and Coexistence MA program. Other universities and global initiatives offer certificates in trauma studies, disaster mental health, and global health, such as the University of South Dakota's Disaster Mental Health Certificate. For a more complete list, readers may also consult the psychology degree guide at https://psychologydegreeguide.org/specialty/international-psychology and the APA graduate study guide (https://www.apa.org/pubs/databases/gradstudy).

ENTERING THE FIELD OF HUMANITARIAN SERVICE IN GLOBAL PSYCHOLOGY

Before contemplating humanitarian service in global psychology, it is important to reflect on one's motivations for undertaking this work, as well as relevant factors that may bear on the long-term sustainability of one's initiatives and efforts. As a psychologist, your direct service clinical expertise may not be what makes you most useful in the field. Many of the challenges in providing global humanitarian service are around an organization's local capacity and logistics: Training a local cohort of providers is more impactful than parachuting in and providing direct care to beneficiaries. You need to know how to organize, train, supervise, and adapt interventions so they are culturally informed and evaluate the utility and impact of your programing. Above all, you need humility. You need to recognize that you are a foreigner in somebody else's world—that they're the experts, by virtue of their deep immersion in their local context. Diplomacy is essential. Change is not made by being bullheaded or adventurous. It is made by collaborating with the people who will live with the consequences of the crisis long after you leave.

Advice for Psychologists Who Want to Work in Global Humanitarian Service

A decision to embark on a career move in the area of global humanitarian service should involve both research and introspection. The next section includes a series of key points to consider when considering such a move.

Assess Your Personal Fit

Humanitarian service work often involves personal and financial investment. When considering personal motivations, it is important to examine one's own short- and long-term goals, both positively and negatively. There are a variety of issues to consider, from managing one's living situation and bills to the affordability of being away and possibly not earning income while doing so. In particular, one may wish to contemplate professional and personal questions such as the following: How long will your humanitarian service experience or contract work last? How long might a sponsoring organization provide support overseas (e.g., housing, meals, stipends)? Is there a faculty mentor or professional peer who would be able to discuss goals and who could help along the way (e.g., through existing service-learning programs in the university or elsewhere, through independent study)? How might the humanitarian service experience be relevant to one's larger educational and/or professional goals? Is there adequate time and flexibility in life—both at the personal and professional level—to engage in this work? If relevant, how will business associates, professional colleagues, or students manage in your absence? If you have dependents, how will they manage financially or otherwise? Would a partner, spouse, or family members come along? If so, how might they feel about doing so? Or, if leaving loved ones "behind," how would they—or you— feel about your absence? This situation may lead to sadness, loneliness, anger, and resentment, along with attendant impacts on relationships. Factors such as these should be weighed frankly and considered well before serving.

Reflect on Your Expectations and Motivations for Providing Humanitarian Service

It is important to consider one's expectations and motivations for wanting to serve in humanitarian settings. Historically, some individuals may be like commandos in their zeal to fix things, whereas others may be more like Mother Teresa at a motivational level. While it is understandable to be proud of one's work in this domain, it is often invisible to others—do not expect medals and plaudits. Insofar as possible, the impetus for humanitarian service work should spring from a genuine desire to learn, grow, and meet needs that are evident to you. In this regard, a good sign of motivational clarity— at whatever stage of one's professional education and development—is when the population or issue addressed has a deep emotional effect and is difficult to "compartmentalize away." From our perspective, in this day and age, when we seem to have all manner of means for distracting ourselves from the needs that are "out there" in the larger world, the fact that one "can't stop thinking" about certain issues, situations, or populations may actually be a sign of humanity and a core motivation for humanitarian service work.

Even so, we encourage you strongly to reflect deeply on the nature and etiology of your motives and consult with others whom you trust and respect, lest you leap into a noble cause without sufficient reflection on why you are doing so. Presuming one undergoes a sustained process of reflection, it should be recognized that providing global humanitarian service may have substantial short- and long-term professional benefits for you. Although benefits should not be the main or primary reason for engaging in humanitarian service work, it is important to balance possibilities of hubris with the "purer" goal of advocating for a legitimate cause.

Identify Your Focus for Humanitarian Service

Practically speaking, it is worth asking which populations (e.g., children, adolescents, adults, older populations) and in what context or situations (e.g., postconflict, postdisaster, poverty stricken) you envision serving in. In considering questions such as these, weigh the possible populations and areas that are accessible, as well as aligned with your interests and training, from displaced refugees, women, and children, to the aged, mentally ill, physically ill, to victims or survivors of violence, torture, or natural disasters, and to many other populations or areas of potential focus. Will you need additional training, or would it be appropriate for you to gain training and expertise "on the job"? In reflecting on such matters, it should be emphasized that some humanitarian service may include work with healthy and nontraumatized people who happen to live in poor and underserved places, which represents a deep need where psychological expertise may be powerfully relevant, if sensitively delivered.

Determine Where to Provide Humanitarian Service

When considering "where" to provide humanitarian service, it is tempting to think of regions or countries. This is perfectly appropriate and fitting. However, global humanitarian service work also may be done locally, without a passport or plane ticket. To take but one out of innumerable examples, in some areas of the United States, there are displaced refugee populations, which are served by local agencies that may be stretched and could benefit from a psychologist's expertise. It is also important to match your linguistic skills with the service location. The most effective humanitarian service will require fluency in the local language. Other issues to consider along these lines include the culture, politics, climate, and health needs that are evident in a given locale, as well as your own personal safety.

As previously noted, variables such as length of service and point of career in which service occurs are both worthy of consideration. That is because some volunteer opportunities may be completed while one is a student in an educational and training program or simply as an "independent" volunteer as part of a bona fide service group tour. Others, perhaps in a time of career (e.g., retirement) or life transition (completion of a terminal degree), may allow for a longer stint of months or even years. Other humanitarian service psychologists may opt for a paid full-time position working for an organization. Such terms of service need not be mutually exclusive (e.g., it may be possible to engage in international experience on internship, or as part of a degree program, which then leads to a career in international service). For example, we know a Fulbright scholar who worked in Nepal as a postgraduate and then again 30 years later as a retiree. In short, you may consider engaging in humanitarian service at different times in your career and for varying lengths of time, as a student, early career professional, mid-career psychologists (e.g., through a sabbatical or research stint), or during retirement. And, of course, some may regard service not in volunteer terms but as a career choice, which offers a wonderful set of experiences—as well as a salary.

Ways to Engage in Humanitarian Service

Large-scale (as measured by their size of staffing, budget, or worldwide presence) organizations involved in humanitarian service work (e.g., Red Cross or Red Crescent, Doctors Without Borders, World Health Organization, the United Nations) offer excellent opportunities for international service work. However, a great deal of the work in the humanitarian service field is undertaken by smaller, often local, NGOs (Easterly, 2007), often in collaboration with larger organizations. There is general agreement in humanitarian service community that the most successful psychosocial interventions are those that are locally based and built within the communities they seek to service (Jacobs, 2007). Thus, to enhance the success of their programs, larger global humanitarian service organizations often partner with local NGOs to provide funding, training, mentoring, or consultation. Smaller and local NGOs often are grassroots nonprofit organizations that work on a particular issue, in a circumscribed geographical location, and in response to a particular need. For example, the psychologist-founded and led SAFE Coalition for Human Rights, which has a focus on human trafficking, started exactly in this way. Ideally, they are founded and led by deeply embedded members of local communities who are able to ensure that cultural and contextual hurdles are not impediments to processes of program implementation. Because these individuals serve as experts and ambassadors to their communities, their role in humanitarian service aid is vital to their organizational and intervention success. In short, NGOs may be very small (e.g., two or three individuals) or quite large (e.g., 50 or more), with talented and dedicated individuals working in difficult situations. Thus, they are invaluable to the work of humanitarian service psychologists (Stout, 2009).

As always, searching the internet is often the most efficient way to identify specific opportunities to engage in humanitarian service work. Some organizations—two examples, among many others, are Global Volunteers (https://www.globalvolunteers.org/) and World Advocacy (https://www.worldadvocacy.com/index.html)—offer searchable databases by which to identify international service work opportunities.

As noted earlier, the APA's Office of International Affairs has links to NGOs working internationally in disaster response, which may provide a useful starting list. To take just one example, the Center for Global Initiatives (CGI) was founded by a clinical psychologist working to create self-sustaining programs that improve access to health care in underserved communities throughout the world. Since its inception, CGI provides, without charge, sets of tools that are freely available, as well as downloadable medial libraries and links to Spanish, English, and multilingual medical resources, glossaries, courses, and search engines. In addition, there are tools and information for humanitarian service flight discounts, traveling carbon neutral, luggage requirements, State Department warnings, customs service information, travel document requirements, Federal Aviation Administration travel advisories, and international travel health tips (see http://centerforglobalinitiatives.org/).

EXEMPLARS IN THE FIELD OF INTERNATIONAL PSYCHOLOGY: APA INTERNATIONAL HUMANITARIAN AWARDS

As a tangible example of APA's overarching commitment to international service by psychologists—which, we argue, should receive much more prominent emphasis in the education and training of psychologists—it may be instructive to learn from those that APA has recognized for their international humanitarian work. Since 1999, APA has awarded the International Humanitarian Award. This honor

> recognizes extraordinary humanitarian service and activism by a psychologist or a team of psychologists, including professional and/or volunteer work conducted primarily in the field with underserved populations. "Extraordinary humanitarian services" are defined as professional activities initiated by psychologists, working alone or in association with others, to help alleviate severe stress and restore psychological well-being to a group of people in a variety of difficult circumstances. (APA, 2020b, Description tab)

A list of areas in which past winners have worked includes contextually appropriate psychosocial support in international emergencies (Wessells, 2009), integrating psychosocial programs in multisector responses to international disasters (Diaz, 2008), the development and maturation of humanitarian psychology (Jacobs, 2007), lessons learned in countries of the former Soviet Union and former Yugoslavia with the aim of setting up psychosocial assistance programs (Kapor-Stanulovic, 1999), victims of torture, and global health inequities (Stout, 2004). The 2012 award recipient, John Thoburn, applies his trauma expertise to address issues in disaster-ridden areas, whether natural or man-made. M. Brinton Lykes, the winner in 2013, works to reduce state-sponsored violence. The 2014 winner, Malcolm McLachlan, works to ensure that global health initiatives include minorities, those with disabilities, and those in poverty (APA, 2020b). More recent recipients such as the 2020 winner, Niels Peter Rygaard, PhD, focus on child psychology research, policy, and online training programs for foster care systems globally. And, in 2019, Gargi Roysircar-Sodowsky, PhD, provided mental health and service work with underserved populations impacted by disasters (APA, 2020b). As may be clear, from the standpoint of the APA, international humanitarianism is expressed through a very wide range of commitments and activities, which speaks to the fundamental point that there is no "one type" of international humanitarian service for psychology and psychologists. Even so, two areas in particular—education and mental health—would appear to be especially promising in terms of future directions for humanitarian psychologists (see Chapters 4 and 9, this volume, for more information about intervention and teaching, respectively).

CONCLUSION

Miller's (1969) intention in "giving psychology away" was for psychology and psychologists to galvanize action by offering our knowledge and skills to those who could benefit from such application (e.g., policy makers, educators, the public at large). Such offerings must have practical utility when addressing real-world challenges and opportunities. In addition, global psychology should focus on the needs of the recipient and their community—not the needs of the giver. The "service as charity" model runs the risk of creating a "savior syndrome," leaving those who are cared for in a passive state of waiting for others to alleviate their suffering and intervene to provide outcomes, not the transfer of skills to produce those outcomes (Dalal, 2010). In this regard, anyone embarking on the path of humanitarian service work should reflect on their motivations for undertaking service work, the sustainability of such a career path, and how to understand whether their own goals and values might clash with the needs and desires of those whom they hope to serve (Shealy, 2016).

With evidence-based treatments receiving focus in recent years, the World Health Organization and other funding agencies are lobbying for their global provision (Collins et al., 2011). To date, the dominant paradigm in the global north is often biologically based, with priorities to classify diagnostically, identify universal causal factors and pathways, and seek efficient forms of intervention, which has resulted in nontechnical aspects of care (values, meanings, and relationships) being considered secondary or less important (e.g., Deacon, 2013). This paradigm is based on a set of ontological, theoretical, and empirical or therapeutic assumptions that are historically and culturally contingent and need to be reconsidered if we are truly going to build a globally resonant field and profession of psychology (Stout, 2008, 2009; Wessells, 2009). Toward such means and ends, we are now seeing the deep interconnectedness of the world—be it contagions or commerce. The distinctions of "global" versus "local" are becoming less and less relevant. Likewise, as acknowledgments by APA demonstrate,[1] it is incumbent on us all as citizens of the world to also think and act with an ethic and ethos as psychologists of the world. And, in doing so, we need to bring along a cultural humility in all we do, from clinical services, to consultation, to capacity building.

Finally, many psychologists who engage in humanitarian service work feel it fulfills a deep-seated desire to make a difference in the larger world; however, it is essential they recognize the power and privilege they carry into such work. As part of our own growth and development, humanitarian service may provide a unique opportunity to test the limits of our own training, expertise, and learning, while helping us stretch in ways that are beneficial to self, others, and the larger world. If our education and training are attuned to the needs and opportunities in the larger world, we may, in fact, provide a service that is deeply complementary to, if not unparalleled by, the other helping professions. Yet, humanitarian service, and its transformative power, are activities that most have "discovered" on their own; it is rare for our students to be exposed to this avenue of activity. As such, we strongly encourage our colleagues and programs to emphasize such needs and opportunities at all

---

[1]For example, here are three salient declarations by APA's Council of Representatives: (a) "Apology to People of Color for the Role of the American Psychological Association in Promoting, Perpetuating, and Failing to Challenge Racism, Racial Discrimination, and Human Hierarchy in the United States" (https://www.apa.org/about/policy/racism-apology); (b) "Resolution on the Role of Psychology and the American Psychological Association in Dismantling Systemic Racism Against People of Color in the United States" (https://www.apa.org/about/policy/dismantling-systemic-racism); and (c) "Resolution on Advancing Health Equity in Psychology" (https://www.apa.org/about/policy/advancing-health-equity-psychology).

levels—in high school, as undergraduates, and at the master's and doctoral levels. Our field and profession have enormous potential to impact real human lives in ways that are needed and welcomed. To realize such capacity, we must first expose our students to the realities that are "out there" and all that we might do to help make things better. Such inclinations are in fact core to what draws most of us to our field and profession in the first place, an impulse that should be recognized and fostered—through humanitarian service in global psychology—by all of us as educators, scholars, students, practitioners, and leaders.

REFERENCES

American Psychological Association. (2015). *Board and council actions related to the report of the independent review relating to APA ethics guidelines, national security interrogations and torture.* https://www.apa.org/independent-review/board-council-actions

American Psychological Association. (2017). *Ethical principles of psychologists and code of conduct* (2002, Amended June 1, 2010, and January 1, 2017). https://www.apa.org/ethics/code/index.aspx

American Psychological Association. (2020a). *APA Divisions.* https://www.apa.org/about/division/index

American Psychological Association. (2020b). *APA International Humanitarian Award.* https://www.apa.org/about/awards/international-humanitarian.aspx?tab=4

American Psychological Association. (2020c). *Internationalizing psychology.* https://www.apa.org/international/resources/info

Antares Foundation. (2006, July). *Managing stress in humanitarian workers: Guidelines for good practice* (2nd ed.). https://gisf.ngo/wp-content/uploads/2014/09/0635-Antares-2006-Managing-stress-in-humanitarian-workers-Guidelines-for-good-practice.pdf

Arole, S. R., & Arole, R. S. (2009). Sustainable transformation of communities. In C. E. Stout (Ed.), *The new humanitarians: Inspiration, innovations, and blueprints for visionaries: Vol. 1. Changing global health inequities* (pp. 93–120). Praeger.

Aubé, N. (2011). Ethical challenges for psychologists conducting humanitarian work. *Canadian Psychology, 52*(3), 225–229. https://doi.org/10.1037/a0024342

Azar, B. (2009). *International practitioners.* American Psychological Association. https://www.apa.org/gradpsych/2009/03/cover-abroad

Butterfield, A. K. J., Tasse, A., & Linsk, N. (2009). The social work education in Ethiopia partnership. In C. E. Stout (Ed.), *The new humanitarians: Inspiration, innovations, and blueprints for visionaries: Vol. 2. Changing education and relief* (pp. 57–84). Praeger.

Caldwell, G. (2009). Witness. In C. E. Stout (Ed.), *The new humanitarians: Inspiration, innovations, and blueprints for visionaries: Vol. 3. Changing sustainable development and social justice* (pp. 1–16). Praeger.

Collins, P. Y., Patel, V., Joestl, S. S., March, D., Insel, T. R., Daar, A. S., Bordin, I. A., Costello, E. J., Durkin, M., Fairburn, C., Glass, R. I., Hall, W., Huang, Y., Hyman, S. E., Jamison, K., Kaaya, S., Kapur, S., Kleinman, A., Ogunniyi, A., . . . Walport, M. (2011). Grand challenges in global mental health. *Nature, 475,* 27–30. https://doi.org/10.1038/475027a

Dalal, A. (2010). Psychosocial interventions for community development. In G. Misra (Ed.), *Psychology in India: Vol. 3. Clinical and health psychology* (pp. 361–398). Pearson.

Deacon, B. J. (2013). The biomedical model of mental disorder: A critical analysis of its validity, utility, and effects on psychotherapy research. *Clinical Psychology Review, 33*(7), 846–861. https://doi.org/10.1016/j.cpr.2012.09.007

Diaz, J. O. P. (2008). Integrating psychosocial programs in multisector responses to international disasters. *American Psychologist, 63*(8), 820–827. https://doi.org/10.1037/0003-066X.63.8.820

Drogin, E. Y. (2019). *Ethical conflicts in psychology* (5th ed.). American Psychological Association. https://doi.org/10.1037/0000125-000

Easterly, W. (2007). *The White man's burden: Why the West's efforts to aid the rest have done so much ill and so little good*. Penguin Books.

Fitzduff, M., & Stout, C. E. (Eds.). (2005). *The psychology of resolving global conflicts: From war to peace: Vol. 1. Nature vs. nurture*. Praeger.

Friedli, L. (2002). Editorial. *Journal of Mental Health Promotion, 1*(2), 1–2.

Gewertz, K. (2005, February 17). Psychic healing: Catastrophe survivors don't want to be seen as victims. *Harvard University Gazette*. https://news.harvard.edu/gazette/story/2005/02/psychic-healing/

Giauque, D., Anderfuhren-Biget, S., & Varone, F. (2019). Stress and turnover intents in international organizations: Social support and work–life balance as resources. *International Journal of Human Resource Management, 30*(5), 879–901. https://doi.org/10.1080/09585192.2016.1254105

Inter-Agency Standing Committee. (2007). *IASC guidelines on mental health and psychosocial support in emergency settings*. https://interagencystandingcommittee.org/iasc-task-force-mental-health-and-psychosocial-support-emergency-settings/iasc-guidelines-mental-health-and-psychosocial-support-emergency-settings-2007

International Federation of Red Cross and Red Crescent Societies. (2019, June 21). *Thousands of volunteers from 140 countries celebrate 100 years of humanitarian action* [Press release]. https://www.ifrc.org/press-release/thousands-volunteers-140-countries-celebrate-100-years-humanitarian-action

International Union of Psychological Science. (2008). *Universal declaration of ethical principles for psychologists*. https://www.iupsys.net/about/governance/universal-declaration-of-ethical-principles-for-psychologists.html

Jacobs, G. A. (2007). The development and maturation of humanitarian psychology. *American Psychologist, 62*(8), 929–941. https://doi.org/10.1037/0003-066X.62.8.932

Jacobs, G. A., Gray, B. L., Erickson, S. E., Gonzalez, E. D., & Quevillon, R. P. (2016). Disaster mental health and community-based psychological first aid: Concepts and education/training. *Journal of Clinical Psychology, 72*(12), 1307–1317. https://doi.org/10.1002/jclp.22316

Kapor-Stanulovic, N. (1999). Encounter with suffering. *American Psychologist, 54*(11), 1020–1027. https://doi.org/10.1037/h0088215

Keyes, C. L. M. (2007). Promoting and protecting mental health as flourishing: A complementary strategy for improving national mental health. *American Psychologist, 62*(2), 95–108. https://doi.org/10.1037/0003-066X.62.2.95

Kronenberg, P., & Savaiano, P. (2009). Braille without borders. In C. E. Stout (Ed.), *The new humanitarians: Inspiration, innovations, and blueprints for visionaries: Vol. 2. Changing education and relief* (pp. 1–14). Praeger.

McCormack, L., Joseph, S., & Haggar, M. (2009). Sustaining a positive altruistic identity in humanitarian aid work: A qualitative case study. *Traumatology, 15*(2), 109–118. https://doi.org/10.1177/1534765609332325

Miller, G. A. (1969). Psychology as a means of promoting human welfare. *American Psychologist, 24*(12), 1063–1075. https://doi.org/10.1037/h0028988

Mollica, R. F., McInnes, K., Poole, C., & Tor, S. (1998). Dose-effect relationships of trauma to symptoms of depression and post-traumatic stress disorder among Cambodian survivors of mass violence. *The British Journal of Psychiatry, 173*(6), 482–488. https://doi.org/10.1192/bjp.173.6.482

Shealy, C. N. (Ed.). (2016). *Making sense of beliefs and values: Theory, research, and practice*. Springer Publishing.

Sphere Association. (2018). *The Sphere handbook: Humanitarian charter and minimum standards in humanitarian response* (4th ed.) [ebook ed.]. Practical Action Publishing. https://spherestandards.org/wp-content/uploads/Sphere-Handbook-2018-EN.pdf

Stevens, M. J., & Gielen, U. P. (Eds.). (2007). *Toward a global psychology: Theory, research, intervention, and pedagogy.* Lawrence Erlbaum Associates.

Stout, C. E. (Ed.). (1996). *The integration of psychological principles in policy development.* Praeger.

Stout, C. E. (2004). Global initiatives. *American Psychologist, 59*(8), 844–853. https://doi.org/10.1037/0003-066X.59.8.844

Stout, C. E. (2008). Psychology, social justice, and global works. *The California Psychologist, 41*(6), 6–9.

Stout, C. E. (Ed.). (2009). *The new humanitarians: Inspiration, innovations, and blueprints for visionaries: Vol. 1. Changing global health inequities.* Praeger.

Tabit, M. B., Legault, L., Ma, W., & Wan, K. P. (2016). In search of best practices for Multicultural education: Empirical evidence from the Forum BEVI Project. In C. N. Shealy (Ed.), *Making sense of beliefs and values* (pp. 175–204). Springer Publishing.

Weine, S., Danielli, Y., Silove, D., Van Ommeran, M., Faribank, J., & Saul, J. (2002). Guidelines for international training in mental health and psychosocial interventions for trauma exposed populations in clinical and community settings. *Psychiatry, 65*(2), 156–164.

Welton-Mitchell, C. E. (2013, July). *UNHCR's mental health and psychosocial support.* United Nations High Commissioner for Refugees. https://www.unhcr.org/afr/51f67bdc9.pdf

Wessells, M. G. (2009). Do no harm: Toward contextually appropriate psychosocial support in international emergencies. *American Psychologist, 64*(8), 842–854. https://doi.org/10.1037/0003-066X.64.8.842

World Health Organization. (2001). *The world health report 2001. Mental health: New understanding, new hope.* https://apps.who.int/iris/bitstream/handle/10665/42390/WHR_2001.pdf?sequence=1&isAllowed=y

Zetter, R. (1999). International perspectives on refugee assistance. In A. Ager (Ed.), *Refugees: Perspectives on the experience of forced migration* (pp. 46–82). Continuum.

Teaching

Opportunities and Recommendations for Internationalizing Psychology Education

Richard Velayo, Sherri McCarthy,[1] and Lee Sternberger

In 2007, the Education Leadership Conference (ELC) of the American Psychological Association (APA) proposed globalization as a compelling force in the 21st century, with implications for internationalizing the psychology curriculum in the United States. The following year, the ELC focused on globalizing psychology education, involving 159 psychologists from 16 national groups of psychology academic leaders at different levels of education and training, 11 psychological associations apart from the APA, 27 divisions and 15 governance groups from the APA, and several individuals from other countries. Since that time, there have been further conferences, publications, and calls for internationalizing psychology's knowledge base and education (e.g., Gross et al., 2016; Leong et al., 2012; Rich et al., 2017; Takooshian et al., 2016).

Professional interests, conferences, and scholarly outputs highlight two overarching realities. First, internationalization within the field and profession of psychology, and in the teaching of psychology in particular, are both necessary and inevitable given increasing global interconnectedness and the needs and aspirations of today's students (e.g., Cranney & Dunn, 2011; Institute for Innovative Global Education, 2022; Silbereisen et al., 2014). Second, because psychological expression and explanatory models differ around the world, a truly global discipline of psychology requires attention to cultural

---

[1]Sherri Nevada McCarthy was lost in a tragic accident in 2017. Please see APA PsycNet (https://psycnet.apa.org/record/2018-33351-020) for an account of her many accomplishments.

https://doi.org/10.1037/0000311-010
Going Global: How Psychologists Can Meet a World of Need, C. Shealy, M. Bullock, and S. Kapadia (Editors)

and international variation. This means we must, as teachers, reach broadly to include theories, constructs, and psychological research data that go beyond the ethnocentrism of those derived solely from small or selective samples from Western, educated, industrialized, rich, and democratic (WEIRD) countries (e.g., Henrich et al., 2010). To build a truly international approach to education in psychology—indeed, to education in general—it is necessary to reflect deeply on the knowledge, skills, and values we hold as educators. Two fundamental principles are necessary in this regard:

1. We need to be cognizant of how our own educational backgrounds and professional allegiances create a lens through which we perceive, evaluate, and manage reality (e.g., beliefs regarding why we are who we are as human beings as well as the models and methods that are and are not acceptable for making such judgments or facilitating change in self or others; Bullock, 2012; Burgess et al., 2004; Shealy, 2016).

2. Internationally minded psychologists should prepare their students to become informed, responsible, engaged, and effective global citizens (Stevens, 2009; Stevens & Gielen, 2007; Takooshian et al., 2016).

Regarding the first principle, we must commit to ongoing and globally minded exploration, expansion, and enrichment of our perspectives regarding human behavior, development, functioning, and change and apply this approach to ourselves, our students and colleagues, the field and profession, and the public. In short, internationally minded psychologists seek to identify and illuminate the underlying assumptions and epistemologies that exist within all cultures and contexts—including their own—thus affording students of all ages and levels the opportunity to examine and engage different versions of reality for themselves (e.g., Bullock, 2012; Burgess et al., 2004; Morgan-Consoli et al., 2018; Shealy, 2016; Velayo, 2015).

This task may become more difficult if dominant theoretical propositions, epistemological frameworks, meaning-making systems, methodological approaches, programs of research, or ways of understanding and facilitating change are internalized as true or better than others without sufficient awareness of possible confounds (e.g., alternative worldviews; problems with generalizability; cultural, economic, language, or political variables that affect the dissemination of knowledge). Psychologists educated and trained from a Western perspective may be particularly susceptible to these problems because so much of what is known or conveyed about psychology is derived from the West. At the same time, evidence suggests, in fact, that all human beings are potentially influenced by versions of reality that prevail in their culture and context and thus become central to their own sense of personal and professional identity. As such, we suggest that internationally minded psychologists neither reflexively embrace nor reject models, findings, or applications simply because of their origins (e.g., cultural, historical, national, regional; e.g., Chakkarath, 2005; Deacon, 2013; see also http://div52.net/wp-content/uploads/2020/01/D52-Bylaws-final-Oct-2020.pdf).

Regarding the second principle, global action on overarching initiatives, such as the United Nations' Sustainable Development Goals (see https://sdgs.un.org/goals) or attention to behavioral effects on climate change—just to name a few areas where psychology can and should play an important role—require a globally informed approach to education and training in psychology. Such emphases are congruent with broader trends in higher education, which underscores the need to develop a globally competent citizenry (Cranney & Dunn, 2011; Silbereisen et al., 2014; SummitX, 2022; Wang et al., 2020).

Consistent with these two overarching principles, in this chapter, we argue that now is the time to foster international perspectives in psychology teaching, training, and education at the high school, undergraduate, and graduate levels. In addition to expanding upon the "why" of internationalizing psychology education, we will also offer a how-to of practices by discussing specific issues, strategies, and resources that may further facilitate the internationalization of psychology education within the United States and globally.

INTERNATIONALIZATION IN HIGHER EDUCATION

For decades, higher education institutions (HEIs), national organizations, government agencies, industry leaders, and the popular press have engaged in discussions about the internationalization of colleges and universities. The American Council on Education, the Association of American Colleges and Universities, the Association of Public and Land-Grant Universities, and the International Association of Universities are among the organizations that have called for the comprehensive internationalization of community colleges, 4-year institutions, and research-intensive universities in order to provide today's students with the knowledge, skills, and values to meet the global needs and opportunities of the 21st century (Bartolini et al., 2009; SummitX, 2022).

In response, many professional organizations now list the internationalization of higher education as a central aspect of their missions and activities, including but not limited to, the Forum on Education Abroad, National Association of International Educators, the Association of International Education Administrators, the European Association of International Education, the International Education Association of Australia, and the Asian Pacific Association of International Education. Along similar lines, the International Association of Universities identifies institutional agreements, networks, research collaboration, visiting scholars, and mobility opportunities for students, faculty, and staff as common elements of an internationalization policy and strategy (see https://www.iau-aiu.net/). Many current strategies also frame internationalizations efforts within the umbrella of Sustainable Development Goals (see https://sdgs.un.org/goals; e.g., Ramaswamy et al., 2021).

In fact, international education organizations have long urged HEIs to adopt a more global focus in their own mission statements, strategic plans and priorities, faculty and student recruitment strategies, curriculum and cocurricular programming, and models and methods of assessment (Sternberger et al., 2009). Programmatic and survey research have been conducted to assess current practices and provide blueprints and best practices for internationalization, including in the field of psychology (e.g., https://www.acenet.edu/About/Pages/default.aspx). Overall, HEIs have been encouraged to initiate activities that infuse global perspectives into teaching, learning, and research to build international and intercultural competence among students, faculty, and staff and to establish relationships and collaborations with people and institutions abroad. They are also encouraged to foster student mobility and to adopt technologies that facilitate international engagement among students, faculty, and institutions, such as virtual exchange and collaborative online international learning or COIL (e.g., see https://www.kansai-u.ac.jp/Kokusai/IIGE/; https://coil.suny.edu/).

To operationalize these aspirations—and to demonstrate the very real nature of such work—consider the Aurora Network of Universities, Applied Global Studies Association, and Institute for Innovative Global Engagement as three examples of how such work is currently happening around the world. First, the Aurora Network of Universities (2022), a "platform for European university leaders, administrators, academics, and students to learn from and with each other" (Dedicated to Difference section), focuses on four key themes: (a) diversity and inclusion, (b) societal impact and relevance of research, (c) students, and (d) innovation of teaching and learning. As such, the Aurora Network pursues a range of real world deliverables, as indicated in Figure 9.1.

Relatedly, the Applied Global Studies Association brings together universities around the world with a shared mission to

> produce self-reflective, socially aware, and globally engaged leaders who have the necessary dedication, knowledge, skills, and experiences to make a demonstrable difference in the world through the application of informed scholarship and thoughtful practice across one or more of the following five areas of concentration: 1) Conflict Resolution, 2) Global Education, 3) Human Rights, 4) Religious and Cultural Understanding, and 5) Sustainability. (International Beliefs and Values Institute, 2022, para. 1)

As indicated in Figure 9.2, participating universities operationalize this mission in a wide range of ways, which further the eight components of the Applied Global Studies model (e.g., Ikeda et al., 2020, 2022).

As a third example of internationalization processes of higher education, consider the mission of the Institute for Innovative Global Education (IIGE), based at Kansai University in Japan, a grant-funded entity by the government of Japan, which

> aims to build new ties and strengthen those existing between Japanese and higher education institutions all over the world. Using widely-available technology, students and faculty will work together across borders by applying the Collaborative Online International Learning (COIL) method. IIGE will serve to generate new partnerships by introducing this mode of virtual collaboration, in particular with higher education institutions in the United States through the U.S.-Japan COIL Initiative. (Institute for Innovative Global Education, 2022, para. 2)

FIGURE 9.1. Key Deliverables and Activities of the Aurora Network of Universities

KEY DELIVERABLES / ACTIVITIES

Aurora Competence Framework, to equip a diverse student population with the skills and mindset to make them social entrepreneurs and innovators, willing and able to tackle the major challenges of our societies.

Aurora Education Area, giving students a meaningful international experience through embedded mobilities.

Aurora Cocreation and Topical Platforms making inclusive collaboration with external stakeholders and students regular practice in education, research, and outreach—at local, national, European, and global levels.

Aurora Capacity Development Support, contributing to an even distribution of higher education & research excellence across all regions of Europe.

Aurora Sustainability Pioneers, with Aurora SDG (Sustainable Development Goals) Research and Education dashboards, Alliance-level SDG education and a jointly implemented Aurora Sustainable Campus plan.

Note. Image courtesy of the Aurora Network of Universities (https://www.aurora. network-global).

Through a network of universities in Japan and around the world, the IIGE advances international higher education by bringing together associates with expertise in the following areas, as indicated in Figure 9.3: (a) training programs and quality assurance, (b) research, (c) promotion, (d) program advancement, and (e) development.

As these three examples illustrate—and there are many more—this is the world of international higher education now, not in some distant future. Therefore, as psychology educators who wish to "go global" and "meet a world of need," two fundamental questions are before us: (a) How familiar are we with innovative, integrative, and international educational programs like these? and (b) Are we helping our students engage with such international education opportunities as well as with their peers around the world who are already doing so? In many ways, this chapter is designed to provide substantive answers

FIGURE 9.2. Eight Learning-Based Components of the AGS Model

Through eight learning-based components, the AGS Model helps students gain the confidence and competence necessary to become successful change agents across a wide range of local and global settings.

- **Challenge-Based Learning**
- **Depth-Based Learning**
- **Evidence-Based Learning**
- **Field-Based Learning**
- **Media-Based Learning**
- **Project-Based Learning**
- **Student-Centered Learning**
- **Technology-Based Learning**

Note. Image courtesy of the Aurora Network of Universities (https://www.aurora. network-global).

FIGURE 9.3. Components of the IIGE Approach

Note. Image courtesy of the Institute for Innovative Global Education, Kansai University (https://www.kansai-u.ac.jp/Kokusai/IIGE/about/).

to these questions so that our teaching is responsive to, and embracing of, a globalized world that the next generation is inheriting now.

INTERNATIONALIZATION IN PSYCHOLOGY

Within psychology, attention to a more global perspective may not be surprising given that people from cultures throughout the world interact with one another and seek to do so in ways that facilitate mutual understanding (McCarthy et al., 2009). A more internationally focused curriculum fosters knowledge and skills that help students respond effectively while raising awareness of our global interconnectedness and mutual accountability and lowering the tendency toward prejudice and stereotyping (McCarthy, 2002). Given that many students who study psychology will not become psychologists, and because psychology is likely to remain one of the most popular areas of college and university study, we who teach psychology should be concerned with helping students at all levels deepen their understanding of self and others within an increasingly global society. At the same time, those who do continue past the baccalaureate degree to become psychologists in the United States as well as in other regions of the world are increasingly likely to work in varied contexts and with highly diverse populations. Cultivating the capacity to transcend national perspectives, boundaries, and presuppositions within all of our students—regardless of their career aspirations—will promote their ability to apprehend and approach the inevitable cultural complexities they will face with awareness, sensitivity, and skill (e.g., Gross et al., 2016; Silbereisen et al., 2014; Takooshian et al., 2016; Velayo, 2012; Wandschneider et al., 2015; Wang et al., 2020).

At the same time, psychology programs in many areas of the world that have traditionally been dominated by Western (primarily U.S.) psychology models are struggling to make their curricula more locally relevant. As Bullock (2012) noted, expanding and contextualizing the psychology curriculum may be more a process of "nationalization" in those countries dominated by imported curricula as opposed to "internationalization" in the United States and other Western countries. As such, internationalization must embrace a genuine interplay between general, global, or universal perspectives on the one hand with local, particular, or contextualized perspectives on the other, particularly when developing and disseminating teaching and training materials.

PURSUING INTERNATIONALIZATION IN PSYCHOLOGY EDUCATION

Concomitant with the processes of curricular internationalization, there is a growing recognition of cultural differences in the models or factors that lead to commonalities and differences in human functioning within and across cultures (Silbereisen et al., 2014; Wandschneider et al., 2015). One challenge for psychology instructors is to balance different epistemological frameworks that may describe and explain psychological phenomena in qualitatively different terms (Grenwald et al., 2012; Gross et al., 2016). The first aspect of this challenge is that psychological research from the United States has dominated the psychological literature, at least in the context of English-language publications, which also are the most visible (Leong et al., 2012). The preponderance of U.S.-based work, although well developed and substantive, carries with it an ethnocentric risk of taking the behavioral phenomena, explanatory frameworks, and interventions that characterize U.S. psychology as normative and universal in application.

Thus, best practices in the teaching of psychology—or any discipline—require providing as rich a picture as possible of psychological phenomena and striving to understand social, familial, interpersonal, and individual behaviors within their historical, cultural, and local contexts. As educators, we therefore seek dialogue, self–other awareness, discussion, and sustained engagement to understand and evaluate psychological models and to promote exploration and discussion of similarities and differences within and among cultures.

Fortunately, we see evidence that such good and healthy processes are underway, mainly because perspectives from multiple countries and regions are increasingly available in English publications (Leong et al., 2012). In addition, accessibility to psychology journals and textbooks that are published in languages other than English and written by researchers and authors outside of the United States is increasing with the proliferation of accessible international bibliographical databases such as Scopus (https://www.elsevier.com/solutions/scopus), REDALYC (https://www.redalyc.org), and SciELO (https://scielo.org/). Until recently, it was difficult to engage in international discussions and access international research for a variety of reasons, including language barriers, cost, and availability. Access to internet-based communications has served a crucial role in opening up a world of inquiry and practice, not only in psychology but also across the disciplinary spectrum. At the same time that international accessibility is growing, there is a corresponding increase in attention to Indigenous perspectives as valid forms of psychological inquiry. As a result, many psychologists are reviewing the frameworks and the content that they teach and promote and seeking to expand their scope to acknowledge the epistemologies and scholarly output of different cultures (e.g., Grenwald et al., 2012; Gross et al., 2016; Silbereisen et al., 2014; Takooshian et al., 2016).

Therefore, to go global in the truest and fullest sense, psychological curricula in the United States and many Western or developed countries must increasingly include research and insights from beyond those borders (Leong et al., 2012), just as non-U.S. and non-Western educators and scholars engage in similar processes. As previously noted, this means that international educators must seek out and explore the different ways that reality is perceived, evaluated, and managed. For instance, educators might provide opportunities for students to consider how constructs such as self, family, or personality are understood across cultures as well as how human change processes such as child rearing or social interaction are shaped all over the world by the norms, expectations, and values of the cultures in which they take place. In doing so, it is important to be inclusive regarding the theories, methods, findings, and applications to which students are exposed. Simultaneously, students should be encouraged to evaluate and reflect upon their own worldviews and meaning-making systems vis-à-vis other cultural perspectives or approaches in a curious and open manner. Such ongoing and synergistic engagement is necessary in order to develop a psychology that includes rather than excludes and offers the promise of a truly global field of inquiry and practice (e.g., Bullock, 2012; Burgess et al., 2004; Morgan-Consoli et al., 2018; Shealy, 2016; Velayo, 2015).

The vision for psychology education and training developed by participants at the APA's ELC in 2007 continues to be relevant, as is the International Conference on Psychology Education, which has held several conferences relevant to these issues (Leong et al., 2012; McCarthy et al., 2009). Implementing the recommendations emerging from such conferences requires change to organizational and educational systems at several levels, from classroom activities to institutional involvement and action. We summarize some of these recommendations and best practices next. We then discuss broader ways to internationalize education before concluding with a description of resources that may facilitate the internationalization process.

BEST PRACTICES AND SPECIFIC ACTIVITIES FOR THE CLASSROOM

As we contemplate best practices in the classroom, it may be helpful to ask what exactly is meant by curricular internationalization. Bond (2003) named three approaches to internationalizing the curriculum: add-on, infusion, and transformation. The add-on approach is characterized by including intercultural or international themes or content in the curriculum without changing the original structure or teaching strategies used. Infusion involves the incorporation of content that enhances students' cross-cultural experience and understanding, focuses on the interdisciplinary nature of the curriculum, and exposes students to various international and multicultural perspectives (Bond, 2003). Transformation, which is the least utilized and most difficult to implement, encourages new ways of thinking, incorporates new methodologies, raises epistemological inquiries, challenges assumptions, and considers the plausibility of subjective and new data sources (Bond, 2003; Silbereisen et al., 2014). Many questions follow from this definitional framework. For example, if the goal of curricular internationalization is to change students' epistemological views of psychology and the world, how does such conceptual change occur? Is one model of internationalization more effective than the other? How do we best assess the impact of educational interventions and modify our approaches based upon these results? These questions are among many worth asking as we move toward more international approaches to education, training, learning, and growth (Wandschneider et al., 2015; Wang et al., 2020).

Curricular internationalization also may include exploring the contributions of Indigenous psychologies. Although all local psychologies, even mainstream Western approaches, are Indigenous in a definitional sense—that is, systems of knowledge based on paradigms that originate in particular localities and cultures (Kim et al., 2006)—important psychological models and traditions have existed for thousands of years outside of modern centers of psychology in the United States and Europe; these traditions can offer insights about psychological factors in human functioning. To take a few examples, Confucian scholars such as Yi Toegye developed and debated the "science of mind" in 16th-century Korea (McCarthy et al., 2013). In Malaysia, where the same monarchy has existed uninterrupted for over 3,000 years, many of the codes of conduct accepted within the culture are based on sound psychological principles of communication and relationship building that Western psychologists only uncovered much later (Jaafar et al., 2004). In a similar vein, for over 3,000 years the Hindu tradition has offered philosophical and scientific thought that includes elaborate conceptual frameworks, theoretical analyses of the human personality, and therapeutic techniques to navigate the difficulties of human life to reach higher levels of development (Chakkarath, 2005).

Moreover, such cross-cultural comparisons can be meaningfully engaged across all levels of international psychology. For example, doctoral students in clinical, combined, counseling, and school psychology—which are now recognized as "health service psychology" programs from an accreditation standpoint—could reflect upon the current iterations of the *Diagnostic and Statistical Manual of Mental Disorders* and the *International Classification of Diseases* through different cultural, economic, and epistemological lenses. As an example, the following questions could be asked: How would Hindu culture comprehend matters of mental health diagnosis versus a Judeo Christian culture? What is the nature of reality from each perspective? And how and why do such values and identities matter in theory, research, and practice (e.g., Burgess et al., 2004; Chakkarath, 2005; Deacon, 2013; Wandschneider et al., 2015; Wang et al., 2020)? In short, psychology curricula and programs that prepare students to work with others in the realm of mental health might compare and contrast different Indigenous perspectives—from East and West as well as different cross-cultural or country examples—in order to provide a more complete picture of human behavior and to offer additional perspectives regarding the conceptual and applied nature of intervention delivery (APA Working Group on Internationalizing the Undergraduate Psychology Curriculum, 2005; Gross et al., 2016; Takooshian et al., 2016).

In addition to including diverse content, it is important to attend to the processes of growth, learning, and development, such as reflection and exchange. Reflective activities encourage students to examine how their own cultural backgrounds contribute to their perspectives and actions. These activities may include self/other perspective-taking exercises, engagement in debates regarding cultural research and theory, assessment of self in relation to the larger group or groups in which one is a member, and exchange activities that might include joint assignments with colleagues and students in other countries, or actual travel. Ultimately, such activities should ask students to identify what they believe about self, others, and the larger world; contemplate the implications of such beliefs for actions, policies, and practices in the real world; and question how their perspectives, beliefs or actions have developed and might change from a different cultural perspective (e.g., Iyer, 2013; Wandschneider et al., 2015; Wang et al., 2020).

Next, we offer examples of classroom-based activities, organized under four domains, which may directly help internationalize psychology education.

Introduce International Content Through Guest Speakers, Conference Content, and Use of Relevant Internet Resources and Social Media

Guest speakers who are international—or who specialize in international issues—are a wonderful resource, providing a valuable source of information to facilitate discussion and scholarship of international and global perspectives. Inclusion of such perspectives may be facilitated through individual class lectures or by arranging conferences, student research forums, or panels that feature international speakers, projects, and student work. Typically, the ensuing dialogue among students who participate in such events is lively and compelling. At a complementary level, colleges and universities are likely to have an international office that can help locate international students to visit your classroom; colleagues in your own department or institution also may be able to alert you to international colleagues on campus. Many activities are broadcast as webinars or other media, allowing broad participation.

Internet- and media-based technologies and systems—including but not limited to social media, blogs, wikis, videoconferencing platforms, podcasts, virtual exchange, and COIL—are also revolutionizing the nature and scope of how disciplines may internationalize their programs and curricula (Institute for Innovative Global Education, 2022; Takooshian et al., 2016). YouTube and other internet-accessible videos also may provide a comprehensive source to easily access relevant international content.

Through web-based systems, instructors and scholars from different locations around the globe are able to work together, often in real time, on joint projects and activities. Students are generally well acquainted with these technologies—at times, more than faculty. When thoughtfully and deliberately used, such web-based resources may be invaluable for teaching research, supplementing lessons, improving the quality of collaboration, and pursuing the larger goal of internationalizing programs and curricula. Such technologies may also enhance student willingness to communicate and work together with their peers in different geographical locations while expanding the boundaries of psychological education. For instance, classes at two different institutions based in two different countries can organize to meet each other through video conferencing. Online systems such as Blackboard, Canvas, Zoom, and virtual exchange or COIL technologies, which are now available in most U.S. schools and to students in many other countries, can facilitate web-enhanced classes and allow students from different institutions across the world to hold discussions in real time (e.g., https://www.kansai-u.ac.jp/Kokusai/IIGE/).

Examine Current Issues Through an International Lens

Requiring students to access news outlets or other sources of information from outside the United States facilitates their ability to compare and contrast perspectives across local, regional, national, or international sources. For example, comparing reports of the same event from news channels in different countries can highlight different assumptions and attributions; comparing reports on social issues such as gun violence, early education, corporal punishment, obesity, or mental health prevalence in the United States and another country in relation to laws (e.g., regarding gun ownership for gun violence) could be an assignment that elicits discussion of the role of culture, education, and media vis-à-vis social issues. Course activities and writing assignments that require students to seek and compare information and materials across countries other than their own allow them to understand how sociocultural variables interact with a wide range of issues that are relevant to psychology (Iyer, 2013; Leong et al., 2012). Such activities increase psychological knowledge about the diversity of human behavior across different aspects (e.g., gender, culture, religion, politics). By extension, conversations deriving from these assignments may evolve to include a range of other issues, from concepts of individual well-being to the roles of individual autonomy and social cohesion and the meaning and nature of human rights. Discussions can provide an interesting way to advance international awareness as well as explore how cultural norms and values impact cross-cultural similarities and differences (Leong et al., 2012).

Within the larger institution, students also may be required or encouraged to attend campus forums (e.g., lectures, films) or create new opportunities for international engagement. For example, students may be asked to interview students or faculty from other countries and reflect on what they learned in writing or in presentations. In the "Making Sense of Beliefs and Values" course at James Madison University (JMU), a group of students filmed their own experience in the larger community when they visited restaurants and tasted foods from around the world, and then interviewed those who prepared the food to learn about what they were eating and its meaning in different cultures and contexts (see https://www.jmu.edu/global/isss/get-involved/madison-intl.shtml). Not only are such projects informative and experiential in nature, they also may be highly enjoyable for students and faculty alike (Iyer, 2013; Leong et al., 2012). Likewise, faculty may work with colleagues or campus organizations to promote opportunities for dialogue and exchange about contemporary issues relevant to the role of psychology and psychologists, such as immigration, terrorism, protection of privacy, or cultural beliefs about family and social bonds (e.g., SummitX, 2022). Relevant readings or other materials that could inform discussion and debate can be assigned to accompany these experiences.

Two books are recommended to aid in constructing curricula that help students develop a more international perspective about psychology. One is the book by Leong et al. (2012), which contains information and tools to assist psychology faculty in teaching and training future generations of psychologists with a much more international mindset and global viewpoint. Each chapter gives a detailed description of how the psychology curriculum works in terms of social, developmental, clinical, and counseling courses and other psychology subfields. The other book, by Gross et al. (2016), offers clear approaches to studying psychology across cultures, practical ideas to use in the classroom, resources that connect students to the world beyond their home campus, and expert advice on how to develop and administer study-abroad programs.

Encourage Student Research on International Topics

Students' international awareness may also be strengthened as they learn about the research of others and how to do their own research as well as discover research relevant to their own questions. Students may be encouraged or required to do research that addresses the global implications of their particular interests. For instance, they might be required to describe cultural differences in approaches to or perceptions of their chosen topic, either from the literature or through discussion with students of diverse cultures to provide a platform where international perspectives are encountered and embraced. Faculty may encourage students to find research articles written by non-U.S. authors using data collected from outside the United States.

As students collect data for their own research, faculty should facilitate collaboration with international colleagues and students or encourage students to compare their findings with data collected elsewhere. For example, the APA has a webpage with a list of links to a variety of electronically available psychology data sets (https://www.apa.org/research/responsible/data-links). APA's Division 52 (International Psychology; https://div52.net) and APA's Office of International Affairs (https://www.apa.org/international/) also provide a wealth of information that may be investigated, including conferences, colleagues, and students around the world who are interested in similar issues.

Encourage Study Abroad, Service Learning, and Field Trips

The number of U.S. students who study abroad—whether for a shorter experience, a semester, or a year—is growing (Farrugia et al., 2012), a trend that should be encouraged within programs and departments of psychology. Specifically, according to its recent *Open Doors Report*, the Institute of International Education (2020) reported that the number of students who studied abroad grew by 1.6% to 347,099 over the 2017–2018 academic year. Approximately 11% of students receiving a bachelor's or associate's degree studied abroad.

Furthermore, Open Doors 2020 demonstrates that the profile of American students studying abroad is diversifying. In the 2018–2019 academic year, 31% of students who classified as racial or ethnic minorities studied abroad. In 2008–2009, however, racial and ethnic minorities made up barely 20% of the study-abroad population.

For the fifth year in a row, the number of overseas students in the United States has reached 1 million, growing to 1,075,496; however, this number represents a decrease by 1.8% from the previous year (2018–2019). This drop is likely a reflection of more stringent immigration policies during the Trump administration, the cost of education in the United States, and perceptions of crime or unfriendliness in the country. However, according to the Project Atlas (Institute of International Education, 2019), the United States remains the top destination for international students who choose to study outside of their home country.

Relevant to psychology, 7.9% of study-abroad students have identified the social sciences as their major (Institute of International Education, 2022). Certainly, not all of those students are studying psychology. However, given the popularity of psychology at the undergraduate level, it is likely that many of them are psychology majors.

Study-abroad programs assume many forms. For example, Minnesota State University in Mankato has instituted a summer program where graduate students of organizational psychology combine visits to companies and psychologists abroad with sightseeing opportunities. From our perspective, much more could and should be done to offer educational and training opportunities for master's- and doctoral-level students in order to illustrate the importance of applying their knowledge and skills to a world of need, both at home and abroad. Historically, fewer study-abroad programs have destinations in South America, Africa, the Middle East, or South and Southeast Asia. From our perspective, offerings should be expanded to include destinations for study abroad outside North American and European parameters.

Service activities and class field trips also may facilitate broader internationalization goals. For example, the campus of one of the authors (McCarthy) was near the border with Mexico. To promote internationalization and take advantage of such proximity, over the past decade students and faculty from the closest major Mexican state university regularly joined students and faculty at her university in service activities including seminars, research projects, and events at each other's campuses. One of the student projects examined quality of life via an existing survey that was developed under the auspices of the Oxford Happiness Inventory. This survey has been used by students to gather data in Malaysia, Indonesia, Pakistan, Botswana, Nigeria, and the United States and has served as a basis for student presentations at conferences around the world (Hawkey et al., 2012). These projects allow students to meet and network with others who have common international interests and may be encouraged by granting extra credit or special recognition to students who participate in such activities.

Course credit also may be offered for international education and training experiences. For example, Northern Arizona University's psychology and social work students have courses taught by faculty available during summer sessions in Central and South America (see https://nau.edu/psychological-sciences). Students also may learn more by attending classes at a university in a different country or engaging in service learning courses and experiences, which focus on international populations at home and abroad (Sternberger et al., 2005). Finally, supporting internships abroad also is an effective way to engage with international scholars and practitioners by encouraging graduate students to undertake international service learning projects as part of their training program (Grenwald & Velayo, 2011). At the graduate level, two examples of psychology programs that specifically focus on international education and training in psychology are the Chicago School's International Psychology PhD program (see https://www.thechicagoschool.edu/psychology-programs/international-psychology/) and the William James College's (formerly Massachusetts School of Professional Psychology program) Service Learning and Summer Immersion Program (see https://www.hmhnetwork.org/). If your own unit or department has not developed one or more courses or programs along these lines, it may be time to encourage such a step or to engage those who already are doing so.

PURSUING INTERNATIONALIZATION AT YOUR INSTITUTION

Understanding larger systems of higher education as they function in countries outside of the United States is an important competency for international educators. As the three examples presented earlier illustrated, that is because many HEIs are interconnected, working with partners around the world through student and faculty mobility schemes, joint research, capacity-building projects, dual and joint degree programs, and so forth (Sternberger & Wang, 2015). Such consortia offer dynamic opportunities for psychologists to connect with colleagues around the world inside and outside their discipline and to pursue a range of activities of direct professional benefit (Sternberger, 2005).

Typically, an international office such as an institute for global engagement or similar entity in a college or university can help faculty become aware of these ties. If your institution does not have an institute for global engagement, it would be worthwhile to encourage the creation and development of such a system to promote campus internationalization. Faculty play an especially important role in introducing ideas and potential contacts to their international office, which may benefit not only the individual faculty members and students but also the campus as a whole (Lonner & Murdock, 2012). More specifically, faculty can promote internationalization institutionally in a number of ways (Sternberger & Wang, 2015). We review some of those methods next.

Facilitate Participation in International and Cross-Cultural Awareness Experiences

Promoting educational sessions on international or cross-cultural awareness at your college or university (e.g., developing intercultural experience, understanding local immigrant populations, learning about cultural practices) will enhance the teaching environment by encouraging greater global awareness. For example, through Madison International, a living and learning community at JMU, the entire campus and surrounding community become a laboratory through which students become more culturally aware by explicitly encouraging them to encounter cultures different from their own and report back to the larger system (Iyer, 2013). Along these lines, faculty who are interested in promoting internationalization should deliberately provide incentives to their students to attend such experiences, both on and off college grounds. For instance, many universities and colleges host an "international week," which includes cultural programming, student debate or discussion, and academic presentations (e.g., https://www.utoledo.edu/cisp/iew/). If you are part of an HEI that does not yet feature such an event, consider approaching other faculty, students, and administrators about the possibility of developing your own "I-week." If your institution already hosts such activities, encourage your students to become involved by including this experience in relevant syllabi or other program requirements.

Encourage International Faculty Exchange

From the standpoint of internationalization, it is often in the best interest of institutions to support the active presence of their faculty at other institutions around the world. For example, one of the authors (McCarthy) taught online classes for her university while participating in faculty exchanges in Russia, Brazil, and Malaysia. This arrangement facilitated links between students and faculty that have proved important for future research and teaching projects. Similarly, hiring faculty from outside the country to teach web-based courses (e.g., as adjunct faculty) and encouraging engagement by nonenrolled students in such courses or program experiences (e.g., in a partner institution) can be a relatively inexpensive and high impact practice. Policies that work against such practices should be revisited, as they are not conducive to overarching processes of internationalization. According to Harden (2006), arrangements between psychology schools in different countries can be made to (a) facilitate sharing of learning resources on various topics from different perspectives; (b) establish an "ask the expert" tool with online access to students, faculty, and professionals in different countries; (c) facilitate student-led online forums and discussions between students from different countries; and (d) develop an example bank that underscores the sociopolitical and cultural analysis of particular problems.

The Fulbright International Education Administrators awards program (https://www.cies.org/iea) also provides an opportunity for travel abroad, which is designed explicitly to introduce higher education faculty or administrators to the culture and higher education systems in other countries through campus visits, meetings with foreign colleagues and government officials, attendance at cultural events, and briefings on education. Through such experiences, participants gain new perspectives on the opportunities and needs to internationalize U.S. campuses as well as how such goals may be achieved. For faculty, the Fulbright Program (https://eca.state.gov/fulbright) offers both teaching and research grants, ranging in duration from a few weeks to a year. Likewise, hosting Fulbright scholars from other countries while encouraging faculty to accept Fulbright fellowships outside the United States helps internationalize the university. Fulbright funding covers the cost of travel for current Fulbright scholars in the United States to serve as guest lecturers on other campuses. In addition, university faculty exchanges between U.S. and non-U.S. institutions substantially increase the internationalization of psychology curricula by sharing perspectives among institutions, students, and colleagues. Collaborating with an institution's international office, such exchanges can be developed at the institutional level, which may include research, teaching, and practical experiences. An alphabetical list of exchange programs (for non-U.S. and U.S. citizens) by the U.S. Bureau of Education and Cultural Affairs may be accessed online (https://exchanges.state.gov/us/alphabetical-list-programs).

Promote Recruitment of International Students for Graduate Programs

The presence of international students plays a powerful role in creating a more globalized culture and curriculum. At the graduate level (master's and doctorate), students have a deep experience base that leads to cogent observations vis-à-vis U.S.-based curricula, theory, and practice, which may be quite illuminating and thought provoking for students, faculty, and administrators alike. Also, graduate students with assistantships may help to internationalize teaching, research, and service by bringing their own perspectives to the classroom. For example, JMU's Combined-Integrated Doctoral Program in Clinical and School Psychology has made a deliberate effort to attract highly qualified international students for many years, aiming to enroll at least one international student on average for each entering class of six students. The presence of such students has enhanced the depth and breadth of discourse (e.g., adding an international dimension to conversations), facilitated additional activities (e.g., increased participation in an on-campus international learning community), and has been instrumental to the overall internationalization and diversity of the doctoral program and the larger department (Burgess et al., 2004).

ENCOURAGE GREATER INTERNATIONAL AWARENESS OUTSIDE OF YOUR INSTITUTION

Given the importance of providing a more international curricular experience to students at one's own institution, collaborative efforts between institutions and other outside organizations can further enhance internationalization efforts. Much can be gained by promoting international engagement outside of one's institutional home. The following strategies demonstrate how promoting the integration of off-campus cross-cultural, international, and multicultural experiences and perspectives allow psychologists to augment campus-based activities and open up a world of possibility for their students and colleagues.

Encourage Students to Engage With International Mentors

As a discipline and profession, psychology offers a rich array of resources that allow students to engage in international activity and seek mentors who can help them gain their global footing over time. A prime example was the APA Division 52 Heritage Mentoring Project in 2011 (see https://www.apa.org/international/pi/2012/06/div-52), in which a psychology graduate student in the United States interviewed a scholar based outside of the United States (generally via electronic means) and wrote an article about their work, assisted by a mentor. Resulting interviews were featured in the Division 52 newsletter, *International Psychology Bulletin* (see https://div52.net/publications/newsletter/).

To take just one example, a graduate student from a school psychology program in Maine interviewed a well-known Indonesian psychologist (Kesel & McCarthy, 2013). Likewise, the Fast Connect program from APA's Division 52 has graduate students, early career psychologists, and senior psychologists all interview one another and write up the results in a brief format, which is also published online and in the *International Psychology Bulletin*. As a final example, the International Congress of Psychology has developed a young scholars program, which connects burgeoning psychologists with established scholars to support their development over time. Faculty and administrators are encouraged to familiarize themselves with programs like these and support greater engagement between their own students and colleagues around the world.

Collaborate With Colleagues and Institutions in Other Countries

One of the most obvious, dynamic, and surprisingly accessible strategies for internationalizing your own activities as an instructor and researcher is to establish collaborative relationships with colleagues who share similar interests but work in different countries. Ideally, such activity should be centered on research or other professional work, establishing a foundation that can be built upon over the years. The good news is that information regarding the work of international colleagues is readily available through web-based searches for colleagues working in allied areas. Moreover, most major psychology conferences within the United States have a strong international presence. Reviewing conference offerings is a relatively easy way to identify international colleagues who are working in areas of common interest; they can then be contacted in advance of attending a conference in order to arrange on-site meetings.

Skype, Zoom, Facetime, and other forms of web-based communication can also facilitate the sort of dialogue that may culminate in a deeper understanding of each other's research as well as the possibility of engaging in joint activities. Similarly, a review of preconference materials will illustrate the breadth of international partnerships that are already flourishing, many of which began simply by two or more colleagues reaching out to one another. Such collaborations are likely to thrive even more if students (undergraduate and graduate) are involved. Continuing advances in internet-based exchange opportunities—for example, COIL—also provide excellent opportunities for faculty and students to develop accessible and affordable course and program partnerships between partner institutions around the world (e.g., COIL does not require a physical presence in another country as part of the learning experience; see https://www.kansai-u.ac.jp/Kokusai/IIGE/).

Finally, when reaching out to international colleagues, consider domestic colleagues who already may have such relationships established and might welcome your participation or who might like to join you in some outreach effort in the context of a specific project (e.g., research paper, grant application). Ultimately, your teaching will benefit from bringing back home the results of such collaborations while modeling and illustrating the many benefits of such arrangements to the future psychologists who are now in your classroom.

Attend International Conferences

Multitudes of psychology conferences happen around the world (e.g., https://www.allconferencealert.com/psychology.html, https://www.apa.org/international/resources/events, https://psychologyconferences.com, https://waset.org/psychology-conferences). Many of these conferences include sessions or programming streams that focus on new teaching methods, classroom demonstrations, issues of assessment, and recent developments and advances in specific subfields of psychology. Attendance at these conferences can involve extra expenses that your department and institution may or may not be able to cover. Demonstrating that you have papers and presentations accepted in such venues may be an added inducement to help defray travel costs. An international office at your institution may also be able to help. If an institution has a process for internationalization underway, it is more likely that resources will be available for faculty and students to attend international events. Travel grants may also be possible through various professional organizations (e.g., an APA grant to cover up to $400 of registration fees at conferences outside the United States and Canada). Further, most international conference organizers offer travel grants to early career scholars (e.g., International Society for the Study of Behavioral Development, Society for the Study of Emerging Adulthood, International Council of Psychologists). You may also offset some conference expenses by taking on volunteer roles within the conference organization or an associated international organization (e.g., serving on committees or serving in an elected office). By bringing conference events and opportunities to the attention of your home institution—and becoming actively involved as a presenter or member of leadership—faculty demonstrate their commitment to international activities and are in a position to communicate the benefits of doing so. To identify promising international venues, good resources include the international calendar developed by APA's Office of International Affairs (see https://www.apa.org/international/resources/events.aspx).

Reach Out to Psychology Groups Outside of the United States

As noted earlier, students, early career, and established psychologists have many opportunities to create connections with allied groups outside of their home country. The APA Office of International Affairs offers valuable resources in this regard (see https://www.apa.org/international). At a complementary level, many divisions of APA have made efforts to recruit and include members and affiliates worldwide (see https://www.apa.org/about/division/). As a result of these emphases, and other globalization trends already noted, APA annual convention programming has become quite international. Along these lines, national psychology associations should emphasize the work they do with international associations and make their members more aware of international opportunities relevant to psychology. The Committee on International Relations in Psychology and the APA Office of International Affairs organize these efforts within APA and provide directories of contact information for national and international psychology organizations in other countries. Regional organizations (e.g., Western Psychological Association) are also starting to promote regular international programming at their conferences. In short, fostering collaboration between American and other psychological associations is creating a greater network for internationalizing psychology, which offers multiple opportunities for professional collaboration.

Encourage Publishers to Increase International Content in Textbooks

Creating a clearinghouse of psychology resources from various countries that may be electronically accessed via the web is a worthwhile step toward the broader goal of internationalizing psychology (e.g., Velayo et al., 2012). In addition, instructors can help by reviewing and promoting textbooks that have significant international content as well as involving others (e.g., colleagues and graduate students) in such processes.

Promote Internationalization by Collaborating With Regulators, Institutions, and Disciplines

If the internalization of psychology curriculum is to be sustained, it needs to become a guiding value of accreditation bodies as well as institutions. That is, program evaluation and accreditation processes must be connected to these efforts and these results (e.g., by explicitly recognizing international diversity as integral to multicultural diversity among other criteria for accreditation at all levels of education, from high school through undergraduate and graduate education). Efforts in this direction are supported by APA's adoption of a policy to infuse an international perspective in psychology (Clay, 2017), new multicultural guidelines (APA, 2017), and the development of guidelines for fostering international competencies (e.g., Morgan-Consoli et al., 2018). In addition to relevant entities in the United States endorsing such developments—particularly APA's Commission on Accreditation—international organizations as well as national professional and academic organizations based in other countries can garner similar support (e.g., see websites for the International Association of Applied Psychology—https://www.iaapsy.org—and the International Union of Psychological Science—https://www.iupsys.net).

Concomitant efforts should also be directed to HEIs in order to help administrators, faculty, and students as well as external policy makers realize the importance of internationalizing the curriculum in order to modernize education, enhance professional mobility and competitiveness, and make educational degrees in psychology optimally relevant within an increasingly global economy. Because psychology is one of the most common courses taken by students from all majors at HEIs across the United States and in other countries, psychologists are in a good position to promote such processes while influencing other disciplines and departments as well (Leong et al., 2012; Marsella & Pedersen, 2004).

CONCLUDING THOUGHTS

To internationalize the psychology curriculum on a widespread and substantive level, multiple actions are needed to address the instruction of psychology at educational institutions throughout the country that simultaneously assists departments to develop globally applicable, multiculturally sensitive, and international curricula, programs, and policies. The good news is, as illustrated by the many resources and ideas described in this chapter, the scope of psychology education and its attendant practices have dramatically expanded over the past few decades. Increasing international connections among psychologists, joint research, and projects across national and international boundaries, along with technological advances that facilitate communication, have all enhanced the potential for psychology to be a truly global discipline. As a consequence, cultural diversity and the global dimensions of psychology education will remain prominent and continue to thrive in the future.

In the final analysis, the inexorable forces of globalization are here to stay and will only become more prominent in the years to come. Thus, for psychology and psychologists to meet a world of need, we must strive as educators to apprehend and contribute to this ongoing evolution in ways that are meaningful and add value for our students, institutions, professional organizations, and the local and global citizens to which we ultimately are accountable. Certainly, our human interest in psychology transcends national boundaries and may be used as a way to understand and work not only with our species but with all living systems in order to help protect our planet and ensure a more viable future for us all.

REFERENCES

American Psychological Association. (2017). *Multicultural guidelines: An ecological approach to context, identity, and intersectionality.* https://doi.org/10.1037/e501962018-001

American Psychological Association Working Group on Internationalizing the Undergraduate Psychology Curriculum. (2005). *Report and recommended learning outcomes for internationalizing the undergraduate curriculum.* American Psychological Association. https://www.apa.org/ed/precollege/about/international.pdf

Aurora Universities Network. (2022). *Aurora Universities Network* [Home page]. https://aurora-network.global

Bartolini, L., Gharib, A., & Phillips, F. (2009, July). Internationalizing psychology courses. *Psychology International, 20*(3). https://www.apa.org/international/pi/2009/07/courses.aspx

Bond, S. (2003). *Untapped resources: Internationalization of the curriculum and classroom experience: A selected literature review* (CBIE Research Millennium Series No. 7). Canadian Bureau for International Education.

Bullock, M. (2012). Internationalizing resources for psychology programs through professional organizations. In S. McCarthy, K. L. Dickson, J. Cranney, A. Trapp, & V. Karandashev (Eds.), *Teaching psychology around the world* (Vol. 3, pp. 462–467). Cambridge Scholars Press.

Burgess, G. H., Sternberger, L. G., Sanchez-Sosa, J. J., Lunt, I., Shealy, C. N., & Ritchie, P. (2004). Development of a global curriculum for professional psychology: Implications of the combined-integrated model of doctoral training. *Journal of Clinical Psychology,* *60*(10), 1027–1049. https://doi.org/10.1002/jclp.20033

Chakkarath, P. (2005). What can Western psychology learn from Indigenous psychologies? Lessons from Hindu psychology. In W. Friedlmeier, P. Chakkarath, & Beate Schwarz (Eds.), *Culture and human development: The importance of cross-cultural research to the social sciences* (pp. 31–51). Psychology Press.

Clay, R. (2017, February). Weaving an international view into psychology education. *Monitor on Psychology, 48*(2), 60. https://www.apa.org/monitor/2017/02/international-view

Cranney, J., & Dunn, D. S. (Eds.). (2011). *The psychologically literate citizen: Foundations and global perspectives.* Oxford University Press. https://doi.org/10.1093/acprof:oso/9780199794942.001.0001

Deacon, B. J. (2013). The biomedical model of mental disorder: A critical analysis of its validity, utility, and effects on psychotherapy research. *Clinical Psychology Review, 33*(7), 846–861. https://doi.org/10.1016/j.cpr.2012.09.007

Farrugia, C., Bhandari, R., & Chow, P. (2012). *Open Doors 2012 Report on international education exchange.* Institute of International Education.

Grenwald, G., Oberlechner, T., & Velayo, R. (2012). Internationalizing postsecondary education in psychology: A global endeavor. *Psychology Learning & Teaching, 11*(3), 359–364. https://doi.org/10.2304/plat.2012.11.3.359

Grenwald, G., & Velayo, R. (2011). Internationalizing your psychology course: Preliminary survey findings. *International Psychology Bulletin, 15*(2), 53–58. https://www.researchgate.net/publication/324113642_Internationalizing_Your_Psychology_Course_Preliminary_Survey_Findings

Gross, D., Abrams, K., & Enns, C. Z. (Eds.). (2016). *Internationalizing the undergraduate psychology curriculum: Practical lessons learned at home and abroad.* American Psychological Association. https://www.apa.org/pubs/books/4316169.aspx?tab=2

Harden, R. M. (2006). International medical education and future directions: A global perspective. *Academic Medicine, 81*(12, Suppl.), S22–S29. https://doi.org/10.1097/01.ACM.0000243411.19573.58

Hawkey, K., McCarthy, S., Zubair, A., & Jaafar, J. (2012, July). *What is responsible for happiness? Cross-cultural comparison of quality of life indicators* [Conference session]. International Union of Psychological Sciences International Congress of Psychology, Cape Town, South Africa.

Henrich, J., Heine, S. J., & Norenzayan, A. (2010). The weirdest people in the world? *Behavioral and Brain Sciences, 33*(2–3), 61–83. https://doi.org/10.1017/S0140525X0999152X

Ikeda, K., Christersson, C., Dirkx, J., & Shealy, C. (March, 2022). *Applied global studies: Connecting international students through a virtual bridge* [Panel presentation]. Annual Conference of the Asia-Pacific Association for International Education, Vancouver, Canada.

Ikeda, K., Shealy, C., & Chistersson, C. (October, 2020). *Applied and engaged global studies: A virtual bridge to connect international students* [Panel presentation]. Annual Conference of the European Association for International Education, Virtual Convening, Institute for Innovative Global Education. https://www.kansai-u.ac.jp/Kokusai/IIGE/

International Beliefs and Values Institute. (2022). *Applied global studies: Preparing agents of change to meet a world of need.* http://www.ibavi.org/content/applied-global-studies.php

Institute of International Education. (2019). *2019 Project Atlas infographics.* https://www.iie.org/Research-and-Insights/Project-Atlas/Explore-Data/Infographics/2019-Project-Atlas-Infographics

Institute of International Education. (2020). *Open Doors 2020 fast facts.* https://opendoorsdata.org/wp-content/uploads/2020/05/Open-Doors-2020-Fast-Facts.pdf

Institute of International Education. (2022). *Open Doors.* https://www.iie.org/en/Research-and-Insights/Open-Doors

Institute for Innovative Global Education. (2022). *About IIGE*. https://www.kansai-u.ac.jp/Kokusai/IIGE/about/

Iyer, C. (2013). *Assessing and engaging beliefs and values in a learning community of U.S. and international students: Implications and applications from the forum BEVI project* (Publication No. 3592877) [Doctoral dissertation, James Madison University]. ProQuest Dissertations and Theses.

Jaafar, J., Kolodinsky, P., McCarthy, S., & Schroder, V. (2004). The impact of cultural norms and values on moral judgment of Malay and American adolescents: A brief report. In B. N. Setiadi, A. Supratiknya, W. J. Lonner, & Y. H. Poortinga (Eds.), *Ongoing themes in psychology and culture* (pp. 399–414). Selected papers from the Sixteenth International Congress of the International Association for Cross-Cultural Psychology, The International Association for Cross-Cultural Psychology.

Kesel, D., & McCarthy, S. (2013). Sarlito W. Sarwono: A force for developing psychology in Asia. *International Psychology Bulletin, 17*(1), 44–47.

Kim, U., Yang, K. S., & Hwang, K. K. (Eds.). (2006). *Indigenous and cultural psychology: Understanding people in context*. Springer.

Leong, F., Pickren, W., Leach, M., & Marsella, A. (Eds.). (2012). *Internationalizing the psychology curriculum in the United States*. Springer. https://doi.org/10.1007/978-1-4614-0073-8

Lonner, W., & Murdock, E. (2012). Introductory psychology texts and the inclusion of culture. *Online Readings in Psychology and Culture, 11*(1), Article 1. https://doi.org/10.9707/2307-0919.1115

Marsella, A., & Pedersen, P. (2004). Internationalizing the counseling psychology curriculum: Toward new values, competencies, and directions. *Counselling Psychology Quarterly, 17*(4), 413–423. https://doi.org/10.1080/09515070412331331246

McCarthy, S. (2002). Preventing future terrorist activities among adolescents through global psychology: A cooperative learning community. In C. Stout (Ed.), *Psychology of terrorism: Vol. 4. Child, family, and adolescent issues*. Greenwood-Praeger.

McCarthy, S., Jaafar, J., Kamal, A., & Zubair, A. (2013). *Psychology at work in Asia*. Cambridge Scholars Press.

McCarthy, S., Karandashev, V., Stevens, M., Thatcher, A., Jaafar, J., Moore, K., Trapp, A., & Brewer, C. (Eds.). (2009). *Teaching psychology around the world* (Vol. 2). Cambridge Scholars Publishing.

Morgan-Consoli, M. L., Inman, A. G., Bullock, M., & Nolan, S. A. (2018). Framework for competencies for U.S. psychologists engaging internationally. *International Perspectives in Psychology: Research, Practice, Consultation, 7*(3), 174–188. https://doi.org/10.1037/ipp0000090

Ramaswamy, M., Marciniuk, D. D., Csonka, V., Colò, l., & Saso, L. (2021). Reimagining internationalization in higher education through the United Nations sustainable development goals for the betterment of society. *Journal of Studies in International Education, 25*(4), 388–406. https://doi.org/10.1177/10283153211031046

Rich, G. J., Gielen, W. P., & Takooshian, H. (Eds.). (2017). *Internationalizing the teaching of psychology*. Information Age Publishing.

Shealy, C. N. (Ed.). (2016). *Making sense of beliefs and values: Theory, research, and practice*. Springer Publishing.

Silbereisen, R., Ritchie, P., & Pandey, J. (Eds.). (2014). *Psychology education and training: A global perspective*. Psychology Press. https://doi.org/10.4324/9781315851532

Sternberger, L. (2005). Partnering for success. *International Educator, 14*(4), 12–21.

Sternberger, L., Ford, K., & Hale, D. (2005). International service-learning: Integrating academics and active learning in the world. *Journal of Public Affairs, 8*, 75–92.

Sternberger, L., Pysarchik, D., Yun, Z., & Deardorff, D. (2009). Designing a model for international learning assessment. *Diversity and Democracy: Civic Learning for Shared Futures, 12*(1), 7–9.

Sternberger, L. G., & Wang, F. (2015). Higher education: Partnership for the future. In N. Jooste, H. De Wit, & S. Heleta (Eds.), *Higher education internationalization in the developing world* (pp. 83–93). Nelson Mandela Metropolitan University.

Stevens, M. (2009). Education and training of international psychologists: The current status of internationalization of the psychology curriculum. In S. McCarthy, V. Karandashev, M. Stevens, A. Thatcher, J. Jaafar, K. Moore, A. Trapp, & C. Brewer (Eds.) *Teaching psychology around the world* (Vol. 2, pp. 39–59). Cambridge Scholars Press.

Stevens, M., & Gielen, U. (Eds.). (2007). *Toward a global psychology: Theory, research, intervention, and pedagogy.* Lawrence Erlbaum.

SummitX. (2022). *Cultivating the globally sustainable self: How the human species might fulfill its potential.* https://summitx.org/cultivating-the-globally-sustainable-self-how-the-human-species-might-fulfill-its-potential/

Takooshian, H., Gielen, U. P., Plous, S., Rich, G. J., & Velayo, R. S. (2016). Internationalizing undergraduate psychology education: Trends, techniques, and technologies. *American Psychologist, 71*(2), 136–147. https://doi.org/10.1037/a0039977

Velayo, R. S. (2012). Internationalizing the curriculum. In J. E. Groccia, M. A. Alsudairi, & W. Buskist (Eds.), *Handbook of college and university teaching: A global perspective* (pp. 268–278). Sage. https://doi.org/10.4135/9781412996891.n18

Velayo, R. S. (2015). *Internationalize undergraduate psychology.* American Psychological Association. https://www.apa.org/education/undergrad/internationalize.aspx

Velayo, R. S., Grenwald, G., & Manfred, M. M. (2012, Fall). How psychology instructors internationalize their courses: Strategies, perspectives, and implications. *International Psychology Bulletin, 16*(4), 48–53. https://internationalpsychology.files.wordpress.com/2012/12/ipb_fall_2012-10-06-4_final_revised.pdf

Wandschneider, E., Pysarchik, D. T., Sternberger, L. G., Ma, W., Acheson, K., Baltensperger, B., Good, R. T., Brubaker, B., Baldwin, T., Nishitani, H., Wang, F., Reisweber, J., & Hart, V. (2015). The forum BEVI project: Applications and implications for international, multicultural, and transformative learning. *Frontiers, 25*(1), 150–228. https://doi.org/10.36366/frontiers.v25i1.350

Wang, F., Pait, K., Acheson, K., Sternberger, L., Staton, R., & Shealy, C. N. (2020). Beliefs, Events and Values Inventory assessment of global identity: Implications and applications for international, cross-cultural and transformative learning. In J. Frawley, G. Russell, & J. Sherwood (Eds.), *Cultural competence and the higher education sector* (pp. 83–113). Springer. https://doi.org/10.1007/978-981-15-5362-2_6

10

Concluding Thoughts on *Going Global*

How Psychologists Should Meet a World of Need

Craig Shealy, Merry Bullock, and Shagufa Kapadia

We've come to our concluding chapter of *Going Global*, but in truth, this journey was underway long before us and will continue to be chronicled long after we're gone. Human beings have always "gone global," whether that meant the next village, country, continent, or planet, beyond the horizon we knew or imagined was "out there." We are going to find out what's out there; we always have and always will. When Wilhelm Wundt established the first psychology laboratory in 1879 at the University of Leipzig in Germany, he could not have imagined how psychology, as a discipline and profession, would traverse the world in the years to come.

Think about it. Over the past 150 years, we psychologists have expanded our scope from basic laws of sensory experience to models of group action to directing our accumulated knowledge and skills toward the most pressing issues of our day, all over the world. Along the way, we've developed sophisticated theories, research methods, and practical applications that address countless aspects of human form and function. From inventing procedures for selecting military personnel in both of the World Wars, to developing successful models for treating serious psychopathology, to helping lawmakers and the judiciary understand that separate is not equal because of how prejudice is internalized, we psychologists have provided voluminous evidence about how to optimize humanity's potential as a species. We've shown the importance of early attachment, illuminated how language develops, and demonstrated how trauma affects the brain, even across generations. And we've done so much

https://doi.org/10.1037/0000311-011
Going Global: How Psychologists Can Meet a World of Need, C. Shealy, M. Bullock, and S. Kapadia (Editors)

more. From astronauts and athletes to zealotry and zoophobia, psychologists are interested in, well, everything, and for good reason. Our discipline and profession are about humanity, all of us, all over the world: who we are, where we came from, where we are going, and how we might get there. And not just us, but other living things, their relationships to us, and our responsibilities to them.

Do we always get it right? No. As our authors rightly document, we have failed, sometimes grievously, particularly to value the voiceless, learn from the marginalized, and protect the most vulnerable among us. At our worst, we have colluded with and perpetuated racist concepts, some of which were responsible for reprehensible practices like eugenics and forced sterilization. Likewise, we still have a long way to go to integrate notions of what it means to be human from countries and cultures very different from psychology's roots in the West. Rectifying these acts of commission and omission are not trivial matters and must be pursued with passion and persistence if we are to fulfill our potential to become a truly global field of inquiry and practice.

As psychology becomes more global, we will become more able to recognize and respond to global needs, as exhaustively documented across multiple literatures, including those presented in the Introduction to this volume and the previous nine chapters. One does not have to be a psychologist to feel and see the urgency of these matters: from the reasons why human beings continue to deny climate change—the most serious existential threat we face as a species—and wanton acts of violence we perpetrate against one another, to vexing quandaries like how different religious systems can coexist while maintaining that theirs is the only "true faith," to the overdue delivery of delayed justice for those who have been marginalized and oppressed. Humanity's problems are ineluctably psychological in nature. Therefore, psychology and psychologists need to be part of the solution.

The chapters in this book describe the scope and nature of problems and solutions that call for the application of our expertise across nine areas of emphasis: advocacy, assessment, consultation, intervention, leadership, policy, research, service, and teaching. As we have seen, each of these domains provides abundant opportunities to meet a world of need, a process that is already advanced by our colleagues through venues all over the world, both locally and globally (e.g., https://www.unpsychologyday.com/). So, rather than summarizing what already has been written in the preceding chapters, we thought it might be helpful to conclude with some "notes from the field," or big-picture perspectives regarding what it really means for psychology and psychologists to meet a world of need. Our purpose here is not to review more literature or point the way forward within a specific area of inquiry or practice. That already has been done. What we want to do here is speak from experience, and from the heart, about what it is really like to walk this talk—questions to consider and points to ponder—both locally and globally. As psychologists who still want to make a difference in the world, these are the sorts of perspectives we wish we had heard when we were just getting started or became lost along the way. As you chart and navigate your own life path, we hope these notes from the field are helpful for you.

MEETING A WORLD OF NEED: FOUR QUESTIONS TO CONSIDER

From our perspective, at least four fundamental questions should be asked if we want to "go global" and "meet a world of need":

1. Can we believe in something bigger than ourselves?
2. What is our capacity for complexity?
3. Can we cultivate mind and heart?
4. What will we do with our lives?

Question 1: Can We Believe in Something Bigger Than Ourselves?

If you are called to try and "move the needle" on issues that matter deeply to you, it is very important to recognize that you can only do so much alone. This observation is especially salient for students of psychology—as we all continue to be—because so many of us are attracted to this field and profession to help others. It is tempting to deride this intention as naïve, but we feel the opposite. Listening to our colleagues over the years, we regularly hear versions of ourselves: wanting to make a difference and trying to figure out how best to do that. In our view, this wellspring of hope emanates from deep within us. Through this book, it is our wish to provide navigable maps to canalize the flow of these essential waters.

One privilege of living a relatively long life is that you discover how to do what you want to do more effectively. You become more strategic and realistic while hopefully remaining connected to your capacity to care and inclination to act. Along the way, you learn about constraints, contingencies, systems, and structures. You may become cynical or wary after being ensnared in the ambitions of others or seeing how power is misused to virtue signal, stave off threat, enhance ego, or diminish opposition. On the other hand, you might be fortunate to have observed the use of power in a way that is wise, compassionate, and humble—a model worth emulating in your own life and work. Finally, in your professional life, you may witness the stark contrast between disturbed and disturbing political, personality, and group dynamics and the hopeful arcs we so often experience in young people: to be and become agents of change. That keeps you going.

Despite accumulated wariness as the years roll on—from battles waged and forgotten, lost and won—if you continue to strive for learning and growth, soldiering on with a true heart and open mind, the most important lesson you may learn is that you are not alone. If you are genuinely kind to others, cultivating the capacity to really listen and care, you will find that the inner student is often alive and well in self and other. We hear this hope in our valued colleagues who still strive to be global psychologists and citizens of conscience when they let down their guard over a glass of wine and feel safe enough to say what they really feel. They are often tired from fighting the good fight for so many years. But with kindred spirits, the longing to make real that which should be is an animating force that ascends from deep within us, binding us together in common cause and commitment. In those moments, we take courage and heart from the Welsh poet and writer Dylan Thomas's (1937/1971) poem "Do Not Go Gentle Into That Good Night." We feel the wisdom of his words in our own lives and work.

All that said, it also is important to recognize that being and becoming an effective agent of global change is often mediated by both (a) meritocracy, or the power one accrues as a result of ability directed and effort expended over an extended period of time; and (b) fortuity, consisting of where one is born, and to whom, as well as the circumstances and privileges that comprise one's lot in life. It is easy to attribute your success to your efforts alone, just as it is easy to attribute the success of others to the privilege they inherited. Don't make either mistake because life is typically not so simple. Meritocracy and fortuity interact to produce the life trajectories, processes, and outcomes that are variously deemed to be "successful" or not.

Question 2: What Is Our Capacity for Complexity?

The journey of putting together *Going Global* has spanned years, for reasons that were anticipated and many more that were not. Throughout this process, what has been most interesting to us as editors and authors are the deflection points of consilience and contention that emerged along the way. Perhaps not surprisingly, especially in a book grappling with international and multicultural implications and applications, one of the most complex issues we encountered exists along the etic–emic cultural continuum (e.g., Fetvadjiev & van de Vijver, 2015). Derivative from the study of linguistics and anthropology, and highly relevant to psychologists who are interested in going global, Segall et al. (1990) offered the following explanation of these terms:

> This distinction between culture-specific and universal behaviors is one version of what has been come to be known in cross-cultural psychology as the "emic/etic" distinction. . . . We can say, for example, that if there is a universal behavior, like aggression at a high level of abstraction, that behavior is an "etic." We would refer to a specific variety of aggressive behavior, one that might be peculiar to a given society, as an "emic." We are here suggesting that there are two different levels of analysis in the study of human behavior—emic or etic . . . [and] that a combined emic–etic approach be used. (pp. 53–56)

Other scholars and practitioners agree that the etic–emic distinction may represent an artificial dichotomy and should instead be seen as a continuum. As Fetvadjiev and van de Vijver (2015) observed,

> the emic–etic distinction has been redefined as referring to endpoints of a continuum that ranges from cultural specificity (emic) to universality (etic). In this new approach, emic and etic aspects can coexist and work together because many phenomena studied in cross-cultural research have both universal and culture-specific aspects. (pp. 752–753)

As may be clear, the etic–emic question has profound relevance for psychology and psychologists because our answers determine whether, and to what degree, we (a) believe that our models and methods have applicability across cultures and contexts when they did not emerge from within them and (b) recognize that psychology as it is taught in the Western world is essentially a Euro American construction.

We agree that etic–emic matters are best considered along a continuum, but as is often the case, the devil is in the details, as became clear in some of our internal dialogues, including discussions we had about the relevance or appropriateness of various findings and theories across cultures and contexts. Such considerations are expressed through a myriad of terms, such as "intercultural sensitivity," "privilege," "generalizability," "diversity," "equity," "inclusion," "indigenization," and "de-colonization." Constructs like these are designed to challenge, but they also must bear scrutiny, particularly if they are applied indiscriminately or discriminatorily. Points and points of view relevant to these constructs emerged time and again in the book's nine topical chapters, and we will not reiterate what has already been written. Rather, we think it would be most useful to illuminate the nature of our own thought processes as we grappled with these complexities, since that is where "the rubber met the road" from an editorial perspective.

Although there are many different ways to understand the implications or applications of terms and constructs referring to an etic–emic continuum, a common consideration for us concerned whether, how, and to what degree theories, findings, or practices developed in one culture or context are in fact (a) valid within a different culture and context; or (b) should be examined and revised or discarded in favor of local, within country, or Indigenous understandings, findings, or practices. Obviously, these issues are highly complex and often must be considered on a case-by-case basis, but we were seeking a degree of conceptual consensus among us (i.e., how to think about such matters).

After much back-and-forth dialogue over the years, prompted in no small part by the perspectives raised by chapter authors, we find ourselves in accord that psychological findings, theories, and practices should be evaluated and reevaluated in light of cultural exigencies (i.e., we agree with the emic stance in this regard). However, we also agree with the value of striving for appropriate levels of generalizable models and methods—that is, that the relevance of theories and applications should not be rejected, wholly or in part, solely on the basis of who developed them, in what period of time, or in what country or region (i.e., we agree with the etic stance in this regard). This middle ground, as Shagufa dubbed it, calls for considerable capacity to hold complexity and seems like a good and grounding principle to us (see also Berry, 1999; Fetvadjiev & van de Vijver, 2015). Such a perspective also seems highly congruent with the following fundamental point from the vision statement of the American Psychological Association's (APA's) Division of International Psychology, which contends that psychologists and psychology should

> openly explore and engage a globally inclusive and epistemologically diverse understanding of psychology as a discipline and profession, while a) respectfully

and credibly appraising established and emerging models, methods, and world-views from the Global North, South, East, and West and b) eschewing the reflexive and superficial embrace or rejection of any particular paradigm or approach, regardless of origin, culture, or context. (APA Division of International Psychology, 2022, Section 2.2)

We concur and offer such a perspective to our readers as we grapple together with these complex and fascinating issues that are, and should be, of relevance to everyone.

Question 3: Can We Cultivate Mind and Heart?

As psychologists, in addition to believing in something bigger than our-selves and expanding our capacity to hold complexity, it also would be good if we could value the cultivation of kindness as much as the acquisition of knowledge. In this regard, it can be disheartening to behold otherwise brilliant colleagues—who find themselves in positions of authority, influence, or leadership—ignoring or dismissing the deleterious impact of their care-less words and deeds on others. Such conduct manifests in multiple forms, such as (a) overlooking the diminishment or disenfranchisement of others as a result of what we say and do, or what we don't say and don't do; (b) seeing the world in black and white rather than in shades of gray; and (c) becoming smitten with our talent and predilection for arguing each other into sub-mission. That is what we mean by "privileging mind over heart." Although various etiologies exist for this way of being, one that we psychologists excel at is intellectualization. We are also exceptionally capable of condemning others who do not meet whatever standard we—and our theoretical or applied tribe—have deemed to be appropriate or correct.

Of course, we acknowledge the many instances of constructive and collab-orative dialogue that characterize our work and relationships, so we are simply advocating for an ever-richer ratio in that direction in order to model such conduct for ourselves and for our students. In this regard, we believe APA's five Ethical Principles—Beneficence and Nonmaleficence, Fidelity and Responsi-bility, Integrity, Justice, and Respect for People's Rights and Dignity—provide powerful guidance and inspiration regarding our conduct and relationships as psychologists, both locally and globally (see https://www.apa.org/ethics/code).

The point is, when conflict arises—as it will—perhaps we can agree to take a deep breath, turn down the temperature, and see each other not as inten-tionally acting poorly but as flawed human beings who are all trying to reach greater understanding. We believe such actions and values are much more likely to get at "the truth," which often lies somewhere in between the extremes but too often gets shouted down by the loudest voices, which are "vexations to the spirit" as *Desiderata* reminds us (https://mwkworks.com/desiderata.html).

The same admonitions apply more generally to conflicts in our field, wher-ever they occur, and particularly between the scientific and humanistic end-points of Kimble's (1984) "two cultures." Wouldn't it be nice to stop shouting at each other—in our meetings and in print—and start listening more with an open mind and heart? Likewise, could we attend more to questions concerning "why" in addition to "what," by examining not just what we believe to be good and true, or bad and false, but why we hold the convictions and commitments we do in the first place? In short, perhaps we could step back a bit more, consider explanations as well as conclusions, and embrace each other as fellow humans who strive to find meaning and purpose, feel that we are known and have value, and see and believe that we matter?

Question 4: What Will We Do With Our Lives?

The precise wording is disputed (Elms, 2001), but Sigmund Freud would likely have resonated with a quotation that is often attributed to him: "Love and work . . . work and love, that's all there is." Likewise, although we might quibble over the parameters of this assertation, lived experiences suggest that much of human existence is devoted to this twin pursuit. So, if one wants to meet a world of need, it is worth reflecting persistently on the values that propel us forward each day of our life. In this regard, it may help to reflect often on Jacob Marley's admonition to Scrooge in Charles Dickens's *A Christmas Carol*, that wealth or power are not the marker of success. As the ghost of Marley repentantly avows, "Mankind was my business. The common welfare was my business; charity, mercy, forbearance, benevolence, were all my business. The dealings of my trade were but a drop of water in the comprehensive ocean of my business."

Perhaps our education and training programs in psychology could set aside some time to focus on such matters, and not just when discussing our philosophical roots or the historical schools of thought that built our foundations. Yes, it is necessary to expose our students to great theorists and theories, but it is not sufficient if we are to meet a world of need. We also need to consider why, how, whether, and to what degree such people and perspectives advance the common welfare. Along with prowess and competence, we need to emphasize compassion, humility, engagement, and service because these values are all integral not only to our discipline and profession but also to what we do and whom we become. For if we don't draw such linkages for our students, why should we be surprised if they don't do so in their own lives and work?

From the standpoint of education, training, and credentialing—particularly in light of our accreditation, licensure, and continuing education systems—we tend to focus a lot on the trees of foundational areas (e.g., abnormal, behavioral, biological, cognitive, cultural, developmental, educational, experimental, motivation, personality, social) and applied areas (e.g., clinical, counseling, evaluation, forensic, health, industrial and organizational, school, sport, statistics), rather than how our forest—psychology—is part of a larger system of interdisciplinary and intercultural groves. Although we psychologists live in our own woods, we also share many interests and goals with colleagues who inhabit other forests. It is important for our students to know that, so their gaze is lifted up to the canopy and the wide world beyond even as they stand upon interconnected roots that are communicating away in the substrate below. Without such awareness, they won't know where they are grounded, or what is beyond them, and may be prone to set their gaze and life's work on one specific tree without awareness of its place in the global forest. Whether one strives to become a generalist (the forest) or specialist (the tree)—or to move back and forth between these levels of analysis—it is important to understand (a) how and why one's life's work fits into the larger ecosystem and (b) on the basis of such understanding, be optimally reflective regarding the allocation of time and effort through one's career.

To be clear, we value theoretical, scholarly, and practical advancement for its own sake. However, we are suggesting there is merit in asking our students and ourselves to think about the purpose of living and the meaning of life, for such questions—more than the answers—are likely to shape and enrich our personal and professional endeavors. What if we actively listened to the wants and wishes of others, imagining that their vision of the greater good may be just as valid as our own? What if we prized people who exemplified empathy for the human condition and the natural world? What if we privileged projects that were about equity, justice, and empowerment? What if we set aside time to talk about the news—what is happening locally and globally—and how our discipline and profession might respond? What if we valued collaboration— the process of joining together—rather than going it alone? What if we focused on the facilitation and evaluation of transformation—individually, relationally, communally, nationally, and globally? What if we embraced the arts and humanities as well as the sciences and social sciences? What would our students be and become, and how would they spend their lives, if values like these were voiced and lived, albeit imperfectly, by us? In short, to meet a world of need, we acknowledge the wisdom of Reinhold Niebuhr's (1952) contention that "anything worth doing takes more than one lifetime," to which we would humbly add, "and more than one life."

GOING GLOBAL: CLOSING PERSPECTIVES ON MEETING A WORLD OF NEED

In the introductory chapter of *Going Global*, we offered the following inspiration from Lao Tzu: "The journey of a thousand miles begins with a single step." Although expressed over 2,500 years ago, that perspective seems timely and bears repeating as we close this book by inviting you to write your own chapter wherever you are in your life and career, whether a beginning student taking your first introductory psychology course or an established professional heading toward retirement. In our experience—knowing and working for decades with psychology students, colleagues, and friends all across the lifespan and all over the world—it is never too early or late to take that single step forward as you navigate your own life journey in our fascinating field of inquiry and practice. To help, we thought it would be good to conclude by asking a number of us, starting with authors and ending with editors, to answer the following question, which captures the letter and spirit of this book: In order to go global and meet a world of need, what recommendations would you offer to psychology and psychologists? We hope the responses that follow offer a final measure of inspiration as you walk your own journey of a thousand miles.

PSYCHOLOGISTS GOING GLOBAL: CONCLUDING THOUGHTS FROM CONTRIBUTORS AND EDITORS

Thema Bryant-Davis

Going global requires a sustained commitment to cultural humility, decolonial psychology, and Indigenous psychology. Before we go out into the world as psychologists, we must look within to examine our biases, assumptions, and privileges as individuals and as a field. When we seek to serve globally without introspection, we can engage in harmful practices based in the false belief that psychologists from the West are the experts who are going to save people who lack knowledge or skills. This falsehood doesn't honor the voices, wisdom, and rights of international communities to shape and define themselves. Lack of humility disrupts the possibility of trust and collaboration with the global community. Cultural humility is a stance that resists a one-size-fits-all approach based on interventions and studies conducted with a narrow population.

Additionally, going global requires a decolonial approach to psychology. While Western psychology often focuses on the individual's symptoms of distress, a decolonial approach attends to context, including the sociopolitical factors that affect people's lives both past and present. Finally, we need an indigenizing psychology that acknowledges, appreciates, and appropriately integrates the cultural resources and wellness practices that predate the field of psychology. Many needs face our world, and we can be part of the solution if we participate with cultural humility, a contextualized perspective, and an appreciation for diverse pathways. It is also important to note that Western society has problems that need to be addressed. Western psychologists are part of the global community but not separate from it.

William E. Hanson

With increased globalization, extensive cross-national test use, and widespread crisscrossing around the world, we psychologists must first do no harm. We must also act in good faith, with a crystal-clear understanding of cross-cultural assessment issues, including those related to psychological testing, measurement, and program evaluation. Fortunately, psychologists are leaders in this regard. Given their leadership and expertise in assessment, they make meaningful and measurable differences in the lives of many. However, to go global, psychologists are encouraged to think complexly about assessment issues around the world, act flexibly, and become intimately familiar with published resources, international organizations, and various emic and etic practices globally.

Psychologists are also encouraged to immerse themselves in different cultures. Immersion and exposure are critically important aspects of becoming multiculturally competent and providing culturally sensitive and responsive assessment services. As always, psychologists are also encouraged to maintain scientific attitudes and mindsets, that is, being curious and open-minded while simultaneously asking, "Where's the evidence? What's its quality? And is it appropriate to culture and context as well as ecologically valid?" Additionally, psychologists are encouraged to work collaboratively and empathically, whether locally or abroad. Finally, and perhaps most important, psychologists are encouraged to become deeply reflective and highly self-aware, particularly regarding assessment-related biases, personal beliefs and values, and worldviews. In so doing, psychologists will continue meeting—and positively affecting—a world of need.

Connie Henson

In the past several years, disparity in access to resources, health, and fundamental freedoms has increased for many people. Those without access also experience reduced recognition and respect for their diverse ways of learning, thinking, and being in the world. This disparity is not just between high- and low-income countries but also within nations. The accumulated wealth and privilege in many high-income countries masks the poverty and deprivation experienced by minority segments of the broader population of these countries. Moreover, the concentration of power in many countries has resulted in many peoples, cultures, and needs being invisible to the wider population. As such, consulting psychologists must see what is not seen by acquiring competencies, such as self-awareness and the ability to question assumptions and expectations.

Likewise, consulting psychologists learn how to collaborate with people who are different from themselves to achieve mutually agreed positive change. All of these skills and practices are essential for addressing the worsening inequity between and within national boundaries. Now more than ever, consulting psychologists can use our knowledge and our practices to address disparities found in virtually all aspects of our work. In a world that is becoming more inequitable, it is not enough to just not be racist, elitist, or misogynistic. Leadership carries the responsibility to be active in antiracism and antielitism and profeminist in our lives and work in the world. Consulting psychologists are well positioned to contribute.

Laura Johnson

Can psychology interpret the magnitude of the present moment and realize its full potential to heal a world in need? Nature provides a clear and scoping view of our challenges, guideposts for the necessary effort, and a promise for adaptive resilience through our collective efforts to advance wellness in the world.

Wake Up to the Anthropocene

Will psychologists wake up to our true situation with a clear view of ourselves, society, and planet Earth? We have entered the Anthropocene, a time when humankind has left an indelible mark on the geological record and enacts a daily toll. A sustainable psychology necessitates a sustainable planet. With an eye to sustainable development goals, human rights, and social justice, psychologists can find ways to align their efforts toward a just and sustainable future.

Think Like a Mountain

"Only the mountain has lived long enough to listen objectively to the howl of a wolf" (A. Leopold, 1986). I invite psychologists to come outside to play. It is time we leave our isolated, disciplinary-bound silos of operation that lead to individual professional gains. Systems thinking promotes a deeper understanding, ever-widening circles of possibility, and a greater moral commitment to address complex challenges of our children's time. A diversity of perspectives, that includes the most marginalized, can catapult psychologists' potential for meaningful impact.

Follow the Fungi

Through complex underground networks of mycelium, fungi engage in symbiotic relationships with plant roots, resulting in interplant communication, sharing resources, and other adaptive behaviors. Adaptation and resilience, in plants and among people, can be cultivated through collective effort.

Sandra Shullman

The COVID-19 pandemic has clearly shown that the world's health, economy, climate, and general well-being are pointedly interdependent. Yet, much of Western-based psychology and psychologists operate from a limited Eurocentric view of psychology. In the United States, for example, global psychology issues are often addressed as special topics and often conceived as how Western concepts can be applied elsewhere. For psychology and psychologists to truly go global and meet a world of need, we must first recognize that context is critical to psychology and that other parts of the world have a great deal to teach us about psychological issues and other contexts. To make psychology a truly global discipline, we must consider doing the following:

- developing better avenues for accessing and integrating research from other countries and cultures, such as global research and intervention networks and global, interdisciplinary research and intervention teams;

- asking broader questions and seek broader, global samples or populations;

- adopting a global population health model of intervention;

- working with psychology training councils to integrate global curriculum;

- routinely putting a global lens on all policy, intervention, and research questions;

- leveraging national memos of understanding to create multinational research and intervention structures;

- getting major funders in resourced countries to support principal investigators who partner with researchers in less resourced countries;

- streaming global and national conferences and national psychological association meetings to create real global access and incorporate topics and presenters globally;

- training our practitioners to think globally as they address issues of immigration, international populations, and social justice issues, such as conflict, climate change, racism, poverty, and health equity; and

- actively seeking cross-national and cross-cultural mutual learning experiences.

Above all, we must come to view all of psychology and all psychologists across the globe as learning partners, developing mutually respectful professional relationships. Global learning partnerships and strategies will engender global psychology solutions. As Walt Disney so eloquently stated, "You can't learn from experiences you aren't having."[1]

Lee Sternberger

Although I am trained as a clinical psychologist, I have worked in the administration of international education for my entire career. I didn't study abroad until I was in my mid-30s, and my daughter was 2-and-a-half years old. I can still remember my first trip to London as a graduate student (again) when I went back to school to earn a master's degree in architectural history. My life path changed over those months, and I've never looked back. Since then, donning my administrator and psychologist hats, I've witnessed and researched the profound impact of international experiences on students, both undergraduate and graduate. Through mixed methods assessment all over the world, we see empirically that students demonstrate through a myriad of modalities—from study abroad and service learning to internships and travel— the transformative nature of interacting with and learning from the contexts and cultures of others.

The world has already gone global, and psychology must continue to do so as well. The pandemic of 2020 and 2021 has reshaped our lives, at least

---

[1]Quote attributed to Walt Disney in a seminar attended by Randall P. White at a Disney University Backstage event. See also Izard, R. (1967). Walt Disney: Master of laughter and learning. *Peabody Journal of Education, 45*(1), 36–41.

temporarily. And while life will return to a semblance of normalcy, I hope some aspects of our present reality will remain. For example, I've always been a big believer in distance learning, and the era we are living through has taught us how nimble and creative we can be as teachers and supervisors in this digital age. In particular, virtual exchange (VE) and collaborative online international learning (COIL) are here to stay. Through paradigms and technologies like VE and COIL, students and faculty can have profoundly meaningful and academically rigorous experiences working internationally. As global psychologists, we need to explore and embrace methodologies like these. They provide options for students who may never study abroad, since many, if not most, of our students will never leave their country of origin due to financial exigencies or practical matters beyond their control. So, if we're really committed to diversity, equity, and inclusion, let's champion models and methods like VE and COIL, which make that which is global, local. In the final analysis, whether virtually or in person, after immersion in someone else's world—when the heartfelt act of saying goodbye encounters a newfound hope to say hello again—we are realizing a time-tested way go global and meet a world of need.

Merry Bullock

We are drawn to psychology for many reasons, and for many reasons, some of us choose to go global with our scholarship and activism. For me, those reasons changed over time. I was initially drawn to psychology for its certainty. It was the age of behaviorism, and the promise was that a science of behavior would tell us all we wanted to know about why and how humans worked. Culture, if it was mentioned at all, was simply another stimulus variable. My own subsequent development mirrored some of the sea changes in psychology. Our ways of reconciling our own human experience and our observations as psychological scientists began to include the mind, motivation, social behavior, and a constructive view of consciousness and experience. Yet psychology was still, to me, a science of universals.

In many ways, I became a global psychologist accidentally as an unanticipated consequence of living and working in universities in multiple countries. After completing all my education in the United States, I moved progressively farther away—to Canada, then to Germany, and later to Estonia. My experiences as an initial outsider, in places that many see as functionally equivalent in terms of Western culture, shook my assumptions of what was normative, assumed, and presumably obvious both in everyday life and in professional approaches in psychology.

When I returned to the United States, it was a time of attempted global inclusiveness with the mantra "We are all the same." But my own experience was that we were fundamentally not the same and perhaps not the same because of the differences in sweeping expectations, norms, language, customs, history, and styles that—at least in my experience—varied with geography. At the same time, my own work in psychology was slowly becoming broader.

I began as a scholar in basic developmental science, but was soon involved in more applied work elicited by the questions my students and ultimately my employers asked: How do things work in application, and how do we take basic research to be useful in real-world applications? How can our science make the world a better place? And how does culture underlie our differences in perspective and identity?

Those of you who are going global now are doing so in a profession that approaches global action and culture in more sophisticated ways, and you are doing so in a world that offers many more opportunities for interaction, engagement, and collaboration. But even though the world offers more opportunities, I believe the challenges of engaging in that world remain the same as they have been since international collaboration began. The challenges are that international work is slow, it must be meticulous, and it requires an extraordinary level of curiosity, self-reflection, humility, and deep listening. Being effective also requires building broad learning partnerships with local experts. Meeting some of these challenges is straightforward—we can all learn patience and to be careful in our work—but it requires putting your ego on hold and being a quiet observer, even if you are present as a putative expert. As an outsider to any culture, you cannot know the errors you will make and the nuances you will miss (how can we know what we do not know?!), but you can be willing to err, willing to be corrected, and humble about listening to, reflecting on, and accepting the perspectives of others. I am not sure we can ever stand in another's shoes, but we can learn to recognize that they are not our own shoes and that the person in those shoes may have a perspective more valid than our own.

The chapters in this book offer some extraordinary insights into ways that psychologists can go global. As you read through them, you may be inspired by the opportunities. As editors, we hope you are. But my admonishment stands: this work is hard because there is no clear road map, there are few easy inroads, and there is much uncertainty. But the rewards are strong, too: connecting with others, being useful, and for me—and I suspect for most authors in this book—doing the work that makes your heart sing.

Shagufa Kapadia

I respond to this question from the vantage point of a scholar who was initiated into psychology and human development by reading theory and research that essentially originated in the Western world. Engaging with the brilliant and fascinating scholarship on human development was a joy, and yet, I often observed a niggling disjunct between what I learned in class with my experiences in real life; it was kind of like "now I see it, now I don't." This feeling especially came to the fore during an undergraduate course focusing on adolescence, titled "Understanding One's Own Self." Among other theories, we learned about G. Stanley Hall's famous dictum "sturm und drang," and much as I tried to identify with it, it just seemed to elude me.

Seeds of discontent were sown and stayed with me for a few years until I was introduced to the concept of indigenization and cross-cultural approaches to understanding human development. A kind of relief swept over me to learn about the culture–development interface. The subdiscipline of cross-cultural psychology (despite its primary interest in peeling away culture to arrive at core universals), and even more so cultural psychology, was appealing in its assertion and empirical demonstration that culture shapes development. I share here some contemplations that I think we need to reflect upon together, through dialogue, discussion, and collaboration rooted in sensitivity and compassion. The head and the heart must work together.

At the outset, I invoke Wilhelm Wundt, the architect of modern Western psychology. In learning about his work, what many of us seem to have overlooked is his recognition of two complementary traditions in psychology: the natural science tradition and the cultural science tradition. The former somehow overshadowed the latter, rendering modern psychology largely divested of culture. I bring up this point in our journey toward a global psychology because it may be worthwhile to pause and look back on ideas of scholars past.

Today, psychology is undergoing a transformation anchored in two dimensions: one is toward greater culture and context sensitivity, and the other is applicability to global problems (Kapadia, 2011). Non-Western academic contexts of psychology in particular are grappling with yet another transition that involves a process of discovering, relearning, and integrating concepts, theories, and methods that likely make more sense in their cultural contexts.

As psychologists, we need to develop the patience and perseverance to observe, understand, and, whenever possible, even engage with alternate perspectives. At the same time, we need to guard ourselves against over-simplifying characterizations of "other" societies (for instance, the individualist/collectivist, or I/C, dichotomy, which is a dominant reference in cross-cultural research). Attributing broad, monolithic labels to cultures and societies precludes attention to variations and inequities (e.g., gender, ethnicity, class, caste) within culture, which are critical as they mediate situational variables (e.g., nature of parenting, access to health care facilities) that constrain or facilitate well-being.

We know that cultures differ in their ways of making sense of this world. Some prefer binaries, whereas others are more comfortable with options and possibilities that hover in the gray zone or even a coexistence of contradictions. Exploring other worldviews and models of psychology bears immense potential for discovering psychological concepts and variations that may not be part of one's cultural repertoire (e.g., the Buddhist concept of mindfulness or the Hindu-Indian model of *panch koshas*, which emphasizes self-realization in terms of knowing oneself as a part of universal consciousness), all in favor of broadening our understanding of human behavior and its potential.

Importantly, we need to accept that the workings of mind and behavior are largely embedded in context. Even today, we find that psychology leans more toward the positivist paradigm that privileges a decontextualized, individualistic model of human development. This may well be one reason why it remains largely disconnected with lived realities. Greater attention to individual–context interface may also help us to overcome the oft experienced dissonance between the formal academic study of psychology with the psychology that unfolds in our everyday lives. Only then can the discipline become a catalyst for positive and equitable social change on the ground. The onus is upon us to devise approaches that allow us to probe into and unveil the intricacies that people experience in their everyday lives as therein lie the real stories. And unless we know these stories, we may be able to do little to help.

Most of all, we need to shift away from the tendency to treat other world-views or concepts as "add-ons" or "boxes of exotic interest" and instead move toward keeping an open mind and generating models that truly include diversity as a central element of human life and living. It would bode well to expand the boundaries of psychology to invite other traditions and approaches of understanding the human mind and behavior, which may lead us to dis-cover a more comprehensive and pluralistic universal, if that is the quest.

Here, I draw an analogy between the current state of psychology and the Indian parable of the blind men and an elephant. A group of blind men have never encountered an elephant before. They are learning to conceptualize it by touching it. Each blind man feels a different part of the elephant's body and describes it from his particular perspective. Obviously, their descriptions are rather different from each other. Each one is describing the reality that he is feeling, and yet the concept of the elephant as a whole remains elusive. It is only by understanding the description of the others and collectively making sense of how the parts integrate to form a meaningful whole can they comprehend the real image of the elephant. The parable illustrates well how our culturally subjective realities can be true and yet fall short of other realities.

As a community of psychologists who share a common goal, we need to reach out to each other and make attempts to understand and embrace each other's emic, dialogue and argue about the etic, and strive to honor both to the extent possible. Our psychological world is a kaleidoscope with infinite patterns that change with each turn of the instrument.

My ongoing academic journey has been enriching in the challenges it poses in making sense of multiple, often vastly different perspectives on human development and behavior. Most of all, it is a journey laced with much hope, for deep down, I believe that we are all striving toward a common goal, which is to understand and enhance the lives of individuals and families within our own contexts as well as across the world's societies. That going global to meet a world of need is sine qua non has been reinforced more than ever in the context of the enduring pandemic, with future surges looming large. Also, that we have come together to discuss and write about going global signifies that we have already embarked on the journey of discovery that promises much excitement, enrichment, and fulfillment as scholars and as human beings.

In ending, I invoke a quote from the *Upanishad* (a Vedic Hindu text) that I think resonates well with our collective goal:

> You are what your deep, driving desire is.
> As your desire is, so is your will.
> As your will is, so is your deed.
> As your deed is, so is your destiny.
> (*The Philosophy of the Brihadaranyaka Upanishad*, 2019, Chapter IV, 4.4.5)

Craig Shealy

In 2004, while completing a 5-year stint as training director of a doctoral program, I was ready, for many reasons, to focus more explicitly on my long-term research and applied interests in beliefs and values.[2] In particular, with the 9/11 terrorist attacks in the United States still vivid in the minds of many, I had begun meeting with a group of interdisciplinary colleagues to try to understand the nature and form of belief systems that would compel people to fly airplanes into buildings, killing themselves and thousands of others in the process. Dissatisfied with the proclaimed explanations of etiology at the time (e.g., "they attacked us for our freedom"), we spent a lot of time at the outset discussing how our scholarly and professional activities were relevant to these and other real-world events. As our conversations evolved, it seemed to us that far too much of our research was intended for consumption by a relatively narrow group of like-minded colleagues in still smaller subfields within our individual academic disciplines. Rarely did we seek out the perspectives of colleagues from fields other than our own; seldom did we attempt to engage the public or policy makers in anything approximating open dialogue, where we had as much to learn as we did to teach.

Although we lamented the apparent conclusion by nonacademics that the academy was removed from such real-world issues and concerns, we ultimately concluded that this perception, by the public and policy makers, was largely of our own making. What could—what should—we do about this state of affairs? After much deliberation, and a number of false starts, we ended up creating a nonprofit and nonpartisan entity called the International Beliefs and Values Institute, or IBAVI (see https://www.ibavi.org).

With its mission to "explore beliefs and values and how they influence actions, policies, and practices around the world," the IBAVI (2022) has engaged thousands of colleagues and students in various projects, collaborated with a wide array of institutions and organizations in the United States

---

[2]Portions of this section are reproduced from *Giving Away a World of Psychology* (https://www.apa.org/international/pi/2007/09/shealy), *Still Giving Away a World of Psychology* (https://www.apa.org/international/pi/2015/03/world-psychology), and Shealy, C.N. (2017, August). *Our future is global: How psychology and psychologists can meet a world of need.* Presidential Address for the Division of International Psychology at the Annual Convention of the American Psychological Association, Washington, DC.

and internationally, and developed an association of IBAVI chapters in countries around the world in order to broaden our collaborative capacity and scale up our work. Since our inception in 2004, the IBAVI has included many psychologists in various initiatives but many more nonpsychologists, which has compelled me at times to comment, in various venues, that "I am a clinical psychologist in recovery."

In offering this observation, I mean no disrespect to my field, which I have been honored to engage for over 30 years, but rather to make a threefold observation. First, I spend a lot of time working with nonpsychologists, who—through no fault of their own—have relatively little understanding or appreciation for who we are and what we do as psychologists. Second, as much as I value my discipline and profession, it does not always know whether or how to involve our own colleagues or students—much less those in other fields or the public at large—when grappling with problems like environmental sustainability, religious and cultural understanding, or human rights. Fortunately, this state of affairs is changing (e.g., https://www.unpsychologyday.com/) but not nearly fast enough to respond to the challenges and opportunities before us. Third, because of the two previous factors, psychological expertise is generally not seen as essential to addressing or resolving big picture issues (e.g., the sustainable development goals), which often include phenomena that are fundamentally psychological in nature (e.g., climate change denial, attitudes about gender, religious and cross-cultural understanding, conflict resolution). Speaking personally, these three observations are at the very heart of why I hoped we could come together and write this book.

So, at the conclusion of this venture, I find myself reflecting again on the threefold impetus for *Going Global*, the powerful contributions of my esteemed coauthors, the hundreds of colleagues I have been privileged to engage over the years, and my own life and career. For me, all of these forces and factors inform and affirm my response to the overarching question before us as we bring this volume to a close: In order to go global and meet a world of need, what recommendations would you offer to psychology and psychologists? I offer my response in the form of seven questions that may be worth asking, 10 lessons learned, and five points to ponder.

Seven Questions Worth Asking

1. Why do you care?
2. What matters most?
3. Who are your champions?
4. Where are you now?
5. What are your strengths?
6. What is your desired destination?
7. How will you know that you have arrived?

Ten Lessons Learned

1. Quality is more important than quantity.
2. Do something that really matters.

3. Pick your partners well.
4. Listen, learn, travel, care—eschew indifference.
5. Seek synergy, collaborate often, cultivate self and other.
6. Good people and systems often will help if you ask.
7. You very likely have something of worth to say.
8. Be kind (insofar as possible).
9. Find at least one sane, supportive, and wise mentor (and strive to be the same for another if asked).
10. You're only schlepping around the planet for a while.

Five Points to Ponder

Think Globally, Act Globally. Whatever your particular goals and objectives, if you aspire to work internationally, it is necessary but not sufficient to act locally. Review and get involved with international organizations and initiatives within our broader field and profession, such as the activities of the APA's Committee on International Relations in Psychology (https://www.apa.org/international/governance/cirp), APA's Office of International Affairs (https://www.apa.org/international), or APA's Division 52, International Psychology (see http://internationalpsychology.net/home/). In going global, I'd also strongly encourage you to join at least one international organization (for possibilities, see https://www.apa.org/international/networks/organizations/international-orgs). There are many other resources as you've seen from the preceding chapters, so take the time to dive deep into these diverse worlds, which illuminate a rich array of pathways and possibilities for thinking and acting globally.

Live and Work Outside the Box. Psychologists' knowledge, skills, and values have relevance to a wide range of issues and applications around the world. Consider the following competencies as examples: strategies for emotional and behavioral change; crisis intervention with individuals, families, groups, and communities; knowledge of program development and evaluation; familiarity with research design and methods; consultation, supervisory, and leadership skills; and ability to understand, mediate, and resolve conflict. Such competencies are needed more than ever around the globe, and as psychologists we must imagine and create more opportunities for ourselves, our field and profession, and especially our students if we are to engage in a more culturally sensitive, effective, and relevant manner with these real-world needs and issues, and translate our expertise into ecologically valid actions, policies, and practices.

Prepare to Learn From and Play Well With Others. If you are interested in working globally, and want to learn how you may be of service, it will help to approach your experience and process with a beginner's mind. You may not know what you do not know; your theories, interventions, and solutions may not be relevant or appropriate. The epistemologies that are inculcated in you from your training and culture may inadvertently limit your skill and effectiveness. Finally, although you may be given great deference because of your title or degree, do not assume such behavior from others has anything to do with you personally—it may be culturally mediated—or worse, that it is justified. You are first and foremost a guest in another culture and context. In the end, through your words and deeds, take every opportunity to refute the lamentable stereotype of the "ugly American" (or any other nationality) who always knows best. Actively seek out collaborative opportunities with international psychologists and kindred spirits from across the interdisciplinary spectrum, and you, your work, and our current students and future leaders will be immeasurably enriched. As ambassadors for our wonderful field and profession, we have much to teach and even more to learn from our global encounters.

Cultivate Patience, Perspective, and Perseverance. The core contention of Reinhold Niebuhr—"anything worth doing takes more than one lifetime"—seems pretty right to me, particularly when working toward large-scale global change. At the same time, although a single lifetime may not be sufficient, it most certainly is necessary. That is because, as Lao Tzu reminds us, "The journey of a thousand miles begins with a single step." Thus, to become an agent of global change, it is necessary to cultivate patience, perspective, and perseverance, knowing that, fair or not, roadblocks and setbacks are inevitable and our work never will be completed fully in our own lifetime, for such work really is not our own alone, but an enduring and collaborative preoccupation that is of import to us all. Effective and reflective global change agents learn to accept these inevitabilities, acknowledging that we are, after all, the beneficiaries of those who came before us. Their exertions and convictions constructed the trails we now walk, whether or not we recognize this debt. So, with grit and gumption—and surrounded by kindred spirits who help us along our way, just as we help them—let us strive to blaze paths of promise for those who follow long after we depart.

Keep the Faith. Finally, it is worth asking, what motivates us in the first place? At our best and not our worst (since such factors often are determined for, rather than by, us), why would we strive to leave the world a little better than we found it by the time we die? Like so many of us, such essential questions of existence, meaning, and purpose have occupied me for as long as I can remember. For my part, these strivings are an expression of who we are fundamentally as a species; they are our evolutionary legacy, just as they may be a manifestation of processes that remain veiled and ineffable during our time on Earth—at least for me, since I am not personally authorized to refute such prospects, which long have been putative for billions around the globe.

In the final analysis, from my perspective, all we can do is mightily seek our own vision, refine it deeply, openly, and persistently, and hopefully find ourselves expressing an affirmative faith in life and living to the larger world. Although I consider myself a scientific-humanist, and have spent my life learning from and honoring colleagues around the world who have assumed a similar mantle in the past and present, I also know as a clinician and human being that the theories and data we produce ultimately are subordinate to that which we long for most: a sense that we matter, that we exist for a reason, and that we can—we must—do more to make things right here on Earth. In that spirit, I wish you reasoned and abundant faith in the integrity of your own life and the story you tell in order to light a promising path that the rest of us may follow.

REFERENCES

American Psychological Association Division of International Psychology. (2022, January). *Bylaws of the Division of International Psychology.* http://div52.net/wp-content/uploads/2021/08/BYLAWS-OF-THE-DIVISION-OF-INTERNATIONAL-PSYCHOLOGY-july2021.pdf

Berry, J. W. (1999). Emics and etics: A symbiotic conception. *Culture and Psychology, 5*(2), 165–171. https://doi.org/10.1177/1354067X9952004

Elms, A. (2001). Apocryphal Freud: Sigmund Freud's most famous "quotations" and their actual sources. *Annual of Psychoanalysis, 29,* 83–104.

Fetvadjiev, V. H., & van de Vijver, F. J. R. (2015). Measures of personality across cultures. In G. J. Boyle, D. H. Saklofske, & G. Matthews (Eds.), *Measures of personality and social psychological constructs* (pp. 752–776). Academic Press. https://doi.org/10.1016/B978-0-12-386915-9.00026-7

Kapadia, S. (2011). Psychology and human development in India. Country paper. *International Society for the Study of Behavioral Development Bulletin, 2*(60), 37–42.

Kimble, G. A. (1984). Psychology's two cultures. *American Psychologist, 39*(8), 833–839. https://doi.org/10.1037/0003-066X.39.8.833

Leopold, A. (1986). *A sand country almanac* (7th ed). Ballantine Books.

Niebuhr, R. (1952). *The irony of American history.* Charles Scribner's Sons.

Segall, M. H., Dasen, P. R., Berry, J. W., & Poortinga, Y. H. (1990). *Human behavior in global perspective: An introduction to cross-cultural psychology.* Pergamon Press.

The Philosophy of the Brihadaranyaka Upanishad (3rd ed.). (2019). (Swami Madhavananda, Trans.) [Ebook]. Advaita Ashram. (Original work published 1934) http://www.upanishads.kenjaques.org.uk/Ebook_Download.html

Thomas, D. (1971). *Do not go gentle into that good night.* Poets.org. https://poets.org/poem/do-not-go-gentle-good-night (Original work published 1937).

INDEX

ABOUT THE EDITORS

Craig Shealy, PhD, is a professor of psychology at Western Washington University and the executive director of the International Beliefs and Values Institute (IBAVI), which coordinates an array of scholarly, grant, educational, and service activities in the United States and internationally. Dr. Shealy's research on the Beliefs, Events, and Values Inventory (BEVI) has been featured in multiple publications. A licensed clinical psychologist, he is a Fulbright specialist in Japan, fellow of the American Psychological Association (APA), past president of APA's Division of International Psychology, a Nehru chair at MS Baroda University in India, and a National Register Legacy of Excellence Psychologist.

Merry Bullock, PhD, is secretary-general of the International Council of Psychologists and cochair of the Global Network of Psychologists for Human Rights Steering Committee. She has served in leadership roles in many psychology organizations, including APA (senior director of the APA Office of International Affairs for over a decade), the International Union of Psychological Science (deputy secretary-general), and APA's International Division (president). Dr. Bullock's research and scholarly writing explore early cognitive and motivational development, scientific reasoning, policy applications, and internationalization. She is the recipient of awards for distinguished contributions to psychology from national, regional, and international organizations.

Shagufa Kapadia, PhD, is a professor in the Department of Human Development and Family Studies and former director of the Women's Studies Research Center at The Maharaja Sayajirao University of Baroda, India. Her scholarly interests are cultural and cross-cultural perspectives in human development, particularly adolescence and emerging adulthood. She has researched cultural dimensions of socialization, morality, social support exchange, identity, and hopes and aspirations. Dr. Kapadia has been a recipient of the Fulbright Senior Research Fellowship and the Shastri Indo-Canadian Faculty Research Award. She serves as the India coordinator of the International Society for the Study of Behavioral Development (ISSBD).